THE EMPIRICAL GAP IN JURISPRUDENCE: A COMPREHENSIVE STUDY OF THE SUPREME COURT OF CANADA

In jurisprudential writing, single decisions are often held up as representative without any evidence to support this claim. In order to address this problem, Daved Muttart has made a systematic study encompassing every judgment of the Supreme Court of Canada between 1950 and 2003.

Muttart analyses almost 5000 Supreme Court decisions to determine whether they overruled precedent, the extent to which they were decided on fact, law, or policy, and the legal and extra-legal modes of reasoning utilized by the Court. Muttart uses the results of this comprehensive examination to test the validity of extant jurisprudential theories. Ultimately, he concludes that the Court's method of operation is evolving as it moves into a new century. While its reasoning is becoming less foundational, the Court remains a predominantly legal, as opposed to political, institution.

Filling an important niche in the study of jurisprudence, *The Empirical Gap in Jurisprudence* demonstrates that systematic studies based on large samples of cases will yield many insights that could not be gleaned from prior efforts that relied on small, hand-picked samples.

DAVED MUTTART obtained his PhD and conducted post-doctoral studies at Osgoode Hall Law School, York University.

DAVED MUTTART

The Empirical Gap in Jurisprudence

A Comprehensive Study of the Supreme Court of Canada

UNIVERSITY OF TORONTO PRESS
Toronto Buffalo London

ISBN-13: 978-0-8020-9159-8
ISBN-10: 0-8020-9159-8

Printed on acid-free paper

Library and Archives Canada Cataloguing in Publication

Muttart, Daved, 1955–
    The empirical gap in jurisprudence : a comprehensive study of the
Supreme Court of Canada / Daved Muttart.

    Includes bibliographical references and index.
    ISBN-13: 978-0-8020-9159-8
    ISBN-10: 0-8020-9159-8

    1. Judicial process – Canada.   2. Prospective overruling – Canada.
3. Canada. Supreme Court.   I. Title.

    KE8244.M88 2007   347.71′035   C2006-904663-8

University of Toronto Press acknowledges the financial assistance to
its publishing program of the Canada Council for the Arts and the
Ontario Arts Council.

University of Toronto Press acknowledges the financial support for
its publishing activities of the Government of Canada through the
Book Publishing Industry Development Program (BPIDP).

Contents

Tables and Figures

Preface

The first seed for this project was planted during the second year of my undergraduate law degree whilst I was flush with the majesty of the law in general and the common law in particular. My father had the audacity to complain that justice suffered, and suffered badly, when judges were bound by precedent. He felt that it was more important to render justice in the particular case and that any other concern was immaterial. I was of course offended by this frontal assault on my chosen discipline and profession.

In this frame of mind, I was pleased to encounter *Paquette* (1976), which reformed the felony murder rule. Here was the Supreme Court of Canada changing a nonsensical law to render justice, not only in the individual case, but in all other cases where justice required that the pronouncements in *Dunbar* (1938) be adjusted. The legal system had successfully weathered my father's frontal assault. The law could be changed when absolutely necessary, but otherwise precedent provided justice, not to mention stability. At the time, I was unaware of any other common law rules requiring adjustment.

Many years later, after almost two decades of practising law in the trenches, I returned to academe and obtained my master of laws degree. This failed to satisfy my intellectual curiosity, so I began the process of applying to the doctoral program. Ultimately, I submitted four proposals. At that point, my favoured and ultimately accepted proposal, 'Styles of Reason and Logic in the Supreme Court: Evolution or Paradigm Shift?' was based on *Paquette*, one or two other cases that had overruled precedent, and Kuhnian epistemology. My jurisprudential worldview held that the outcomes of the vast majority of cases were determined by legal rules. Judges conducted themselves in an intellectually honest positivist fashion. Only in a small set of extra-ordinary cases – which, using Justice Sopinka's term, I labelled 'radi-cal departures' – were decisions based on pragmatic, result-driven criteria.

In conducting this investigation, I was acutely aware of the tension between the need for certainty in the law and the historical example of Islamic law, which dangerously stultified progress when it proclaimed that the door of interpretation (*ijtihad*) was closed.

In the late spring and early summer of 2002, I began to survey cases decided by the Supreme Court of Canada from 1970 to date. I was pleased to learn that there was no published summary of overrulings by the Court, which meant that I had a golden opportunity to add to knowledge of its functioning. I had only a vague idea of the prevalence, or lack thereof, of overruling in the Court's jurisprudence. Justice Sopinka's use of the term 'radical departure' in *Central Alberta Dairy Pool v. Alberta* (1990) to describe overruling was exceptionally intrigu-ing and reinforced my view that radical departures held the key to jurisprudence.

Ultimately I surveyed all the reported decisions of the Supreme Court of Canada from 1950 to 2000 for the purpose of tracking over-rulings and divisions on the Court. Professor Allan Hutchinson of Osgoode Hall Law School helped refine my thinking on hard distin-guishing and provided a helpful suggestion on conducting future sur-veys on a smaller sample of the Court's decisions. I ultimately selected years ending in '2,' a sampling that I referred to as 'the terrible twos.' The terrible twos were used to attempt to directly measure founda-tional in contrast to non-foundational reasoning on the Court.

As my surveys moved into the mid-1980s, I began to notice indica-tions that *Charter* cases were different from non-*Charter* cases. I there-fore separated the former from the latter. These differences provided many important insights into the Court's level of activism.

As I progressed through this study, I began to feel self-righteously indignant at the lack of empirical rigour that characterized jurispru-dence. However, towards the end, I was overwhelmed by the number of variables that seemed to affect both the overall work of judges and the deciding of each individual case. I oscillated between euphoric discovery and despair at the scope of what I was attempting.

Once the survey was completed, I used its findings to attempt to test several of the leading jurisprudential theories. I hope readers find this attempt interesting and useful.

The introductory chapters of this book–describe the empirical gap in jurisprudence and some of the problems arising therefrom. I outline my effort to close the gap and provide some background on the Supreme Court of Canada. I will introduce the importance of overruling to understanding of the Court's jurisprudence and contrast it with the doctrine of *stare decisis*. I summarize the theories of jurisprudence and delineate a continuum of theories of judicial behaviour. The behaviour of judges relative to overruling and hard distinguishing is discussed. I analyse critiques of current legal methodology and highlight the key features of my methodology. Finally, I review current theoretical debates to set the stage for the chapters that follow.

Chapters 4 through 7 and 9 contain the results of my survey, largely in the form of graphs compiled from the data I amassed. Chapter 8 contains other findings, largely statistics compiled by other investigators. Chapters 10 and 11 analyse several extant jurisprudential theories, utilizing the results of my survey of more than 4,800 Supreme Court of Canada cases. Chapter 12 uses new data to determine the level of the Court's activism.

Some of the terms used in the introductory chapters are defined in the endnotes, especially where I have coined a new term or used an existing term in a new or specific way. Fuller definitions are contained in later chapters and in the glossary. Typically, I refer to Supreme Court of Canada cases using an abbreviated case name followed by the year in which the case was decided. Usually, only cases that are quoted have full citations in the endnotes. The Court's cases are easily located in the Supreme Court Reports, on QuickLaw™, on e-Carswell™, or on the Lexum website.

In this book, the term *Justices* refers to Justices of the Supreme Court of Canada or, where specifically indicated, to Justices of the United States Supreme Court. The term *judges* is used generically and refers to all judges, trial and appellate.

This study will examine the behaviour of the Court as a single entity. The work and views of individual Justices will be referred to primarily to shed light on the functioning of the Court as a whole. While occasional efforts at prediction will be attempted, the focus will be on describing judicial decision making.

This study was designed to survey the literature to compile a list of as many jurisprudential questions and theoretical propositions as possible. It then attempts to answer these questions and to test these theoretical propositions. This study will, of course, fall somewhat short of this goal; no study, even a wide-ranging empirical one, can hope to answer all questions. But by adopting ambitious goals, this study provides many useful insights, points out interesting questions for further study, and demonstrates the feasibility of the type of empirical study undertaken herein.

Acknowledgments

This book would not have been possible without the intellectual stimulation and timely comments of Professors Allan Hutchinson (my supervisor) and Liora Salter (who assisted during Professor Hutchinson's sabbatical).

Osgoode's library staff were wonderful, especially John Thomas, who always did his best to help me out. Maureen Boyce and Mandy Zwarenstein consistently frustrated my efforts to name a document they could not find.

My wife, Arpi Panossian-Muttart, as well as Dr Razmik Panossian, Michael Gosling, Professors Shelley Kierstead, and Rebecca Johnson made many helpful suggestions. My mother, Kay Muttart, Ani Koulian, and latterly Barbara Tessman were relentless in removing the many errors that crept into this manuscript. Any errors that remain are mine alone (except for the insertion of commas and periods inside quotes for which Ms. Tessman must take full responsibility!).

I would like to thank Professors Hutchinson, Bruce Ryder, Marilyn Pilkington, Peter Russell, and Ian Greene, who, together with Dean Patrick Monahan, served on my committee.

Virgil Duff at the University of Toronto Press provided indispensable assistance as he shepherded the manuscript through the publishing process. I would also like to express my gratitude for the many helpful suggestions provided by the (anonymous) reviewers.

SECTION I

Setting the Stage

1 Introduction

Jurisprudential theories are typically based on anecdote, superficial observation, and the undocumented impressions of individual authors. In jurisprudential writing, single instances are regularly held up as being representative without any evidence being offered in support of their representativeness. Theorists indulge in normative prescription without first describing the work, behaviour, and capacities of judges. Taken together, these shortcomings constitute a serious empirical gap in jurisprudential scholarship. The hallmark of this gap is the chasm between theory and verification.

Closing the empirical gap will require legal scholars to become more thorough and systematic in their examination of the caselaw and of other aspects of judicial behaviour. This book begins to close the gap by analysing almost five thousand cases decided by the Supreme Court of Canada.

At present, jurists routinely describe judicial behaviour without having first conducted a study to verify the accuracy of their descriptions. Legal philosophers habitually advocate changes to the form of judicial method and process without prior study of the actual behaviour of judges. For example, H.L.A. Hart, in *The Concept of Law*,[1] discusses only four cases in the main body of his text and only two more in his postscript. The notes to this text cite an additional eleven cases. Ronald Dworkin, in *Law's Empire*,[2] cites a total of fifty-one cases but discusses only a handful of these in any detail. In both texts, the cases cited lack any apparent pattern: they are trial and appellate, British and American. There is no indication in either of these seminal texts that any procedure was used to ensure that the cases chosen were representative of the tens of thousands of cases decided during the period. Apologists for the status quo point out that learned authors such as Hart and Dworkin have read a wide range of cases and that they are merely citing illustrative examples of trends which they believe they have observed. But disputation between Hart, Dworkin, and their respective disciples has raged for decades. Resolution of these controversies requires empirical investigation; the endless parsing of contending theories has proven grossly inadequate.

The limited samples of cases cited by jurisprudes have resulted in most jurisprudential theories being constructed upon weak foundations. A well-supported superstructure is lacking. Jurisprudential writing is too often characterized by allegation without verification, by idiosyncratic impression instead of rigorous research, by small and selective sample instead of systematic study. This approach foments errors and prevents their correction. Debates proliferate *ad infinitum*, descending into ever-deeper levels of obscurity. The investigation of actual judicial behaviour constitutes the first step towards closing the empirical gap.

Jurisprudence has been notoriously feeble in supporting its philosophical analysis with empirical research. There is thus a gap – what I call the empirical gap – between what judges actually do and what jurisprudential writers say they do. This book makes an initial effort to remedy this deficiency in regard to courts' use of legal reasoning. Systematic sampling of the reasons for judgment rendered by the Supreme Court of Canada furnishes the basis on which to test several theories of legal reasoning and to document trends in the jurisprudence of the Court.

An Empirical Approach

Empirical research is only starting to become established as a typical mode of scholarship in the legal academy.[3] Standards are just beginning to be set.[4] As such, studies that attempt empirical legal research should be creative while taking care to ensure that their methodology is sound. But a lack of methodological standards should not be used as an excuse for timidity. We should go forth with courage to investigate reality with our own eyes.[5] As legal scholars we have a distinct advantage over other disciplines: regular grappling with issues of proof, during which we have formulated rules of evidence, has prepared us to formulate appropriate methodological guidelines for empirical research.

What, then, is the state of jurisprudence?

Orthodox theories of jurisprudence have maintained that legal adjudication is a distinct decision-making process entirely separate from politics. These foundationalist theories hold that law yields much more objective results than those of the political process. For example, Ronald Case states that 'judicial application of law, properly conducted, requires that judges conform to prescribed modes of reasoning,' which are based largely on the application of legal precedent. He cites the writings of the most prominent positivist theorist, Herbert (H.L.A.) Hart in support of this assertion.[6]

Powerful critiques have been launched against these orthodox theories, most notably by Allan Hutchinson, who asserts that considerations beyond the narrowly legal affect judicial decision making,[7] and by anti-foundationalists, largely as part of the Critical Legal Studies movement.[8] Ronald Dworkin propounds a semi-foundational regime under which judges should add coherent moral principles as part of the foundation for their reasoning processes.[9]

This is jurisprudence today: none of the above authors attempt to advance any evidence in the form of a systematically gathered sample of judicial behaviour in support of their theories. Exceptional cases are held up as being representative of all cases. Authority is cited in place of investigation.

The study described in this volume was designed to resolve, or at least clarify, one or more of the current debates between jurisprudential theorists. It analyses the extant theories of jurisprudence and of legal reasoning that I believe to be sufficiently evolved to be tested empirically. The data for the tests included *all* the reasons for judgment of the Supreme Court of Canada rendered between 1950 and 2003. This large sample allowed several important trends to be tracked and quantified. Qualitative analysis, including hermeneutics, will also be applied to the Court's reasons. Where anecdotal accounts of judicial behaviour were available, I accessed them in an effort to provide evidence to confirm or contradict my survey findings. Empirical research requires the evaluation and weighing of all available data, be they quantitative, qualitative, or narrative in nature.

This study takes the view that the task of jurisprudence is to accurately describe and, if possible, predict the actual behaviour of judges. To do so requires empirical observation. The juxtaposition of unverified theories against each other is to be eschewed.

Methodological Insights from the Study of Science

Mainstream science, and especially the philosophy of science, has provided many valuable ideas for this study of jurisprudence. John Losee, in *Philosophy of Science*, traced the historical steps through which the empirical study of phenomena has progressed. According to Losee, Plato sought to uncover a 'deeper knowledge' of the underlying pattern that lies concealed in nature. Aristotle described induction and deduction. Roger and later Francis Bacon promoted experimental verification. The Church was more interested in saving appearances and maintaining its theological positions than engaging in empirical study. In the twentieth century Karl Popper stated that the scientific method required that theories constantly be exposed to the possibility of being falsified; if they were falsified, they would have to be modified or discarded. Thomas Kuhn described science as working on the verification of a paradigm until anomalous observations compelled a revolutionary paradigm shift during which a new theory would be adopted. Imre Lakatos observed that science typically held onto its core theories but that auxiliary hypotheses were constantly being tested and modified.[10]

The essence of these later developments is the need to test theory through experiment or other observation of phenomena to determine whether the theory is consistent with the observations. Theories lacking in observable implications are of little use.[11] Observations that are capable of either refuting or confirming the theory provide the best experimental instruments. 'Empirical' is not restricted to statistical or other quantitative analyses. A theory often postulates qualitative outcomes, and the presence or absence of these qualitative outcomes either confirm or refute the theory.

Theory may be essential to observation.[12] If one looks without a theory at a field full of seagulls, one sees merely a group of birds, some of which occasionally interact with each other. The interactions appear random and meaningless. However, if one adopts the theory that seagull behaviour is governed by territorial imperatives, competition for food, and the attraction of mates, one no longer sees a field full of seagulls moving randomly about. One sees directed behaviour organized by clear social rules. Suddenly one *understands* seagulls. Theory, in addition to organizing one's observations, permits one to predict future behaviour. Seagull behaviour that conforms to these predictions verifies the theory. Behaviour that does not conform to prediction refutes the theory or indicates that it needs to be modified.

An incomplete or partially inaccurate theory is better than no theory because its ordering of functions and insights allow much more data to be considered at one time. For example, Newtonian mechanics provided useful insights, not to mention practical applications, despite evidence that it was significantly flawed.[13] Furthermore, any theory, even one that is highly problematic, is capable of being the basis for testing designed either to support it or to refute it. The data collected while testing the old theory usually form the foundation for a new theory, one with more predictive power and capable of explaining a broader range of phenomena.[14] Out of the ashes, a new phoenix is born. Copernicus and Galileo would never have seen the sun at the centre of the solar system had Ptolemy not first seen the earth as the centre of the universe. Similarly, the theories of Hart, Dworkin, and Hutchinson, and even those of critical legal scholar Joseph Singer, despite their limitations, organize large swaths of judicial phenomena, enabling improved insight and providing starting points for empirical inquiry.

But before the extant jurisprudential theories are described in more detail, it is worthwhile to pause to consider just what it is that judges do.

What Judges Do

Judges decide. After the evidence has been given and the parties' lawyers heard, the judge must render a decision. As will be seen from the varied hypotheses below, there is widespread debate as to what considerations inform the judge's decisions. Does she apply propositions of law to the facts and decide using simple logic? Does she engage in a particularized process of analogic reasoning? Is her decision the result of idiosyncratic notions of justice? Or does it rest on class politics? Can other bases for her decision be determined? Whatever the decision-making processes a judge employs, they are almost entirely beyond direct study inasmuch as they occur almost exclusively within the private confines of the judicial cranium.

The judge's reasons for judgment may show each step of the judge's reasoning process as he moved towards his decision. More commonly the judge has already reached his decision before writing his reasons. In this case, his reasons merely justify his decision and may only obliquely elucidate the steps the judge took in arriving at his conclusion.

On their face, almost all reasons for judgment indicate that the judge reached his conclusion based on pre-existing legal rules. The reasons will pronounce that these rules directed him to his decision. The extent of judicial deference to extant legal materials is the central axle from which the spokes of legal theory radiate. These spokes seek to answer the following questions: Is the legal rule as clear as the judge asserts, or does he have more discretion than he purports to allow himself? How do authorized rules and legal principles work together? Is the judge bound by existing rules, or can he change them to better accord with changed circumstances? Is the judge free to decide based on his own or society's morality when the law conflicts with such morality? Has the judge decided based on his personal predilections or based on his political views and used his reasons as rhetorical cover? Legal theorists have debated these issues for decades, if not centuries. Almost invariably, each contending proponent has relied on a small, self-selected, and self-serving data set.

To the extent that jurisprudence is prescriptive and normative, it should be grounded in an accurate description of judicial behaviour. Philosophers can then point to what should be preserved and what should change. Accurate description is an essential first step. Some philosophical propositions may resist empirical verification, but testable propositions should be tested.

Adjudication in Context

As we have seen above, the resolution of disputes and controversies is a quintessentially human endeavour. That part of jurisprudence that constitutes the study of dispute resolution by courts through legal means should begin with an investigation as to how humans resolve disputes. We should begin with a study of the behaviour of judges, not with a dissection of philosophical writings and debates. Reified doctrine, a common starting point of jurisprudential discussion, places us at a vantage point considerably removed from the subject of our study.

Judges are human. They are filled with all the ideals and foibles implied by that term. This human element means that any empirically verifiable theory will provide only general predictions of judicial behaviour. Human activity is invariably messy; every theoretical expectation will be beset with exceptions. Furthermore, judges, being human, are capable of error. Jurisprudential theory must encompass all these phenomena. Exact mathematical precision will not be attainable. Yet, human behaviour, including judicial behaviour, is not without substantial order: random chaos does not prevail. Jurisprudence can provide important insights into how courts function.

The following section describes several of the most prominent juris-prudential theories that seek to describe judicial behaviour. This description is the first step in attempting to narrow the empirical gap. The second, outlined in chapters 4–9 consists of compiling data that may be useful in supporting or questioning these theories. The third step, illustrated in chapters 10 and 11, consists of applying these data in an effort to verify or refute the theories. As the empirical gap begins to narrow, each theory will, to a greater or lesser extent, be verified, called into question, or refuted altogether.

A Typology of Theories of Judicial Decision Making

For the purposes of this study, *jurisprudence* is that body of knowledge that seeks to describe the manner in which judges decide cases.[15] It strives to formulate a coherent and comprehensive theory of judicial behaviour.

This book focuses on four prominent theories: those of Hart, Dworkin, Stone/Goodrich, and Hutchinson. It also attempts to determine which of the deliberative tensions postulated by Justice Wilson now predominate in the Supreme Court of Canada. The extent to which law is objective, neutral, and autonomous is discussed. Other propositions advanced by various authors are touched on. As will be discussed below, jurisprudential theories can be described along a continuum with Hart on the left, Allan Hutchinson in the middle, and critical legal scholars such as Singer on the right.

When setting out to describe legal theory, there is no better place to start than with H.L.A. Hart's *The Concept of Law*.[16] This book best describes the prevailing positivist view of judges and lawyers as to law and legal reasoning and is the favourite target of critics of the positivist point of view. Hart describes three types of rules: rules of recognition, primary rules, and secondary rules.[17] Rules of recognition determine which primary and secondary rules will be followed. If something is provided for in the Constitution, it will generally be recognized as valid and authorizing. Primary rules decree what human beings are required to do or what activities they are to abstain from. These rules provide guidelines to govern future behaviour. To function properly, these guidelines need to have certainty and consistency. For example, to preserve consistency of measurement, the metre bar in Paris has been promulgated as the universal and constant standard of length.[18] Secondary rules provide for the introduction of new or the modification of old

Figure 1.1. Continuum of legal reasoning

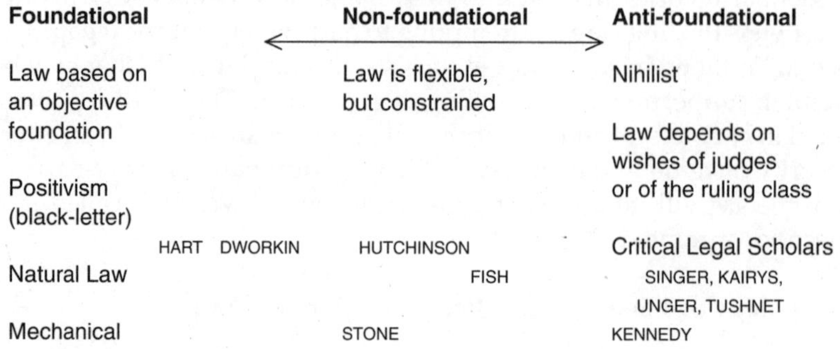

Foundational	Non-foundational	Anti-foundational
	← ⎯⎯⎯⎯⎯⎯⎯⎯⎯→	
Law based on an objective foundation	Law is flexible, but constrained	Nihilist
		Law depends on wishes of judges or of the ruling class
Positivism (black-letter)		
HART DWORKIN	HUTCHINSON	Critical Legal Scholars
Natural Law	FISH	SINGER, KAIRYS,
		UNGER, TUSHNET
Mechanical	STONE	KENNEDY

primary rules. A specific class of secondary rules, rules of adjudication, provides for the interpretation and enforcement of primary rules.

Hart wrote that clear rules easily decide almost all cases. Judges are called upon to make new law only in the small number of hard cases where the law is unclear. Thus law will yield, in almost all situations, a clear and certain result. In short, Hart's theories mirror the practices that many, if not most, lawyers and judges think they are engaged in. These theories are elegant and appear to explain many recurring phenomena. As such, they constitute a powerful paradigm.

The continuum of jurisprudential theories and theorists, shown in figure 1.1, will assist in locating Hart's theories in relation to their competitors. The primary controversy is between foundationalists, such as Hart, who attempt to show that judges employ objective criteria in reaching their decisions; anti-foundationalists, such as critical legal scholars, who maintain that judges decide each case on its own merits without regard to prior decisions; and non-foundationalists, such as Hutchinson, who fall between these two extremes. Foundationalists believe that almost all judicial decisions are decided by the existing law. Anti-foundationalists maintain that almost any decision is possible in any case. Non-foundationalists submit that, while judges have wide discretion, the existing law imposes significant constraints on their decision making.[19]

Foundational theories postulate that judicial behaviour rests on a secure and predictable foundation. It usually relies on a set of specific criteria as specified by the relevant rule. A foundational theory, if its forecasts prove accurate, is thus powerful because it allows perceptions to be ordered and future events predicted. Furthermore, a foundational theory would best support the view that law is autonomous and objective, thus enhancing legal adjudication's claim of legitimacy in society. Non-foundationalism allows judges to consider a wider range of criteria. At the opposite pole, anti-foundationalism, which disputes the determinativeness of legal considerations, denies that any legal theory will be able to predict outcomes. Foundationalism maintains that past rulings control future ones. Therefore, cases where the Court has overruled its own precedent constitute anomalies requiring explanation by Hart's supporters. Changes in the Court's modes of reasoning and the increasing prevalence of policy concerns also cast doubt on the foundationalist theories. Critical Legal Scholars and other anti-foundationalists have described other anomalies in the foundationalist paradigm.[20] One of the goals of this study is to illuminate the extent to which changes in the practices of the Court call the positivist foundational theory into question.

Hartian positivism holds that, in easy cases, judges apply clear rules. In slightly more difficult cases, there may be controversy as to which rule covers the situation. In hard cases, there is no clear rule, and judges must make new law. Positivists believe that existing law easily decides almost all cases and that judges exercise personal discretion only in the small number of cases where the law is unclear.[21] This prevailing paradigm holds that legal reasoning is neutral, in the sense of being free of political and other subjective considerations. Positivism holds that law is determinative, in that legal reasoning will yield, in almost all situations, a clear and certain result. In short, legal reasoning is autonomous.[22]

More recent theorists have criticized Hart's positivistic paradigm on the grounds that it grossly understates the number of hard cases where the law is unclear.[23] This critique states that laws are often promulgated in language which is plurisignative – that is, capable of bearing more than one meaning – especially in the hands of a trained jurist.[24] Laws admitting of polysemy – that is, laws that effectively leave their ultimate meaning up to the judge's choice – contradict the idea that law is an objective enterprise or that legal reasoning is a neutral instrument.[25] The ultimate conclusion of these criticisms leads to a nihilist anti-foundational theory of jurisprudence: judges are entirely free of any constraint and rule as they choose. Judicial reasons are at best *post hoc* justifications and at worst prevarication. Judges enjoy an unfettered discretion; the purpose of their reasons for judgment is to conceal the arbitrariness of their decisions. Yet, contrary to this critique, the behaviour of judges strongly suggests that they believe that they are acting within defined parameters. Their reasons for judgment generally acknowledge constraints and, in many cases, clear directions imposed by pre-existing law. Thus, on the surface, the courts' operating paradigm does not seem to conform to the anti-foundationalists' 'anything goes.' This study attempts to test whether this surface appearance is accurate.

Natural Law, the other major foundational theory, holds that law is based on a set of universal moral standards that are objective and ascertainable. These standards are held to originate with God or to emanate from our essential humanity.[26] To contradict the theory of a singular legal source, critics of Natural Law point to the plethora of different legal systems that have generated vastly different substantive laws. One universal set of moral standards may explain the similarities in legal systems (the law against murder, for example), but it cannot explain the minutiae of real property laws.

Dworkin's theories are slightly less foundational than Hart's. A substantial part of recent jurisprudential debate has consisted of the attempts by Dworkin and his disciples to supplant Hart as the most pre-eminent jurisprude. Where Hart required rules, Dworkin proposes principles. Dworkin's judges – heroic Hercules at the fore – are to apply their moral standards, informed by a holistic interpretation of the co-herent principles contained in legal materials, to the task of adjudica-tion.[27] While Dworkin claims that principles will lead to 'one right answer,' and thus effect more constraint than Hart's rules, it may well be that the preference of principles over rules will lead to more, not less, judicial freedom.[28]

Hart's theories also contrast with non-foundationalist and anti-foundationalist theories. Non-foundationalists concede that there are large areas of determinacy but see law as a continuum between determinacy and indeterminacy.[29] They hold that legal issues regularly drift out of the core and into the penumbra. It is impossible to predict which issue will migrate to the apex of uncertainty.[30] Nihilist anti-foundationalists, whether realists or critical legal scholars, hold that judges decide based on politics, not law.

Closing the empirical gap will result in one or more of the compo-nents of the above theories being supported or undermined.

What Each Theory Predicts

All other things being equal, Hart's theories would predict that cases where the judges disagree among themselves will decline over time.

Overruling should be extremely rare. Most cases should be easy, with the law providing a clear answer. If the non-foundationalists are correct, there will be less formal reasoning (law is 'x,' therefore P wins) than Hart predicts. If anti-foundationalists are right, there will be more overruling and more instances of specious reasoning (often in the form of hard distinguishing[31]). The law will leave a large leeway of choice in the hands of judges. The level of socio-political concerns expressed in the text and subtext judgments will be a useful barometer for determining whether judges are using foundational (less socio-political), non-foundational or anti-foundational (most socio-political) reasoning. The surveys described in this book were designed to measure the above tendencies.

It would be reasonable to expect that courts lower in the judicial hierarchy would most closely reflect the paradigm proposed by Hart: a higher proportion of issues would likely be capable of resolution by established legal rules; most cases would be easy. On the other hand, courts higher in the judicial hierarchy, where the percolation of more difficult issues requires a wider range of judicial activity, would be closer to the wider-ranging style of legal reasoning proposed by Dworkin. Thus if Dworkin's theories are accurate anywhere, it should be at the Supreme Court level. An analysis of Supreme Court decision making should provide a basis for a rigorous testing of Hart's theories.

There are thus, broadly speaking, three possible paradigms or theoretical constructs that we can analyse. The first supports the traditional notion of legal reasoning and judicial decision making: that judges are constrained by existing legal precedent and that their primary technique of legal reasoning consists of an almost mechanical application of law to facts, resulting in an objectively correct decision. Judges employ supplementary techniques when this primary technique is unavailable – for example, when the legal point to be decided is completely novel. The second theoretical construct postulates that judges are, by-and-large, pragmatic – that is, they determine the result they wish to arrive at and then use legal reasoning to justify that already determined result. Here judges rarely use legal reasoning to plot a course to an undefined destination. The third possible paradigm envisions judges as political actors whose decisions are driven by their political and moral beliefs and not by the (pre-existing) law. Judges decide issues based on their ideological views of what is best for society. It is of course possible that each of the three constructs describes some aspect of judicial behaviour.

As the above broadly stroked summary indicates, a central issue is the extent to which judicial behaviour is governed by the law and the extent to which judges exercise an unconstrained (arbitrary) discretion. It therefore makes sense to begin any testing of the theories of jurisprudence with a focus on the foundational theories of positivism. Natural Law will not be studied in any detail. The focus of this study will be on areas of the law where a rule has already been formulated in the precedents. The process whereby judges formulate new rules and standards – an admittedly important subject, but one that would occupy an entire volume in its own right – will be referred to only tangentially or in the context of the overruling of existing precedent.

A Good Theory Describes and Predicts

The law is often said to evolve, evoking comparisons with Darwin's theory of evolution. He described the ways in which most organisms, in response to a changing environment, would adapt and change over time. His theory provided an organizing explanation as to why evolution occurs. The theory of evolution makes it possible to describe in a coherent, inclusive, and meaningful way what organisms are doing. It is now possible to attempt to predict what specific changes an organism might essay in response to environmental change. Once a theory succeeds in describing, it can begin to attempt to predict future events.

Darwin's theory was macro level; predicting specific changes requires a micro-level theory. Unfortunately, micro predictions are more difficult and therefore less accurate. The same might be said about jurisprudence: a systematic theory predicts general judicial trends but will be less successful in predicting what a judge might do with respect to any individual case. Whether faced with a macro question, such as whether the Court will become more and more activist, or with a micro one, such as whether the Court would deem civil unions an acceptable compromise with respect to the issue of gay marriage, a theory that encompasses 'law' as a distinct component of judicial decision making will have greater predictive power than will a theory that restricts itself to 'politics.' A more inclusive model will lead to more accurate predictions. A theory of jurisprudence should therefore include both 'law' *and* 'politics.' Cases in which pressures to modify the law become intense constitute an important intersection between law and politics.

Closing the empirical gap will result in theories which better describe judicial behaviour and which will begin to provide useful predictions of future events.

Summary of Survey Findings

A brief overview may assist the reader in keeping the broader picture in focus. The study of the jurisprudence of the Supreme Court of Canada described herein disclosed the following:

- The behaviour of judges has not remained static. Many texts that describe judicial behaviour tend to describe current behaviour by using old cases. This is usually a mistake. My survey of Supreme Court of Canada cases discloses changes, some of them dramatic, in jurisprudence.
- General trends in the Court's reasons for judgments include the gradual decline in bright-line tests[32] and the increase in open standards.[33] Similar declines also occurred in the use of legal propositions with a concomitant rise in principle-based reasoning. The Court's discourse has become gradually less foundational. More and more of the issues coming before the Court are not determined by clear law but rather require the exercise of choice by the Justices.
- The Court's decisions are based largely on a combination of fact, law, and policy. Gradually since 1950, and especially after the mid-1970s, the facts have determined fewer and fewer of the Court's decisions. The importance of policy implications rose during the same period and has continued to rise to date. Concomitant with the continued increase in the importance of policy, the prevalence of law as a determining force began to proportionally decline after the early 1980s.
- The modes of legal reasoning employed by the Court have also changed. While formal legal reasoning[34] remains the Court's predominant mode, contextual interpretation[35] and doctrinal reconciliation[36] are on the rise.
- Although the raw number of overrulings[37] remains low, the Court is overturning precedent at an accelerating rate. Hard distinguishing,[38] a less forthright method of changing the law, is declining.
- There was a significant crossover in the Court's jurisprudence in the early 1980s. Policy surpassed fact as a factor in the Court's deliberations. The rate of overruling rose above that of hard distinguishing. In addition, contextual interpretation began to rise significantly while formal legal reasoning began to decline. This crossover

indicates an important change in the Court's decision-making processes.

- There are significant differences between Supreme Court reasons for judgment in *Charter* and non-*Charter* cases, in terms of both statistical comparisons and legal reasoning. The trend towards less hard distinguishing is reversed in the Court's *Charter* jurisprudence. This may be a reflection of the Court's ambivalence or uncertainty as to how it should decide these issues. The Court may be concerned with negative criticism of its rulings. A not insignificant number of *Charter* cases are decided by the values held and employed by the Justices.
- Formal legal reasoning is much more prevalent in courts lower in the judicial hierarchy than it is in the Supreme Court. This is an important finding with respect to whether law is capable of functioning as a neutral and autonomous discipline.

To summarize, the Court's behaviour has shifted away from Hartian foundationalism and has become more non-foundational. But the results of my survey provide some evidence supporting, or contradicting, each of the foundational and non-foundational theories.

The Way Forward

The empirical gap results in jurisprudential writing that is usually a meld of portrayal, prediction, and prescription. It is often difficult to determine where description ends and normative advocacy begins. The lack of empirical study results in jurisprudence being almost completely bereft of the systematic description that is the necessary basis for proper analysis of judicial behaviour and the effects of that behaviour. Authors routinely present their idiosyncratic impressions as an accurate portrayal of the process of adjudication. This flawed methodology all but guarantees that these portrayals will be faulty bases for jurisprudential theorizing. To paraphrase the computer system analyst's GIGO acronym, inaccurate inputs lead to inaccurate outputs.

This study attempts to overcome these problems through a more thorough and systematic sampling and analysis. Both the Supreme Court of Canada, the primary focus of my study, and my methodology are described in more detail in chapter 2. Science has expanded our horizons by its use of theory, elaboration, refutation, and verification. Chapter 3 outlines how to use these methods to expand our knowledge of jurisprudence.

2 Possible Solutions: A Case Study of the Supreme Court of Canada

In this chapter, I describe the history and jurisdiction of the Supreme Court of Canada. The description is not intended to be exhaustive, but an overview of the Court will be of assistance in understanding its decision making. After discussing the doctrine of *stare decisis*, I describe the steps I took during my survey of the Court's jurisprudence.

The Supreme Court of Canada

I chose the Supreme Court of Canada because it occupies a middle ground between the final Courts in the United States and the United Kingdom. The period surveyed, 1950 to 2003, includes two decades of *Charter* jurisprudence, which allowed me to study how the Court handled the shift from a largely unwritten constitution to an entrenched bill of rights. The importance of understanding the Supreme Court of Canada is underscored by its power in areas ranging from contract to tort, from fundamental freedoms to zoning bylaws.

History and Jurisdiction

The *British North America Act* of 1867 did not establish a Supreme Court for Canada. Instead, section 101 of the act merely empowered Parliament to create such a court, should it see fit to do so. A bill to create a 'General Court of Appeal for Canada' was first introduced in 1869, but the Court did not come into being until 1875. At that time, the Court was composed of six Justices, who also sat in Exchequer Court. The Court was 'supreme' in name only; its decisions were subject to review by the Judicial Committee of the Privy Council in London. Many appeals came to the Court as of right.

The right to appeal to the Privy Council was not abolished until 1949, making 1950 a convenient starting point for this study. Permission for the abolition had to be sought from the British Parliament, and the constitutionality of the abolition had to be approved by the Privy Council. In Ottawa, the Court had yet to establish a completely favourable reputation; Parliament considered binding the Court to the doctrine of *stare decisis* as part of the Act abolishing appeals to the Privy Council.[2]

In 1949, the number of the Justices on the Court was increased to nine. The Court began to hear more cases, but a significant proportion failed to raise issues of significance. Therefore, in 1975, Parliament altered the Court's jurisdiction by requiring most parties to obtain the leave of the Court before bringing their appeals. The Court also hears matters referred to it directly by the federal government and may hear appeals from references to provincial courts of appeal.

The prime minister is primarily responsible for the appointment of Judges to the Court and care is taken to appoint Judges from each region. While there is now wider consultation before a Justice is appointed to the Supreme Court, the appointment process has been the subject of sustained criticism.[3] Efforts are being made to reform the process, and interim steps have been taken to facilitate more public input. When Justices Abella and Charron were appointed, Justice Minister Cotler appeared before a committee to support their qualifications. The process for the pending appointment of Justice Major's replacement has seen public nomination of suitable candidates, the formulation of a shortlist of six candidates by the justice minister, and a Parliamentary Committee's whittling that list down to three candidates.[4] Most recently candidate and now Justice Rothstein was publicly questioned by an *ad hoc* Parliamentary committee. Nevertheless the final decision continues to rest with the prime minister.

The late 1970s and early 1980s were a period of significant change for the Court. The directions in which Chief Justice Laskin was attempting to lead the Court were becoming clearer. Constitutional turmoil compelled the Court towards creative statesmanship. The Constitution was patriated and the *Charter* entrenched. Rules respecting the intervention of non-parties and the granting of standing were widened in scope. As the Court matured during this period, it significantly altered its modalities of decision making.[5] Although the Supreme Court was not specifically established in the new *Constitution Act*, changes respecting it would henceforth require a constitutional amendment.[6]

As Justice Iacobucci has noted, the Court hears a much broader range of cases than almost any other court of final appeal on the planet:

> Given the Supreme Court of Canada's distinctive tradition and role, it is arguably the most unique among the world's highest courts. First, it is a bilingual court, in that it hears appeals argued in both English and French, and also publishes its decisions and all official documents in both languages. Second, it deals with matters emerging from civil law and common law jurisdictions in the country, and its membership is composed of judges from both of these legal backgrounds. Third, unlike the courts of Europe, the Supreme Court of Canada serves as both a constitutional court and a supreme court for the country. Fourth, in contrast to the United States, the Supreme Court of Canada sits at the top of a unified judicial system, and may hear appeals from provincial and federal courts alike. These cases may involve issues of private law (e.g. torts, contracts and property) and public law (e.g. labour, administrative, taxation and patents). The Court thus has an extremely wide jurisdiction because it may potentially hear an appeal from any court or tribunal in the country.[7]

As the Court entered the twenty-first century, it 'moved from [being] a traditional appellate tribunal to a body exercising a broader supervisory function in the interpretation and application of Canadian law.'[8] It has proclaimed itself the 'guardian of the constitution' as part of the *Charter*'s 'redefinition of our democracy.'[9] Critics of the Court have responded with charges that it is now engaging in unwarranted activism.[10] Whatever one's view, it can no longer be said that the Court plays 'a minor, almost inconsequential role on the national political stage.'[11]

Leave to Appeal and the Decision-Making Process

Prior to the 1975 amendments, anyone with a case in which more than ten thousand dollars was at issue was entitled to appeal to the Supreme Court of Canada as of right.[12] The amendments required almost all prospective civil appellants to first obtain the leave of the Court before bringing their appeal.[13] Some criminal matters could still be appealed as of right, but this was largely restricted by amendments to the *Supreme Court Act* in 1997.[14] Applications for leave now require appellants to convince the Court that their cases raise issues of public importance. Figure 2.1 illustrates that the 1975 amendments resulted in leave being required in the vast majority of cases.[15]

Figure 2.1. Cases on the Supreme Court of Canada docket, 1970–2003*

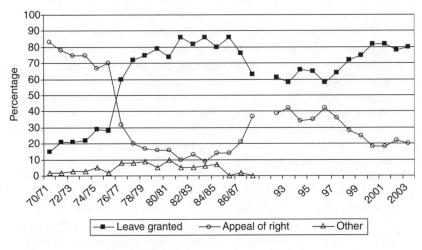

* The break in the data between 1987 and 1993 is attributable to the bane of longitudi-
nal researchers – changes in the way data are reported over time. The Supreme Court
Law Review stopped reporting these statistics in 1987 and the Supreme Court services
report it based on calendar year, not term.
Source: S.I. Bushnell, *Leave to Appeal Applications to the Supreme Court of Canada: A
Matter of Public Importance*, (1982) 3 Sup. Ct. L. Rev. 479; Bushnell, *Leave to Appeal
Applications: The 1985–86 Term*, (1987) 9 Sup. Ct. L. Rev. 467; Bushnell, *Leave to
Appeal Applications: The 1986–87 Term*, (1988) 10 Sup. Ct. L. Rev. 361; Bushnell,
Leave to Appeal Applications: The 1987–88 Term, (1989) 11 Sup. Ct. L. Rev. 383; and
*Supreme Court of Canada, Bulletin of Proceedings: (Special Edition) Statistics: 1992 to
2002* (Ottawa: Supreme Court of Canada, 2003), 5, 8.

The success rate for leave applications had been as high as 30 per cent
in the mid-1970s but has declined since that time. In 2002, approximately 13 per cent of applications for leave were granted. This means
that almost nine in ten persons seeking to have their case heard by the
Court are refused an audience.[16]

Flemming and Krutz found that the Court grants leave primarily on
the basis of jurisprudential concerns, such as whether the case involves
a *Charter* question or an otherwise novel issue. Conflicting opinions in
the lower courts and whether or not a governmental interest is involved
are also important criteria. Appeals solely involved with error correction, those that are fact specific, or those that would likely have limited

relevance to others are less likely to be heard. Non-jurisprudential criteria such as the status of the parties or their counsel have an effect, but these criteria are clearly secondary to the importance of the legal issues.[17] It would thus appear that the leave procedure – whether by design of the Court or of Parliament – results in cases coming before the Court that provide it with the opportunity to decide important issues. This gives the Court opportunities to be activist (or not), with a concomitant increase in the Court's power.

Applications for leave to appeal are initially vetted by the Court's clerks.[18] These clerks are not democratically elected – quite the contrary: their mode of selection ensures that they are not representative of the Canadian population. There is thus a persisting concern that the clerks may have 'an unwarranted influence on which cases' are chosen for hearing by the Court.[19] Leave applications are heard by panels of three Justices. In the event of a substantial breakdown of collegiality, the Court may need to move to the American system, where all nine justices screen the 'cert pool' of cases seeking leave to appeal.[20]

Another way in which persons interested in an issue can voice their concerns to the Court is through intervention in someone else's appeal. Various interest groups have used this avenue to put their submissions before the Court.[21] Approximately 90 per cent of applications to intervene are granted.[22] And more and more cases feature intervenors: under 10 per cent of cases in the mid-1970s compared to almost 40 per cent by 1990.[23] At one level, hearing a wide range of opinions strengthens the decision-making process.[24] But allowing special interest groups access can also make the Court appear political and subject to the influence of elite (left-leaning?) opinion makers.[25] Furthermore, given that the Court grants such a high percentage of intervention applications, refusal can be viewed as a political act, even a pre-judgment of the case. Intervenors often rely on government grants to fund their appearances before the Court; concern respecting activism may lead to increased funding for a different set of interest groups.

Ian Brodie writes that 'the Court uses the legitimacy supplied by interest groups that participate repeatedly in its work to expand its power.'[26] This is a risky strategy; the Court's reputation might suffer along with the reputation of one of these 'allies.' Morton and Knopff base their 'Court Party' critique on the Court's relationship with those seeking to effect change through the courts.[27] Access is power: witness the large amounts of money that can be obtained by granting access to the prime minister at a fundraising dinner. Granting or withholding access is a decision charged with political overtones and political consequences.[28]

Appeals are heard by the Court in panels of five, seven, or nine Judges. Prior to hearing oral argument, the panel members will have received facta (written summaries of the position of each party) together with copies of the exhibits and transcripts of the evidence at the trial court level. Usually they will also receive bound copies of the cases upon which counsel seek to rely.[29] There is often an informal meeting in chambers to discuss the case prior to oral argument. When the Court is in session, it typically hears two cases every day. Counsels' time limits are enforced by a system of lights. One or more Judges usually interrupt counsel to ask questions. After most hearings, the Judges retire to a conference room where each Judge, starting with the most junior, expresses his or her initial view and proposed outcome for the case. Typically, one Judge is chosen to write a draft opinion; if there is to be a dissent, another Judge is chosen to write the dissent.[30] Sometimes there are additional opinions. Drafts are then written, usually with some input from the Court's clerks, and are circulated to the other Justices for their comments. Occasionally a Justice will switch from majority to dissent or vice versa during this process. Where a Justice becomes incapacitated subsequent to the hearing, the Court's decision may be rendered by the remaining Justices or a rehearing may be ordered.

Since the time of Chief Justice Cartwright (1967–70), there have been efforts to control the number of opinions rendered in each case.[31] Academic calls for reform continue to focus on reducing the number of concurring opinions and on rendering the decision-making process more collegial.[32]

The Doctrine of *Stare Decisis*

The doctrine of *stare decisis et non quieta movere*, commonly shortened to *stare decisis*, holds that once a court decides a matter it is bound to decide similar cases in accordance with that precedent. Thus in *London Tramways* (1891), the House of Lords stated: 'A decision of this House once given upon a point of law is conclusive, upon this House afterwards, and it is impossible to raise that question again.'[33] Following precedents leads to certainty in the law; justice favours treating like cases in like manner.[34]

The strictness with which *stare decisis* is followed varies from jurisdiction to jurisdiction. The House of Lords, despite declaring itself free of a 'too rigid adherence to precedent' in its 1966 practice statement,[35] still only rarely departs from its prior decisions.[36] The Supreme Court of Canada departs somewhat more often. When it was first established in 1875, it carefully followed British precedent and studiously abided by the doctrine of *stare decisis*. Gradually, and especially after appeals to the Judicial Committee of the Privy Council were abolished, it showed a willingness to depart from precedent. Courts in the United States are more willing than their counterparts in Canada to overrule prior caselaw.[37] Prior judicial authority plays a less central role in civilian systems, though Quebec has arguably been influenced by its close proximity to the common law.[38]

The policy underpinnings of *stare decisis* rest on the desirability of certainty in the law and in the need for the primary locus of change in democracies to reside in the elected legislators, not with appointed judges. Certainty in the law promotes stability and order.[39] Uncertainty increases litigation and decreases the likelihood that parties will settle their disputes prior to a judicial decision being rendered.[40]

When judges fail to adhere to precedent, they risk usurping the role of the legislature, and government is in danger of being transformed from democracy into oligarchy. For example, the Supreme Court of Canada recently rewrote a portion of Nova Scotia's Workers' Compensation regulations effectively compelling the legislature to spend taxpayers' dollars in accord with the views of the Court.[41]

Issues of both uncertainty and usurpation are raised by *Lawrence v. Texas*, wherein the U.S. Supreme Court struck down a Texas statute that forbade sodomy between homosexuals. In doing so, the Court imposed its will on the democratically elected representatives of the people of Texas. However, if courts attempt to maintain the law static in the face of fundamental social change, they may cause instability instead of certainty.[42] Static law in a changing society will, sooner or later, become asinine. Indeed, U.S. Supreme Court Justice Thomas, even though he dissented in *Lawrence v. Texas*, felt that the anti-sodomy law was 'uncommonly silly.'[43]

Although the Supreme Court of Canada occasionally acknowledges that it makes law, it more typically describes itself as a custodian than as a creator. Thus, at least until recently, the Court has preferred to distinguish inconvenient precedents rather than to overrule them outright. At their worst, these distinctions are open to charges of intellectual dishonesty and prone to causing instability in and disrespect for the law.[44] Even at their best, they fill the law with a plethora of technical details and split hairs.[45]

The dilemma facing the Court lies in determining how long to wait for the legislature to act in the face of injustice. And the dilemma is not answered merely by accurately gauging public opinion: had the Supreme Court of Canada followed public opinion and expanded Mrs. Murdoch's property rights, widespread legislative reform of matrimonial law might not have occurred.[46] At least partly a result of the outcry that greeted *Murdoch v. Murdoch* Ontario passed the *Family Law Reform Act* in 1978 and made major amendments less than a decade later. Such a comprehensive code would have taken the Court half a century to formulate and another half-century to amend.

Notwithstanding these concerns, the Supreme Court of Canada is overturning established precedents more frequently and more rapidly than in the past. The first crack in the bedrock of *stare decisis*, which appeared in *Peda* (1969), was enlarged into a deep and abiding fissure in *Paquette* (1976), when the Court reversed its forty-year-old ruling in *Dunbar*.[47] Major shifts in the law of real estate damages, evidence, and other areas followed.[48] The Court's willingness to reverse its own judgments is not confined to old and hoary precedent; *Morin* (1992) reversed *Askov* (1990), which had been decided less than two years earlier.[49]

The Court's more recent practice of overruling unsatisfactory precedents outright has the advantage of being more transparent, but it calls the whole idea of *stare decisis* into question. The common law is supposed to advance by tiny evolutionary phases – by incremental steps, not by revolutionary moments.

The common law, particularly as described by Hart and his disciples, rests, to a substantial degree, on a foundation of *stare decisis*. But before we start drafting an epitaph for the common law, we would do well to remember that decisions in which the law is overruled outright or distinguished into oblivion are quite rare. These cases constitute less than 4 per cent of the docket of the Supreme Court of Canada. Notwithstanding their rarity, there are two important reasons to study these cases systematically. First, the methods used by the Court to avoid its previous rulings, or to effect a change in the law, are important subjects for study as part of an effort to test or formulate theories of legal reasoning or jurisprudence. Anomalies often yield more insight than do ordinary cases.[50] Second, the fact that the Court is overruling precedents more frequently, and more transparently, has political and constitutional implications.

Steps Taken to Survey Supreme Court of Canada Cases

I surveyed all cases reported in the Supreme Court Reports from 1950 to 2003. My search into the Court's history had indicated that almost all of the Court's decisions were reported in the S.C.R. and that by 1970 all cases were reported in this official reporter, and I confirmed this with the S.C.R.'s publisher. I did in-depth studies on cases reported in S.C.R. volumes for the years 1952, 1962, 1972, 1982, 1992, and 2002. Cases reported in 1987 and 1997 were added to facilitate the comparison of cases where the Court's decision was based on the *Charter of Rights and Freedoms* with non-*Charter* cases. Cases in 1977 were included to complete certain data sets.

I also surveyed the literature, particularly the work of Peter Mc-Cormick, and I have included some of those statistics where relevant. An article by Madame Justice Wilson postulated four sets of adjudicative tensions under which the Court functions; I attempted to determine which tension had the most pull with the court.

The survey was actually three surveys. The first covered all the court's decisions rendered between 1950 and 2002. While initially I was primarily interested in tracking cases in which the Court had changed the law by overruling precedent, I was also making note of other phenomena worthy of study.

During this first survey, I measured the incidence of overrulings, hard distinguishing, and close calls. *Hard distinguishing* refers to cases where the court's reasoning is open to question, and *close calls* indicate substantial disagreement among the Justices. All three terms will be described in more detail *infra*. I noted all criteria that seemed to have had an impact on the result and prepared a description of all prominent criteria and characteristics. When I reached 1980, I started to track those decisions in which the Court was unanimous.[51]

Starting in 1984, when the Court decided its first *Charter* cases, I separated *Charter* from non-*Charter* cases to enable testing of Hart's theorem that the law's hard core would expand and its soft penumbra contract over time. I ultimately decided to extend my study until the end of 2003 to give myself four five-year periods of *Charter* jurisprudence to analyse.

I restricted my subsequent surveys to one year per decade, years ending in '2' – the 'terrible twos.' During the second survey, I analysed the proportion of fact, law, and policy in the Court's jurisprudence as well as the modes of reasoning it employed. I added the Court's decisions in 1987 and 1997 to this survey to facilitate comparisons between *Charter* and non-*Charter* cases. I added cases from 1977 to better pinpoint the period during which the proportion of policy surpassed the proportion of fact in the Court's reasons.

My third survey arose out of a spreadsheet I compiled to compare the various and competing jurisprudential theories. This spreadsheet listed each theoretical proposition along with a prediction of what the indicators I had tracked in the second survey would show. To complete my analysis, I selected five binary sets that would be useful to test which theories, if any, had any empirical validity and the extent of any such validity. These sets were designed to measure the extent to which each pole of the set was present in the Court's reasoning. The sets were: (1) the extent to which the Court propounded and applied *bright line* tests as opposed to *open standards*; (2) the extent to which the Court preferred utilizing narrower *propositions* to more expansive *principles*; (3) the division between *foundational* and *non-foundational* reasoning; (4) the extent to' which issues fell inside the *core* or further out in the *penumbra*; (5) and whether the law provided a *clear answer* or left a *choice* open to the Court. I then repeated my 'terrible twos' decade survey to track these criteria. The categorization of *Charter*/non-*Charter* was used to attempt to contrast the Court's handling of *Charter* issues with more 'traditional' ones.

While some of the variables or indicia of the Court's behaviour tracked in this survey were straightforward, others required a substantial amount of personal judgment on my part. For example, the number of pages of reasons rendered per case required little more than elementary arithmetic, but the calculation of the degree to which policy, as opposed to law, determined the Court's decision required me, based on my knowledge and experience, to asses what the relative determinants were. It is therefore appropriate to briefly describe my background. I graduated from law school twenty-odd years ago and established a successful practice in civil and criminal litigation. The decision of judges, both trial and appellate, daily determined my clients' affairs either directly through their judgments or indirectly through their reasonings about the affairs of strangers. Predicting the behaviour of judges was thus central to my daily activities. In conducting my survey, I pulled back from that experience to study the behaviour of judges from the more theoretical and global perspective of academe. Several of the tests that I formulated as part of the data-collection process arose out of the normative ideals I hold with respect to legal practice. These norms include a belief that transactions should be transparent and forthright (people should mean what they say and say what they mean), that legislatures should, in the absence of clear constitutional restraints, be superior to courts, and that there should be a substantial degree of certainty and coherence in the law.

Close calls required only a simple tally of the proportion of judges in the majority and those in dissent; thus the accuracy of this statistic is not open to question. Hard distinguishing, on the other hand, required me to form an opinion as to whether the Court's reasoning was, or was not, open to question. The task was made all the more difficult by the presumption that the justices who rendered the opinions believed that their reasoning was beyond reproach.

Cases of overruling fall somewhere in the middle. Many instances of overruling are explicitly acknowledged by the judges deciding the case. Others are recognized in subsequent cases or in the academic literature. But where the Court did not explicitly acknowledge the overruling, it was necessary for me to determine whether the judgment constituted an overruling. The Court never acknowledges hard distinguishing but rather attempts to justify these decisions as being in accord with prior caselaw; whether a case constituted hard distinguishing always required the application of judgment. I laboured to be fair, and cases that are arguably on the borderline have been carefully scrutinized. Cases that did not admit of firm characterization were excluded from the study.

In order to guard against my own prejudices, I conducted each survey as a block and did not total up the various types of cases until I had completed each segment of the survey. For example, I did not total the number of cases involving formal legal reasoning until I had surveyed all the cases in 1952, 1962, 1972, 1982, 1992, and 2002 in this regard.

Thus, while many of these categories involve an element of subjectivity, I employed several strategies to make these judgment calls as objective as possible. First, I adopted an attitude of rigorous good faith in that I adhered strictly to my definitions and endeavoured to avoid skewing the results to accord with any of the theories I had studied. Second, I completed each survey in as short a timeframe as possible to ensure that I maintained the same point of view. Third, with respect to overrulings, I compared my findings with reviews of the cases in the literature. Fourth, in several instances my findings were corroborated by other findings in my survey. Fifth, I performed statistical comparisons of *Charter* and non-*Charter* cases to establish the statistical significance of the differences that I had noted. These significant differences buttress the more qualitative differences I noted. Lastly, I selected a very large sample of cases; thus any mistakes should be diluted to the point where they will not influence the overall results.

Because, this study relies largely on the reasons for judgment delivered by the Court, a methodological problem should be borne in mind: it is possible that these reasons do not accurately or completely represent the Justices' reasoning processes. Any deficiency in accuracy and completeness is likely not intended by the Justices. There may in fact be no such deficiency. However, if there is a deficiency, it may mask a variety of phenomena including outright corruption, results-based reasoning, a desire to appear erudite, a striving for acceptance by judicial and legal communities, a desire to veil the Court's activism, and a lapse in logic. I should emphasize that I have nowhere found evidence of corruption on the Court; indeed, much evidence exists indicating that no such corruption exists or has ever existed. On the other hand, many Justices appeared aware of the criticisms levelled at them and at the Court and may have changed their behaviour as a result of such criticsm. Thus, rhetoric, and a desire to shore up the defensibility of its reasoning, may mask the Court's real reasons for its decisions.[52] Justices may decide cases based on certain criteria but explain the decision using different criteria.[53] This lack of accurate articulation often leads to incoherent caselaw, notwithstanding that the actual decisions may have all been rendered on the same (and therefore objectively neutral) bases. I have attempted to avoid this methodological problem in two ways. First, I have used trends from many cases dealing with a wide range of issues. Second, I have compared and supplemented my survey with anecdotal evidence. For example, the recent book by Sharpe and Roach documents a Court wrestling, in good faith, with difficult issues.[54]

Other investigators may make different assessments than I made, especially in individual cases. However, the large sample sizes employed in this survey likely reduced the effect of my individual perspective. If I was prone to see law where others see policy, this tendency should have been as pronounced when I read reasons rendered in 2002 as when I read those rendered in 1952. Since it is primarily trends, and not individual cases, which are being analysed, the fact that the surveyor's knowledge, skill, and point of view have remained constant should ensure a high degree of consistency and reliability.

3 Beginning to Close the Empirical Gap

The Gap and Why It Persists

Examples of jurisprudential allegations include Hart's contention that law is characterized by an expanding core of settled meaning and Roach's conclusion that *RJR-Macdonald v. Canada* (1995) 'did not mark the abandonment of the more deferential approach.'[1] Despite the fact that systematic investigation was available to test these allegations, neither author ventured the attempt. Empirical analysis discloses that Hart's contention is only partially correct and that Roach's conclusion is likely inaccurate.[2]

The empirical gap in jurisprudence persists because jurists claim that empirical analysis is difficult. Some authors cite the overwhelming scope of the task as their reason for not seeking to verify their theorizations.[3] Others cite potential methodological barriers.[4] These concerns ought not to be allowed to prevail. The discovery of rules of genetic heredity required detailed studies over many generations. No Boy Scout would set out without a magnetic compass even though its indications of the direction of the North Pole are imprecise.

The two leading texts cited in chapter 1, Hart's *The Concept of Law* and Dworkin's *Law's Empire*, cite only seventeen and fifty-one cases, respectively. These cases are chosen to buttress the authors' conclusions and are clearly not part of any investigation into judicial behaviour. These small samples are typical of jurisprudential writing. If the behaviour of judges parallels that of most human behaviour, it follows a bell curve with the most frequent behaviours occurring in the centre and the most infrequent behaviours occurring in the tails. There is little in this extant jurisprudential method that would prevent the representation of infrequent, uncommon, and extraordinary judicial behaviour as usual, common, and habitual. Fifty-one cases would fit comfortably in either tail of the bell curve.

Only a large systematic sample is a proper basis on which to describe judicial behaviour, both routine and exceptional. My sample of cases is almost one-hundred times the size of the fifty-one cases cited by Dworkin. In addition, by surveying all the cases from one court, my sample is more representative by several orders of magnitude.

While H.L.A. Hart, like Sigmund Freud, can be criticized for the limited sample upon which he constructed his theory, Hart at least attempted a 'descriptive sociology' of jurisprudence.[5] On the other hand, Joseph Raz, a well-known jurisprude, declined even the attempt:

> My observations are meant to be faithful to the accepted theory of the practice rather than to the practice itself. Their aim is to explain the way judges and legal scholars regard the working of the doctrine of precedent. *Only an empirical study* going well beyond the examination of the law reports could reveal to what extent the actual practice conforms to these theories.[6]

This quote is noteworthy both for its candid admission of the narrow scope and once-removed character of the typical jurisprudential inquiry and for the salutary note of caution at the end.

Note that Raz, like almost all other jurisprudes, does not even attempt a systematic study of the law reports. The empirical gap exists because initial investigatory steps have not been taken. Once the first step is taken, the journey can begin. The first step towards an empirical examination of jurisprudence is to compile and analyse the available evidence. And there is available evidence aplenty in the law reports.

Another problem standing in the way of empirical studies is an excessive concern with methodological purity, which tends to severely curtail the number of empirical legal studies. For example, while Duncan Kennedy concedes the value of the study of appellate decisions, he worries that it will be impossible to establish the true nature of judicial constraint.[7] He is also concerned that it will be extremely difficult to formulate the 'external definitions' necessary for verification and that, even if these can be formulated other jurists will not support his definitions.[8] He therefore eschews the empirical path. Similar concerns must have bedevilled those imprisoned in Plato's mythical cave; their prior experience gave them every reason to fear that any new observations would not be acceptable to the historical ontology of their mates.

To reiterate: I believe that Raz and Kennedy were wrong to decline to apply empirical methods to the study of jurisprudence and wrong to discourage others from the attempt.

I maintain that legal scholars should courageously strike out on the empirical path. If they find something, even if that thing is not crystal clear or permanently definitive, the journey will have been worthwhile. The alternative is to restrict legal scholarship to the 'black letter mentality that ... maintains legal study as an inward-looking and self-contained discipline.'[9] Knees will be skinned, through sometimes stinging criticism, along the path, but legal scholars will pick themselves up again and forge forward.

Overcoming Methodological Pitfalls

While there have been some limited efforts to narrow the empirical gap, most of these have had limited success as a result of several common methodological errors. These errors include the following:

- Many jurists use a small and unsystematically selected sample. This leads to the risk of mistaking cases at the tail end of the bell curve as being representative of the whole universe of cases.
- Authors often fail to cite contrary authority or examples, contrary to the mandates of scientific enquiry and the rules of professional conduct.[10]
- Many jurists neglect to study change over time. Legal reasoning in the 1950s is portrayed as being the same as that in the 1990s.

The last point deserves emphasis. Much jurisprudential writing treats judicial decision making as static. No one has systematically traced the changing trends relative to the manner in which courts decide cases. Courts are often said to rule and reason today in the same manner as they did half a century ago. This is grave error. The manner in which courts resolve disputes has changed dramatically over time. Descriptions that were valid in 1950, or even in 1980, would not accurately represent courts' behaviour in 2003. Today courts use a much wider variety of methods than they did in the past. Some authors perceive differences in the way that different judges decide cases, often pointing to historically exceptional judges such as Learned Hand, Cardozo, Denning, or Holmes.[11] But even here there is no sense that there has been an across-the-board shift in the manner in which courts decide cases. A sense that the context in which issues emerged has changed is somewhat more common, as is an amorphous notion that what passes for 'law' has changed. Historical reviews of jurisprudence, such as Weiler's *In the Last Resort*, often relate an impression of change, but there is nowhere a systematic examination of *how* the Court's decision-making processes have changed over time.[12]

Further methodological pitfalls results from the tendency of investigators to use the tools they are familiar with and to ignore other modes of study. The Arthurs's *Law and Learning* report advocated that legal theory should be examined from numerous perspectives.[13] Carpenters have hammers, saws, and screwdrivers; jurists should also develop a wide variety of tools. Empirical investigation should proceed from as many directions as possible. This will harness synergies and dampen the effect of errors.

Another potential methodological pitfall arises from investigator bias. Robert Moles charged that jurists functioning under Hart's paradigm would ignore important evidence because the presumptions under which they were operating would direct their attention away from important judicial decisions where the law was not 'clear':

> We have seen how someone adopting [Hart's theories] would be required to state that some of the most important decisions in modern jurisprudence are either aberrant or wrong. To put [it] in Kuhn's terms, a paradigm directs the attention of the group which embraces it, and my claim is that for those who embrace the Hartian paradigm, their attention is directed away from those important judicial decisions which have a significant bearing on the direction of law. Just as the natural scientist will fail to observe facts which fail to fit the theory with which he is working, so the legal scientist will either fail to see or will in some other way marginalize those cases which fail to conform to the paradigm with which he is working.[14]

It may well be that paradigm partisanship plays a part in the robust persistence of the Hartian world view. As discussed in the next section, there are good reasons for the persistence of paradigm partisanship in favour of Hart's positivism. Part of the goal of this study is to determine whether this partisanship is warranted.

Other paradigms might skew data in the opposite direction: a non-foundationalist paradigm might downplay the importance of the majority of cases where formal legal reasoning provides a straightforward answer. Anti-foundationalists would ignore the substantial order that law provides to the affairs of the vast majority of citizens such that they can, for the most part, avoid resort to the courts altogether.

But each of these paradigms organizes vast tracts of data; possible paradigm bias ought not to be used as an excuse to forgo the systematic analysis of jurisprudential phenomena. Thomas Kuhn postulated that our habits of scientific perception and thinking would undergo periodic dramatic shifts. These shifts are precipitated when the prevailing paradigm of perception, thought, and habit is challenged by a critical mass of increasingly inconvenient anomalies. This challenge forces a search for, and eventual adoption of, a new paradigm better capable of explaining and ordering the new information represented by the anomalies.[15] These anomalies gain meaning only in the context of the prevailing paradigm. Testing requires something to test.

In Kuhnian terms, foundational positivism is the prevailing paradigm of legal practitioners. Anti-foundationalists and critical legal scholars of one sort or another have delighted in exposing anomalies that cannot be easily explained by the prevailing positivist paradigm. Studies by supporters of the prevailing paradigm have also uncovered anomalies. My survey evidence should either explain some of these anomalies or uncover new ones. These anomalies will indicate areas where theoretical modification (or radical reconfiguration) is called for.

Closing the Gap

Given the advantages of formulating and then testing the most widely entrenched paradigm, my initial approach was to continue the current trend in jurisprudence towards attempting to support an overall foundational theory of legal reasoning. Foundational theories are attractive because they seek to explain a broad range of behaviour and because they have the potential to provide a basis for prediction. In many ways anti-foundationalism is non-theory, is the abandonment of the process of theory formulation. Therefore, at the level of theory, foundationalism will usually prove superior to anti-foundationalism because, as critical legal scholar Duncan Kennedy concedes, 'you can't beat something with nothing.'[16] The scientific method requires that theories be formulated and tested. Non-foundational critiques provide valuable insights into anomalies and other aspects of foundational theory that are most in need of being tested. If the analysis of the evidence only partially supports a foundational theory, it may better support a non-foundational theory. If the evidence supports neither foundational nor non-foundational theories, it will likely describe the extent to which anti-foundationalism is an accurate description of judicial behaviour.

Jurisprudence has generated a large number of well-thought-out legal theories. I submit that it is time to begin the process of putting these theories to the test. Criticism at the level of theory is only the first step. For example, anti-foundationalists have criticized the shortcomings of foundational theory but their analysis has been restricted to the theoretical level. Most views of science described above would prescribe empirical testing as the next step. This second step requires systematically assembling evidence capable of supporting or refuting one or more theories.

The Standard of Proof

Law employs two fundamental standards of proof. In a criminal case, the prosecution must prove, beyond a reasonable doubt, that the accused committed the crime. In civil litigation involving private disputes, a more relaxed standard is employed. Here plaintiffs need merely prove their case on a balance of probabilities. If the version of the facts propounded by the plaintiff is more likely than the version propounded by the defendant, the plaintiff is entitled to succeed. In ordinary decision making, most people use a range of standards: balance of probabilities is fine for choosing a brand of cookies, but there should be no doubt that one's parachute is properly packed.

In this book, I will be employing the civil standard of proof. While some findings, such as the statistical differences between the Supreme Court of Canada's *Charter* and non-*Charter* jurisprudence, are supportable beyond a reasonable doubt, others are not. Overall, our task is to come closer to accurate descriptions and reliable predictions. Empirical methods will accomplish our task more efficaciously than non-empirical ones.

An Empirical Study: Scope and Limits

Some investigators, notably Gregory Sisk and Michael Heise, limit the term *empirical* to quantitative studies.[17] I maintain that all studies that systematically compile and analyse large data sets are empirical. Some of the indicators I studied are quantitative; others have important qualitative components. My study of the Supreme Court of Canada is empirical because it attempts to test theories based on methodically gathered evidence.

Each indicator, such as the rate of overruling, provides a useful tool with which to empirically analyse the Court's behaviour. The weight assigned to each indicator will depend on several factors. Ease of verifiability, most prominent in the arithmetically calculated variables, increases the weight that an indicator can bear. Variables that corroborate each other, such as those that duplicate a crossover or follow a similar trend-line, provide mutual support and thus can collectively bear more weight than each could singly. The weight of each indicator is relevant to whether it has tipped the balance-of-probabilities scale.

My analysis employs each indicator with a view to supporting or refuting a variety of binary opposites. Many theories describe adjudication as a set of nuanced and varied phenomena, but, for the purposes of comparison and testing, it is necessary to formulate binary opposites. When testing theories postulated by various jurists, I therefore utilized Max Weber's concept of the *ideal type* to describe the essential elements of various schools of jurisprudence and the works of its leading philosophers.[18] As such, many works have been stripped of arguably important nuances to facilitate comparisons and empirical verification. This process allowed me to examine the main thrust of theorists, not the many sometimes obscure parsings of their writings. I ask the reader to forgive these binary constructions as I believe them to be essential steps to explaining the rationale for some of the steps in this study. Empirical testing, especially of the quantitative variety, often requires division into black and white. Debate needs to be focused into two, or at most three, opposing propositions to formulate a test. Nuance, or grey, can then be reintroduced into the analysis of the resultant data.

This study goes beyond the scope of writings typified in by Raz above in that it studies the practice of judges rather than contenting itself with a dissection of the accepted theory of that practice. It starts with a broadly based examination of the law reports for the data used to document and analyse jurisprudential trends. It then builds on this examination by combining measurements of a large and systematically selected sample of cases and tracks and analyses trends in legal reasoning. Anecdotal sources are employed to move this study an additional further step beyond a mere examination of the law reports. Research utilizing behaviourism, attitudinalism, and institutionalism is integrated into the analysis.

Examining the Issues, Testing the Theories

To close this introductory section, I outline the major judicial issues that will be analysed in section 2 and the means by which theories of jurisprudence will be tested in section 3. A recurring issue in jurisprudence is the extent to which law is an objective or neutral method of making decisions as opposed to merely a species of political decision-making. Chapter 4 analyses the respective extent to which legal propositions, particular facts, and overarching policy considerations have influenced the decisions of the Supreme Court of Canada. If policy concerns prevail over legal rules, law's claim to autonomy is diminished.

Chapter 5 describes the various modes of legal reasoning employed by the Court. Hartian positivism describes courts as functioning within the parameters of formal legal reasoning. Chapter 5 tracks the extent to which other, less foundational, modes are on the rise. This trend has important implications for legal theory and law's autonomy.

Hart describes legal adjudication as increasing the size of the core of settled meaning. When the Courts overrules precedent, it challenges this notion and raises the spectre that any legal proposition is open to change. Precedent departure is also relevant to the Supreme Court's role in Canadian society, particularly with respect to the issue of judicial activism. Chapter 6 therefore tracks the cases in which the Court has overturned a prior decision.

Precedent departures comprise overruling, hard distinguishing, and, to a lesser extent, ordinary distinguishing. Overruling occurs when the Court declines to follow a prior precedent.[20] Most of the time this is done in an explicit fashion, such as in *Ancio* (1984). When a prior precedent is distinguished, the Court is indicating that it should continue to be followed, subject to the gloss that the distinguishing case places on it. Occasionally the Court distinguishes precedents on bases that are open to question. Differences between the precedent and the case at bar may be difficult to fathom. I have labelled this questionable behaviour 'hard distinguishing' and analyse it to test the soundness of the adjudicative processes of the Supreme Court. Will an analysis of these departures from *stare decisis* support the non-foundational or the anti-foundational thesis, or, in some counterintuitive fashion, will they ultimately support a foundational theory?

Chapter 7 tracks qualitative changes in the Court's reasoning by tracing changes in the proportions of bright-line and open-standard tests, of propositions and principles, of solidly established and penumbral legal issues, and of foundational and non-foundational reasoning in the Court's jurisprudence. The proportion of cases wherein the law appeared to provide a clear answer and those in which new issues were raised for the first time were also traced over time. These trends are relevant to legal theory, law's autonomy (or lack thereof), and the extent to which the Court is free of legal constraints during its decision-making process.

Chapter 8 summarizes Canadian and American investigations of the degree to which judicial decisions are based on the law and the degree to which they are based on the political ideology of individual judges.

The proportion of decisions wherein the Court was unanimous or where it was badly split ('close calls') was tracked over time to determine the Court's cohesiveness and the extent to which its process was providing broadly supported decisions.

There are several important differences in the way the Court treats cases involving the *Charter of Rights and Freedoms* and those that do not involve the *Charter*. These differences, which are described in chapter 9, are relevant to issues relating to legal theory, especially Hart's expanding core of settled meaning, and to the Court's place in the Canadian polity.

The data described in chapters 4 through 9 will be used as the basis for the discussions contained in the concluding section of this book. Chapter 10 discusses the information gathered during this study and uses them to attempt to verify or refute several jurisprudential theories. Can positivism survive as a viable paradigm? If the answer is in the negative, the data should indicate which other theories of adjudication, extant or as yet unformulated, might be capable of surviving critical analysis.

In chapter 11, I use the data to analyse whether law is an objective and neutral process or, as its critics contend, law merely masks the making of political choices.

Chapter 12 will apply the data to the swirling controversy over whether the Court is too activist or whether it is failing to perform its proper constitutional role. The task undertaken is to discover whether empirical study will support or refute the criticisms which have been directed towards the Court.

Whatever their point of view, scholars tend to view their mandate as requiring them to be critical of the Court. Beatty bemoans the Court's timidity in upholding the constitution.[21] On the other hand, Manfredi points to a trend towards 'judicial supremacy.'[22] He worries that the Court

has shown little restraint in building up its own powers of judicial review or in asserting its own pre-eminent authority over the development of

> *Charter*-related constitutional principles ... While it may be appropriate for
> the Court to be final in defining fundamental constitutional principles (a
> proposition which is debatable), it is less clear that it should be final in
> determining the political and policy consequences that flow from those
> principles.[23]

Weiler calls on the Court to show more imagination and to exercise more creativity.[24] Morton and Knopff accuse it of an anti-democratic arrogation of power to itself.[25] Roach recently put the Court on trial and called for a strengthened dialogue between the judicial and democratic branches of government.[26]

The manner in which the Court arrives at its decisions also impinges on the debate over activism. Foundational formal legal reasoning is usually felt to be more consistent with the subordinate role of the judiciary in a democracy: judges should apply the law and leave policy formulation and political choices to the legislature. Non-foundational reasoning would allow the judiciary more input. Anti-foundationalist theories appear to permit judges to disregard the will of the legislature.

As with other areas of jurisprudence, the literature respecting the Court's activism is rife with poorly substantiated opinion. Careful analysis is, more often than not, displaced by polemics. The findings from the surveys described herein, as well as other data specifically collected for the purpose, will be used to analyse the level of the Court's activism and the implications arising therefrom. Chapter 12 thus constitutes a specific example of the value of the empirical study of jurisprudence.

SECTION II

Measuring the Court's Decisions

4 Fact, Law, and Policy

Definitions

There are three primary elements in judicial decision making: fact, law, and policy. The facts encompass what actually happened, especially the acts, deeds, or events in issue. That part of a decision wherein the court is deciding whether the traffic light was green, amber, or red when the defendant entered the intersection deals with fact. A case high in *fact* is one that was decided by its facts. This means that, to the indicated extent, determining what the facts were determined the outcome of the case. To a lesser extent it may also indicate that the special facts of the case (e.g., an especially sympathetic taxpayer) influenced its outcome. In cases high in fact, there is often a dispute among the sitting Judges as to what the facts were. Cases high in fact also read as if they were decisions being rendered by a trial judge: the Court is attempting to determine the facts, and it is clear that this determination will decide the outcome of the case.

The law provides rules that govern our actions. These rules are established in legislative enactment or laid down in caselaw. In this survey, the category *law* indicates the extent to which the Court relied upon the available statutes, prior caselaw, or legal doctrines in arriving at its conclusion. A case high in law is one where the facts were well-established and the application of the law provided a clear answer to the issue raised – that is, once the facts were proved, the law provided an obvious answer. Law in this sense is primarily 'black-letter' law. Law may also involve the interpretation or application of a legal standard. When the Court has to determine what the law is, its decision is usually a mix of law and policy (see the discussion of doctrinal reconciliation and expanded contextual interpretation in the next chapter, pages 51–3, 55, and 60–1).

When the Court ventures into the area of policy, it typically balances a variety of factors as it searches for the general purpose behind the law. In this process, it sometimes disregards the literal meaning of a statute. The category *policy* indicates that the Court arrived at its decision based on the perceived possible impacts of its decision on Canadian society. Policy concerns itself with the way in which the instant decision meshes with other social functions and laws. In such situations the Court is determining what the law should be. Common policies promulgated by the Supreme Court of Canada include the protection of individual autonomy and freedom of contract, the promotion of industrial peace, and the safeguarding of human rights.

Law is a deductive process that looks to past decisions; policy looks forward to future consequences.

Where issues are decided on the basis of mixed fact and law – for example, where the Court is determining whether the defendant was negligent – there will be an apportionment between the fact and law categories. Similarly, where the Court is applying open-ended tests, such as the *Charter* equality test in *Law v. Canada (Minister of Employment and Immigration)* (1999), there will be an apportionment between the categories of law and policy.

Commentators generally assert that the Supreme Court bases its decisions exclusively on law and policy. The continuing intrusion of factual questions into its deliberations calls this assertion into question.

Proportions of Fact/Law/Policy

The results from the completed survey show that the proportion of fact, law, and policy has undergone important changes over time: the proportion of fact has declined while that of policy increased. The relative proportions of fact, law and policy in the Supreme Court of Canada are illustrated in figure 4.1. The declining significance of factual and the rise of policy considerations is even more apparent in figure 4.2. Note, in figure 4.2, the crossover between policy and fact in 1982. To attempt to better understand this finding, I added the years 1977, 1987 and 1997 to the existing data and completed the same survey on all cases in those years. There was relatively little change between 1972 and 1977, making it clear that the crossover happened fairly close to 1982. While the

Figure 4.1. Decade-to decade changes in fact, law, and policy considerations, Supreme Court of Canada, 1952–2002

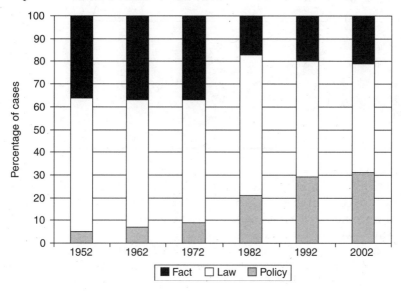

Figure 4.2. Decade-to decade changes in fact, law, and policy considerations, Supreme Court of Canada, 1952–2002

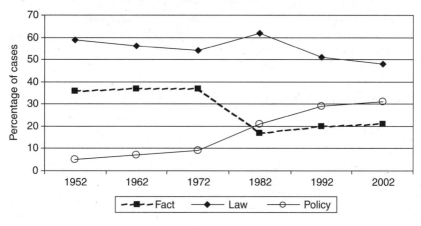

Table 4.1. Fact, law, and policy considerations, Supreme Court of
Canada, 1952–2002, including years 1977, 1987, 1997

	Fact	Law	Policy
1952	36	59	5
1962	37	56	7
1972	37	54	9
1977	36	55	9
1982	17	62	21
1987	15	67	18
1992	20	51	29
1997	18	60	22
2002	21	48	31

results for 1987 and 1997 do not maintain the same division between
policy and fact, it is clear that after 1982 the Court consistently used
policy grounds more than factual ones to decide its cases. The data for
all nine years are reproduced in table 4.1.

Note also the trend between 1997 and 2002, in which the Court relies
more on policy considerations and less on legal precedent. The effect of
this trend is cumulative: once the Court has articulated a policy and
inserted it into the caselaw, that policy becomes enshrined in precedent.
A later Court following the original policy decision would be applying
law, not policy.[1] Therefore figures 4.1 and 4.2 and table 4.1 understate
rather than overstate the role of policy in the Supreme Court of Canada.

As one moves down the judicial hierarchy, there is more reliance on
fact and less on policy in deciding cases. As well, policy concerns in the
two lower courts tend to be more implicit, as opposed to explicit. Figure
4.3 illustrates the differences in the proportion of fact, law, and policy
for the Supreme Court of Canada and two lower courts in Ontario for
decisions rendered in 2002.

Examples in the Caselaw

A good example of a Supreme Court of Canada case in which *fact* was
pre-eminent is *R. v. Cowan* (1962). The Court split 3–2 over whether the
accused solicitor had his client's authority to deal with a cheque. There
was extensive quotation of the trial transcript.

An example of sympathy – apart from personal injury cases, where
the Court's compassion towards the plaintiff is often palpable – is the
income tax case of *Beament* (1952). A solicitor who had volunteered for

Figure 4.3. Proportion of fact, law, and policy, Supreme Court of Canada and Ontario's Court of Appeal and Superior Court, 2002

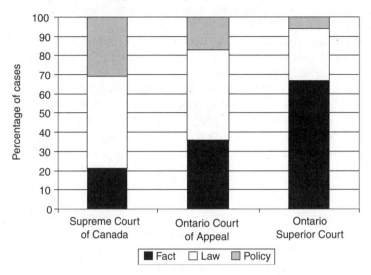

Source: The data for the Ontario Court of Appeal were based on a survey in which I used the QuickLaw Ontario Reports (O.R.) database, which yielded 173 Court of Appeal decisions. This number was reduced to 50, using a random number generator. The decisions in this database have been preselected by the O.R.'s editors, presumably to emphasize decisions featuring points of law and policy and to deemphasize fact. I attempted a similar procedure for the Superior Court but found that QuickLaw's ORP database yielded decisions from the Divisional Court and Small Claims and Family Courts as well as from the Superior Court proper. I therefore chose the Canadian Legal Information Institute's database of Ontario Superior Court decisions for 2002. Regrettably these decisions were not numbered, so a random number generator was not feasible. My sample size thus ballooned to 118 cases. Cases too short for reliable classification were discarded. Most, but not all, motion, application, and appeal decisions were discarded, as I wanted the sample to focus on trial decisions.

military service in the Second World War was held to be ordinarily resident in Canada during a period in which he was in England with his English wife and their children. The taxpayer's military service and the fact that he had left a lucrative legal practice was commented on more than once.

Fact-driven cases continued to be common until the late 1970s. In *Amos v. New Brunswick Electric Power Commission* (1977), the Supreme Court reversed the Court of Appeal and restored a trial finding of negligence. The case turned on whether the defendant should have foreseen that the plaintiff, a young boy, might climb a tree through which an electric cable ran and thus cause one of its branches to touch the cable.

The more recent case of *Gronnerud* (2002) involves a split of 45 per cent fact, 40 per cent law, and 15 per cent policy. The Supreme Court upheld the Court of Appeal's reversal of a trial judgment. The case turned in large part on the wishes of a mother prior to the onset of Alzheimer's disease and the facts surrounding potential conflicts of interest respecting the administration of her estate. In addition, there was an extensive review of the law of guardianship (both litigation and property), and refinements to this law were informed by a policy analysis.

Gronnerud is not a completely isolated instance. In *Housen v. Nikolaisen* (2002), the Court split five-four in reversing the Court of Appeal and reinstating the trial judge's division of liability among the defendants. The issue was one of mixed law and fact; the various views of facts held by the Justices were significant in the outcome of the case. Other 2002 cases where the facts played a significant role in the outcome include *Heredi v. Fensom*, *R. v. Hibbert* and *St. Jean v. Mercier*.

Law continues to provide the Court with the most guidance in arriving at its decisions. For example, in *Registrar of Motor Vehicles (Ontario) v. Canadian American Transfer Limited* (1972), a unanimous Court simply referred to an earlier case delineating the respective federal and provincial jurisdiction over highways in respect of interprovincial trade to interpret the scope of the *Public Commercial Vehicles Act*. In *373409 Alberta Ltd. (Receiver of) v. Bank of Montreal* (2002), the facts were not in dispute and the law of bills of exchange decided the case.

In *R. v. Cook* (1997), the Court was faced with a situation in which the Crown had obtained a conviction despite not having called the victim of the assault as a witness. *Lemay* (1952) had indicated that the Crown was fixed with a duty of fairness in this regard. The court reconciled this duty of fairness with *Charter* jurisprudence respecting the obligation of the Crown to disclose information respecting all known witnesses, and held that the Crown's duty of fairness had been met via disclosure. I found that the result was determined 70 per cent via this analysis of the law, while the facts surrounding the trial contributed 20 per cent, and policy relative to Crown discretion in the conduct of criminal trials contributed the remaining 10 per cent.

The categorization was more evenly split in *Carosella* (1997). A discussion of the law surrounding disclosure in the context of the clinical records of a victim of sexual assault, which had been destroyed by the therapeutic centre, absorbed most of the Court's energy (45 per cent). However, there was a substantial discussion of the policy implications of the therapeutic centre's attempt to shield victims from having their therapeutic discussions revealed to their attackers (35 per cent). The facts of the case, including the centre's policy and the particular victim's willingness to consent to production, also played a part (20 per cent).

In the early 1950s, *policy* concerns played only a very small part in the Court's reasoning, but *Industrial Acceptance Corp. v. Lalonde* (1952) nevertheless provides an early example of a decision dominated by policy considerations. Here, the Court decided that the *Bankruptcy Act*'s policy of facilitating the rehabilitation of the bankrupt required a discharge despite the bankrupt's misconduct.[2]

In *Winnipeg Child and Family Services (Northwest Area) v. D.F.G* (1997), policy considerations suggested that a pregnant woman should not be restrained from ingesting solvents that might harm her fetus. The majority's view was that the policy of a woman's autonomy should have precedence over the welfare of the child, the policy concern favoured by the minority. Fact accounted for 5 per cent, law for 55 per cent, and policy accounted for 40 per cent of the court's reasoning. The issue of abortion provided an important subtext when weighing the rights of a woman and the welfare of the fetus.

Idziak v. Canada (1992) is a case where the result turned on almost equal proportions of fact, law, and policy. The appellant, who was contesting his extradition, presented a sympathetic factual basis for his appeal. This contributed to the Court upholding his right to proceed via *habeas corpus* with *certiorari* in aid on a generous and flexible footing. Law led to the final steps in the decision: (a) the minister had the right to preserve the confidentiality of the memo containing the legal advice that she had received, and (b) she had acted within bounds of the statute. The case is important both for its defence of the right to *habeas corpus* and *certiorari* and for its extradition holding.

By 2002, there were cases where policy concerns outweighed legal authority. In *Krangle v. Brisco* (2002), the Court upheld the lower courts' finding that a doctor was liable for not alerting a pregnant woman of the availability of a test for Down syndrome. But the Court reversed the Court of Appeal's conclusion that the parents should be entitled to have the child cared for in a private facility. It was held that the child should be taken care of by the province's social security arrangements. Fact accounted for 20 per cent, law for 20 per cent, and policy for 60 per cent of the Court's decision. Here the Court's policy concerns of limiting the liability of defendants, first outlined in the 1978 'trilogy,'[3] and the desire to promote government-based social welfare played a major role.

The relative weight given by the Court to policy as opposed to law can sometimes alter the result of the case. In *Hamstra v. British Columbia Rugby Union* (1997), the law clearly stated that the jury should be discharged in the event of the mention in court that one of the parties had an insurance policy. However, the policy of promoting jury trials, in the modern context of almost universal insurance coverage, tipped the scales in favour of continuing with a jury trial.

Methodology

I read each case reported in the Supreme Court Reports for the years 1952, 1962, 1972, 1977, 1982, 1987, 1992, 1997 and 2002. Based on my reading, I characterized the proportion of fact, law, and policy evident in the reasoning of each judgment. I focused primarily on the elements that determined the result of the case. In a very few cases, the apportionment was unclear in which case there was an even three-way split or an equal split between the two competing categories, most often fact and law. A case that merely followed another case had a very high proportion of law. When determining policy, the Court sometimes refers to 'legislative facts,' such as the rise or fall of the rate of inflation. In determining the proportion of fact, law, or policy, I was primarily tracking adjudicative fact, the facts unique to the individual case. I concentrated on the majority reasons for judgment, and my analysis took the reasons for judgment at face value. Where the decision was of insufficient length to allow for an apportionment, it was marked 'short' and was excluded from my survey.

I measured based on proportionality – that is, for example, how much of a role fact, as compared to law or policy, played in the decision. My basic unit of measurement was ten percentage points, which led to divisions, for example, of 20/60/20. Where the division was not so clear, I split the difference and used divisions of five percentage points, leading to divisions like to 25/55/20.

I obtained my list of cases by photocopying the index in the front of each Supreme Court Reports volume. Where these volumes had yet to be compiled (2002), I used the Lexum website for my list of cases. Each case was then accessed for analysis, almost always via QuickLaw™. I performed this analysis at the same time as I was characterizing the mode of reasoning being employed by the Court and the number of pages, Judges sitting, opinions, and dissents in each case. During this stage I also noted whether or not the *Charter of Rights and Freedoms* played a role in the decision.

A significant variable in these studies is thus my personal judgment. My judgment is informed by Bachelor and Masters of Laws degrees, twenty years of practice at the bar and by this study. Since it was my judgment being applied, my judgment is a constant which means that it should accurately measure any trend.

5 Modes of Legal Reasoning

The Supreme Court of Canada's deliberations are now characterized by a wide variety of modes of reasoning, of which formal legal reasoning is the most common. In this mode, analogy predominates, but deduction and induction also play a role. Next in line is a more expansive contextualist mode.[1] This is followed by a mode that seeks to reconcile and rationalize the various doctrines relating to the issues at hand. Less common modes include reasoning based on pragmatic concerns or on principle or values. Cases where the specific facts determine the outcome used to be somewhat common but are now rare.

In parallel with the changing proportion of fact, law, and policy in Supreme Court decisions, discussed in chapter 4, the Court's preferred modes of legal reasoning have also changed over time. At the beginning of the 1950s, formal legal reasoning controlled 90 per cent of cases. Fifty years later, the Court relies on formal legal reasoning to arrive at less than 50 per cent of its decisions. Expanded contextual interpretation now plays a major role in the Court's jurisprudence. Decisions based on the facts of the individual cases are now few and far between.

Definitions for Modes of Legal Reasoning

Formal legal reasoning indicates the application of black-letter law. The Court recites the facts and applies the law to them. The use of legal propositions, from statute or caselaw, is a hallmark of formal legal reasoning. Formal legal reasoning is characterized by a somewhat mechanical appearance. If the facts established that the accused was driving a truck loaded such that each axle bore more than five tonnes, a Court employing formal legal reasoning would consult the *Highway*

Traffic Act to determine the maximum permissible load. If the act prohibited driving with a load of more than five tonnes per axle, the accused would be convicted.

Sometimes the Court extrapolates from existing propositions to arrive at a somewhat new proposition. This is the prototypical way in which Hart's penumbra is shrunk and the core of settled meaning is expanded.

Doctrinal reconciliation has many elements of formal legal reasoning but focuses on the rationalization of various, often competing, strands of caselaw or learned legal doctrine. In such instances, the Court considers the entire corpus of the law, not just the discrete application of one legal proposition. Typically the Court is confronted with two or more cases that seem to point to different directions for the law to take. Existing anomalies must be brought in line with the main body of the law; the creation of new anomalies must be avoided. The Court must also be concerned with the impact of the ruling it is proposing (or resisting) on other analogous areas of the law. For example, a ruling in a theft case may have an impact on the tort of conversion, or vice versa. Thus, the court examines and harmonizes different areas of the law, such as contract and tort or maritime and land-based rules. It seems to be willing to tolerate a certain degree of dissonance between civil and common law doctrine but its tendency is towards convergence. The law in other jurisdictions is frequently canvassed in the process.

Doctrinal reconciliation usually involves an adjustment or reformulation of the law. The Court is striving mightily to restore doctrinal integrity. There is often an historical analysis of where the caselaw has been going followed by a new and comprehensive statement, or restatement, of the law. Doctrinal reconciliation often results in doctrinal change.

Expanded contextual interpretation (or, more simply, *contextual interpretation*) involves the canvassing of a wide range of issues and their multitextured treatment.[2] The Court considers all possible effects and permutations that might flow from several possible solutions. Both legal and non-legal considerations play a role; this is very much a 'big picture,' 'blue sky' analysis. Expanded contextual interpretation most often occurs when a statute is being interpreted, but this mode can also apply to the interpretation of a text, a doctrine, or caselaw. The Court reflects on the entire background, framework, and implications of the situation, including the spirit of what the legislature intended. Legal propositions are merely the starting point for the Court's analysis;

policy considerations almost always play a substantial role in these decisions. Foreign legal materials are often consulted. In this mode 'the Court is not interested in dealing with legal issues in a vacuum, but is interested in evaluating the impact of its decisions.'[3]

The framing of an issue in contextual terms can change the outcome of the case. For example, in *Toronto Area Transit v. Dell Holdings* (1997), the majority determined that the contextual situation of a corporation whose property was being expropriated required that the corporation be compensated for the delays caused by the rezoning and development process. The dissent took a more narrow view and would have restricted compensation to little more than the value of the land and buildings.

Expanded contextual interpretation includes rulings based on the core values of the various members of the Court, most commonly in *Charter* cases. It also includes rulings based on overarching legal principle. Contextual interpretation is the most common mode employed when the Court considers formulating a new legal rule. In such circumstances the Court canvasses the rationale for the old rule and the implications for the new rule it is considering. Formal legal reasoning is usually of little assistance when formulating a new rule, as there are no applicable legal propositions or the available legal propositions are almost always highly unsatisfactory.

A *pragmatic* decision is one that uses common sense to decide the case in a practical and efficient manner. Finding a solution that works in the real world is the goal. Utility governs the outcome; legal propositions and doctrinal elegance take a back seat. No wide context is examined: here the Court is interested in what works, and if the solution is rough-and-ready, so be it. Typically a pragmatic ruling results from a situation where the Court is confronted by an inefficient or counterproductive rule. The Court's answer is typically elegant in an 'on the ground' sense but highly inelegant from a doctrinal point of view. For example, in *Opetchesaht Indian Band v. Canada* (1997), the Court fashioned a practical solution in response to the construction of a hydroelectric line through an Indian reserve. Despite the fact, as argued by the minority, that there was no surrender, as was required for a potentially perpetual grant of property rights, the majority fashioned an easement to exist so long as the line 'is required.' The power line remained – it would have been too expensive and impractical to reroute it – but Aboriginal rights doctrine was thrown into confusion.

Fact driven cases are those in which the facts decide the case. Judgments in this category usually read as if they were being decided by a trial judge. The Court involves itself in determining what the facts of the case are. The law is not in dispute; the success or failure of the appeal rides on the facts. For example, if the Court is arguing about whether the traffic light was red, amber, or green when the defendant went through the intersection, the facts are driving the outcome.

Two other minor modes, or submodes – strands of expanded contextual interpretation – deserve brief mention.[4] *Principle* involves the application of an overarching principle to arrive at a decision. An example of such a principle is, 'No one should be allowed to profit from their crime.' This is the type of legal reasoning advocated by Ronald Dworkin when he calls upon judges to follow Justice Hercules up Mount Olympus.[5] When the Court decides based on the *values* of its various members, the case almost always involves contentious *Charter* issues. Such decisions are based not on law, fact, or policy but upon which competing value is given precedence by the majority – for example, whether it is more important to foster free speech or to protect minorities from hate speech. The incidence of these submodes is sufficiently rare as to make it difficult to track them separately.

The *apparent difficulty* index attempts to quantify how easy or hard it was for the Court to arrive at its decision. (The apparent difficulty index is introduced here to examine how it varies from mode to mode. It is tracked over time in chapter 8, pages 98–9.) The range is from 0 to 1. A score of 0.1 is easy; one of 0.9 is hard. This item of measurement is admittedly very subjective. However, I have tried to be consistent over time, and the fact that I was the sole origin of the indexation will bring some constancy to the measurement. The criteria I used included the extent to which the Court seemed to have to struggle to reach its decision; the number of impediments it faced; how divided, both on quantitative and qualitative bases, the Court seemed to be; how many different ways the Court approached the problem; whether the appeal was being dismissed or allowed; and whether or not foreign caselaw or academic sources were cited by the Court.

Proportions and Trends

As figure 5.1 indicates, formal legal reasoning, although still the predominant mode in the Supreme Court of Canada, is declining while expanded contextual interpretation and doctrinal reconciliation are on the rise. A somewhat different measure of these changes can be seen in

Figure 5.1. Changes in modes of legal reasoning, Supreme Court of Canada, 1952–2002

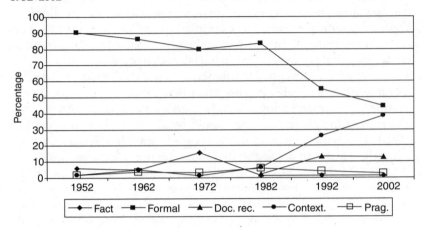

Table 5.1. Percentage of cases by mode of legal reasoning, including submodes, Supreme Court of Canada, 1952–2002

	1952	1962	1972	1982	1992	2002
Formal legal reasoning	90	86	80	84	55	45
Contextual interpretation	2	1	2	6	21	28
Values-based					1	5
Principle		4			3	4
Doctrinal reconciliation				2	13	13
Pragmatic	2	4	3	6	4	3
Fact driven	6	5	15	2	1	1

table 5.1, which also includes two submodes of expanded contextual interpretation.

The crossover evident in figure 5.1 circa 1982 is more vividly illustrated in figure 5.2, where the line representing formal legal reasoning has been removed and data from 1977, 1987, and 1997 added.

Correlation with Other Indicators

Each mode has its characteristic fact/law/policy signature, as figure 5.2 illustrates. There are also important variations in unanimity and dissent. These differences corroborate the above finding that the Court

Figure 5.2. Changes in modes of legal reasoning, excluding formal legal reasoning, Supreme Court of Canada, 1972–2002

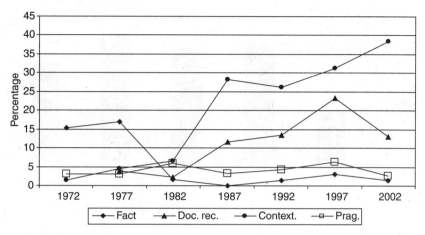

Figure 5.3. Proportion of fact, law, and policy, by mode of legal reasoning, Supreme Court of Canada, 1987–2002

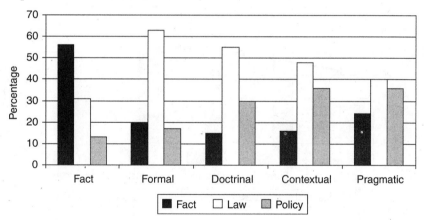

functions within several discrete modes. Note that, in figures 5.3 to 5.4, I have organized the modes so that those that tend to be more foundational are towards the left end of the graph. Note the progressive increase in policy from the left to the right side of the graph.

As figure 5.4 illustrates, contextual interpretation seems to require the greatest number of opinions as a function of the number of judges

Figure 5.4. Opinions and dissents per sitting judge by mode, Supreme Court of Canada, 1952–2002

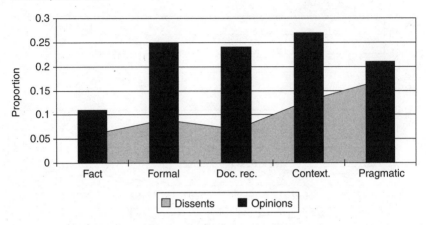

Figure 5.5. Pages and opinions per judge; opinions per case, by mode, Supreme Court of Canada, 1952–1982

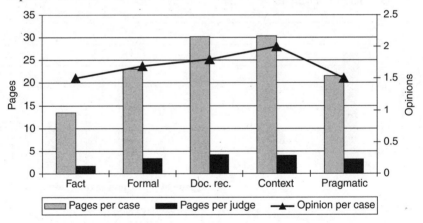

sitting. Pragmatic decisions generate the largest proportion of dissents, followed closely by contextual interpretation.

As figure 5.5 and table 5.2 illustrate, the number of pages in the Court's reasons for judgment also vary by mode of legal reasoning. With the exception of pragmatic decisions, which have fewer pages, there is a similar distribution of pages per judge and opinions per case.

Table 5.2. Papers and opinion per case by mode,
Supreme Court of Canada, 1952–2002

Mode	Pages per case	Opinions per case
Formal	23	1.7
Contextual	30.3	2.0
Values	63.6	2.6
Principle	18.4	1.6
Doctrinal	30.2	1.8
Pragmatic	21.5	1.5
Fact driven	13.5	1.5

Figure 5.6. Unanimity and dissent in the Supreme Court of Canada, by mode of legal reasoning, 1982–2002

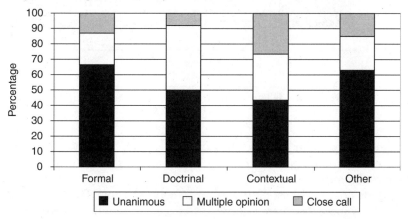

Cases involving contextual interpretation have the highest number of pages. The lower number of pages in fact-driven cases is partially accounted for by the fact that most occurred at a time when the Court's reasons were shorter overall.

As figure 5.6 illustrates, there are variations in the level of unanimity and dissent coincidental with the Court's mode of legal reasoning. *Unanimous decisions* are those in which the Court delivered one set of reasons or where concurring justices satisfied themselves with a simple 'I agree.' Cases of *multiple opinion* are those in which several distinct sets of reasons were delivered. *Close calls* were those in which the Court was sharply divided.[6] Variations in unanimity and dissent have sometimes

Figure 5.7. Modes of legal reasoning in the Supreme Court of Canada, the
Ontario Court of Appeal, and Ontario Superior Court, 2002

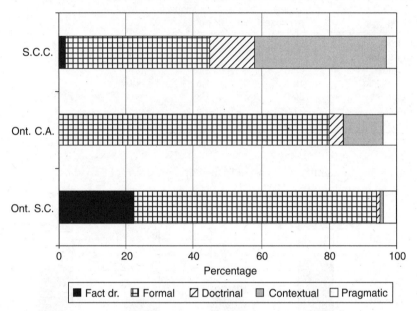

changed from year to year. For example, in 1997 there was a spike in
close calls identified with cases where the Court employed doctrinal
reconciliation.

Modes of legal reasoning vary from court to court. For example, as
figure 5.7 indicates, there is more formal legal reasoning in lower courts
than in the Supreme Court.[7] As we descend down the judicial hierarchy,
the modes that can, generally speaking, be regarded as tending towards
the foundational increase. In particular, note the decrease in contextual
analysis and doctrinal reconciliation as one descends the judicial hierarchy. As is to be expected, many more cases in the Superior Court are
fact-driven. Taken together with the differences in fact, law, and policy
(see figure 4.3), these findings point to substantial differences in functioning among the three courts.

How Many Hard Cases?

Apparent difficulty also varies by mode, with fact-driven, formal legal
reasoning, and principle-based decisions appearing the easiest to de-

Table 5.3. Apparent difficulty* by mode of legal reasoning,
Supreme Court of Canada, 1952–2002

Mode	Apparent difficulty
Formal	0.59
Contextual	0.68
Values	0.88
Principle	0.59
Doctrinal	0.66
Pragmatic	0.65
Fact driven	0.38

*Scores range from 0.1 for the easiest case to 0.9 for the
most difficult.

cide and value-based decisions appearing the most difficult (see table
5.3). As will be described in chapter 8, the apparent difficulty index has
remained fairly steady over the years.

Examples in the Caselaw

The steps typically involved in *formal legal reasoning* are exemplified by
the case of *Fee v. Bradshaw* (1982). The issue was the taxpayer's right of
appeal to the Trial Division. The Court examined the jurisdiction of the
Trial Division under section 18 of the *Federal Court Act* and determined
that its jurisdiction depended on whether the action of the minister in
filing the subject certificate was an administrative action. Upon determination that the minister's action was not administrative, the Court
dismissed the appeal.

  Formal legal reasoning establishes the facts, determines the appropriate test under the law, and applies the law to the facts to arrive at a
decision. Formal legal reasoning is usually mechanical and avoids any
considerations which are not 'law.' Neither the fairness of the result nor
the long-range implications of the Court's ruling are considered. This
mode holds that it is the role of Parliament, not the courts, to change the
law. These issues were canvassed in *Harvard College v. Canada (Commissioner of Patents)* (2002), wherein the majority held that the *Patent Act*
did not permit the patenting of higher life forms. The minority would
have allowed the cancer-prone mouse to be patented, but Justice
Bastarache, for the majority, disagreed, noting: 'In my view, whether
higher life forms such as the oncomouse ought to be patentable is a
matter for Parliament to determine. This Court's views as to the utility
or propriety of patenting non-human higher life forms such as the

oncomouse are wholly irrelevant.'[8] For the majority, the proper method of deciding the case involved a close reading of the provisions of the *Patent Act*.

Expanded contextual interpretation involves the Court's broadening its horizon. The minority in *Harvard College v. Canada* considered the utility of the 'oncomouse,' the extraordinary means that had brought it into existence, the public interest in promoting new inventions, and Canada's international competitive disadvantage. Had the majority adopted this expanded contextual analysis, the decision would almost certainly have been different.

In *Hayduk v. Pidoborozny* (1972), the Court was called upon to determine the identity of the owner of a motor vehicle. Instead of restricting itself to the name on the registration certificate, the Court considered the entire context of the issue, including who paid for and drove the car, the practicalities of insurance, and the protection of users of the highways. A more formalistic reading of the statute could have led to the conclusion that either father or son, but not both, was the owner of the automobile; the Court's contextual interpretation concluded that both were 'owners.'

Babcock v. Canada (Attorney General) (2002) involved the disclosure of cabinet documents. It would have been quite simple for the Court to have held itself bound by the government's certification of cabinet confidentiality. Instead, it carefully examined the issues in the context of the proper role of the Court in relation to the executive branch of government relative to ordinary civil litigation. Despite a certification of cabinet privilege, some of the documents were ordered produced. Had the Court restricted itself to the formal proposition that no cabinet-privileged documents are producible, the result would have been different.

In *A.M. v. Ryan* (1997), the Court used expanded contextual interpretation to formulate a new rule to regulate the disclosure of therapeutic records of rape victims in civil proceedings. The Court considered the relevant Rule of civil procedure, the doctrine of therapeutic privilege, the victim's privacy rights, together with *Charter* cases dealing with similar issues in criminal cases. The all-or-nothing approach followed in the United States was rejected in favour of a procedure that would balance privacy interests against relevance in each case.

The Court used *doctrinal reconciliation* to clarify the effect of an invalid marriage in *Paré v. Bonin* (1977). It examined possible distinctions between 'a marriage which is a nullity, ... a nonexistent marriage, [and] a relatively null or voidable marriage.' The Court explored the practical effects of categorizing a marriage either as void *ab initio* or as being non-existant but still leading to legal effects. It held that in this case the respondent ought to be allowed to keep the property conferred by the marriage, notwithstanding that she could not enter into matrimony because of a mental defect on her part.[9]

Doctrinal reconciliation led to doctrinal change in *R. v. Hill* (1977), when a badly divided Court expanded its jurisdiction to hear criminal sentence appeals. The Court examined prior case law that restricted its jurisdiction and wrang out the change it desired. Conflicting legal propositions meant that formal legal reasoning was inadequate to decide the case.

In *Stewart v. Canada* (2002), the Court was called upon to review a series of cases that had dealt, often unsatisfactorily, with the income tax issue of 'reasonable expectation of profit.' The Court began with its earlier decision in *Moldowan* (1978), which had held that a taxpayer had to have a source of income, or at least a reasonable expectation of profit at some point in the future, against which deductions could be made. Expenses incurred without a reasonable expectation of profit could not be deducted. The court explored the facts in *Moldowan* and highlighted the fact that the earlier case had arisen out of specific sections dealing with hobby farms. In contrast, in *Stewart* the plaintiff was seeking to deduct expenses relating to several condominium units that were generating long-term losses. The Court traced the caselaw both before and after *Moldowan* and described the practical problems generated by the reasonable-expectation-of-profit test. The central problem with the test was that bad investments would not be deductible. The Court restricted the reasonable expectation of profit test to ensure that it properly distinguished between personal and business activities. A decision based on formal legal reasoning would almost certainly have applied *Moldowan* against the taxpayer.

Pragmatic considerations led the Court to modify the law to allow for the joint trial of summary and indictable offences in *R. v. Clunas* (1992). Prior to this case, the law required that two trials, often rehashing exactly the same evidence, be held.

Fact-driven cases include *Freedman v. Côte St. Luc* (1972), where the Court split over whether the defendant driver had kept a proper look out, and *R. v. Saieva* (1982), wherein the Court reversed concurrent findings of fact respecting the date of the theft.

Sub-Modes

The competing *values* of the promotion of democracy and the right of the government to punish felons clashed in the *Sauvé* (2002) elections rights case. The Court split five to four over the appropriate interpretation of the *Charter*'s equality provisions. Chief Justice McLachlin for the majority held that the right to vote is fundamental to democracy and that allowing prisoners to vote would enhance their rehabilitation and reintegration into society. No democracy should exclude a segment of its population. As Justice Gonthier for the minority noted, 'This case rests on philosophical, political and social considerations which are not capable of 'scientific proof.' It involves justifications for and against the limitation of the right to vote which are based upon axiomatic arguments of principle or *value* statements.'[10] He argued that the value judgment of Parliament that civic responsibility is best served with the retributive and denunciatory effects of temporary disenfranchisement ought to be upheld.

The competing values of the promotion of freedom of expression and the suppression of hate speech collided in *Zundel* (1992). Here competing legal propositions rendered formal legal reasoning of little more use than the flipping of a coin. The values are not easily reconcilable, thus making a process of doctrinal reconciliation all but impossible. The Court had to choose which value was the most important in the circumstances.

With respect to the issue of activism it is interesting to note that the Court has adamantly refused to promulgate a hierarchy of values, such that one *Charter* right would trump another. It prefers to decide these conflicts on a case-by-case basis.[11]

The *principle* that an accused must voluntarily commit the crime before he can be convicted determined the result in *R. v. King* (1962). Since the accused's impairment resulted from anesthetic administered by his dentist and the accused was not aware of the state of mind the anesthetic might produce, there was no 'volitive act' on the part of the accused. Crimes require moral fault.

Proportion of Hard Cases

Examples of differences in *apparent difficulty* include *Ahani v. Canada* (2002), rated at 0.2, where the Court merely had to apply its recent decision in *Suresh* (2002), and *Ward v. Canada* (2002), rated at 0.8, where the court had to struggle mightily to determine that harp seals, usually classified as mammals, fell under federal fisheries jurisdiction.

In *R. v. Cinous* (2002), rated at 0.9, the Court reversed the decision of the appeal court and restored the accused's conviction for murder. Three out of the nine Judges dissented, and the majority fractured into two opinions. In the process, the Court considered a wide range of Canadian caselaw along with English and American authorities and eleven texts and academic articles. The decision went on for 73 pages, in which the Court struggled mightily with the doctrine of 'air of reality.'

Methodology

The survey for the modes of legal reasoning was performed at the same time as that for fact, law, and policy, as described in chapter 4. During this survey I also analysed each case to determine whether it was 'hard' or 'easy.'

As I surveyed each case, I made a determination of which mode of reasoning best described the approach of the Court and evaluated the apparent difficulty experienced by the Court in arriving at its decision. The mode of any dissenting Judge was largely discounted and used primarily as a foil to facilitate choosing the mode of the majority, which was effectively the mode of the Court.

Where the majority appeared to use two or more modes of legal reasoning, I attempted to determine which had the most impact on the ultimate decision. In the rare cases where it was not possible to determine which mode predominated, the decision was not included in my analysis. Likewise, if the case was of insufficient length to categorize, it was discarded from the final count.

Pages per case were determined by the number of pages noted in the 'Number of Documents' panel on QuickLaw's search result screen.

I then tallied the results by year using the Excel spreadsheet computer program which also assisted in producing the graphs and tables above.

6 Changing the Law

When one thinks of the law being changed, one thinks first of the legislature. But on occasion the Supreme Court also changes the law and in fact has been doing so with increasing regularity. The Court uses two methods to change the law: outright overruling and the hard distinguishing of prior judicial authority. As with its modes of legal reasoning and the proportion of fact, law, and policy, there was a crossover between these two methods in the early 1980s when hard distinguishing dipped and overruling increased. A full description of my findings in these regards follows the definitions.

Definitions

A decision is *overruled* when the Court declines to follow a binding precedent but instead makes a ruling that would not have been made had that precedent been followed. Overruling results in a change to the law. When the Court overrules, it sets 'aside an earlier decision's authority.'[1] The earlier decision is superseded, annulled, and made void. 'A judicial decision is said to be overruled when a later decision ... expresses a judgment upon the same question of law directly opposite to that which was before given thereby depriving the earlier opinion of all authority as a precedent.'[2]

If a legislative or constitutional change intervened after the binding precedent and the Court changed direction in response to this change, the new decision is not overruling for the purpose of this discussion. Thus, given the intervening enactment of the *Charter of Rights and Freedoms*, *Feeney* (1997) did not overrule *Wray* (1971).[3] On the other hand, if an earlier case held that a farmer who allowed his cattle to stray onto a highway would not be liable to a passing motorist who collided with one of his cows but the Supreme Court now decides that farmers should be liable in this situation, the earlier case has been overruled.

A case is *distinguished* when it appears to have some similarities or relevance to the case being decided, but the Court finds sufficient differences between the precedent and the case under discussion so as not to be bound by the earlier case. When a precedent is distinguished, it remains active law, in contrast to a case that has been overruled.[4] An already decided case is distinguished where the Court points out or clarifies an essential difference between it and the case presently before it.[5]

In *The Authority of Law*, Joseph Raz wrote: '[Distinguishing] is subject to two crucial conditions: (1) The modified rule must be the rule laid down in the precedent restricted by the addition of a further condition for its application, and (2) The modified rule must be such as to justify the order made in the precedent.'[6] For Raz, distinguishing can only narrow rules, it cannot extend them.[7] Thus, the modified rule must be an alternative basis for the original decision. In distinguishing, the court is 'obliged to adopt only that modification which will best improve the rule.'[8] Hard distinguishing usually violates one or more of these rules.

Hard distinguishing refers to cases where the grounds on which the Court distinguishes the precedent are doubtful or not readily apparent.[9] In hard distinguishing, there is no real distinction between the cases. The distinguished case and the newly decided one cannot be logically reconciled with one another.

When using precedent, courts rule by way of analogy. Like cases are treated the same; different cases are treated differently. If there is a feature of the first case that is dissimilar to the second, the judge will have to determine whether the dissimilarity is important; if it is not important, she will distinguish the first case and decide the cases differently. For example, if in the first case, Sam intentionally hit Joe on the nose and that was found to be an assault, then, in the second case, in which Peter intentionally hit Paul on the ear, that would certainly be assault as well. But if, in a third case, Mary's car accidentally rolled down the hill and hit Jane, that would not be assault because Mary did not intend for her car to hit Jane. Intention is important to assault, and thus negligence is distinguished from assault. Yet the exact target of an assault, nose or ear, is unimportant. A judge crafting a definition of assault that attempted to distinguish a precedent based on the target of the assault would almost certainly be engaging in hard distinguishing.

Hard distinguishing is either faulty reasoning or an overruling in disguise. The difference between overruling, sometimes called a 'radical departure,' and hard distinguishing is best illustrated by *Central Alberta Dairy Pool v. Alberta Human Rights Commission* (1990), where the majority explicitly overturned *Bhinder* (1985) but where Justice Sopinka would have preferred a more indirect approach. He chided his colleagues: 'Apart from constituting a radical departure from *Bhinder*, this conclusion requires a rewriting of the statute.'[10] If Justice Sopinka's reasoning – that the existence of a Bona Fide Occupational Qualification was dependent on the employer's ability to accommodate – had been applied in *Bhinder*, Bhinder would have almost certainly won. Justice Sopinka's hard distinguishing would have done indirectly what the majority did directly.

A case has *changed the law* when the pre-existing state of the law would have led the majority of lawyers to give a black-letter legal opinion different from their opinion after the case was rendered. Overrulings will almost invariably change the law.

Any case decided by the Judicial Committee of the Privy Council while it was the final court of appeal for Canada and any case decided by the Supreme Court of Canada will be considered to be a *binding precedent*. This definition is adopted notwithstanding that the Court has, on several occasions, declared that it is not absolutely bound to follow prior cases, even its own or those of the Judicial Committee of the Privy Council.

Explicit overruling occurs where the Court, or some of its members, clearly acknowledges that it is changing the law. In these cases there is a reference to the prior case and a transparent acknowledgement that the Court is declining to follow the prior holding. In cases of *non-explicit overruling*, the Court's opinion is not transparent, but the decision clearly effects a modification in the law. In some cases, the prior case is not cited. However, in the end result, it is clear to a knowledgeable observer that the Court has declined to follow precedent.

Trends in Overruling and Hard Distinguishing

Figure 6.1 shows the percentage of cases in which the Court overruled precedent as well as the percentage of cases featuring hard distinguishing. Figure 6.2 portrays the number of cases involving overruling. There is thus an overall and sustained rise in the rate of overruling. Even though this overall rate remains low, it constitutes an important juris-

Figure 6.1. Percentage of Supreme Court of Canada cases involving overruling and hard distinguishing, 1951–2000

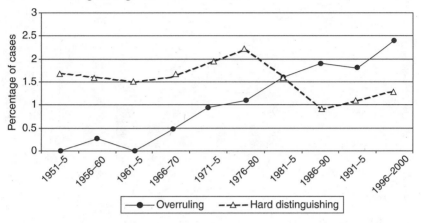

Figure 6.2. Number of cases involving explicit and non-explicit overruling, Supreme Court of Canada, 1951–2000

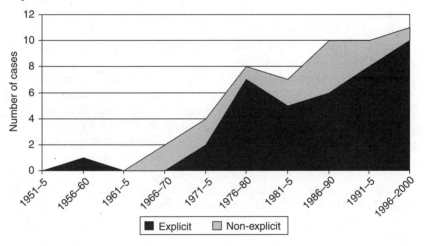

prudential trend. Note also the crossover between overruling and hard distinguishing in the early 1980s. This coincides with the crossovers earlier noted. The rise in overruling coincident with the decline in hard distinguishing indicates that the Court is rendering reasons for judgment that are more transparent and less convoluted.

Figure 6.3. Number of cases involving overruling and hard distinguishing, Supreme Court of Canada, 1951–2000

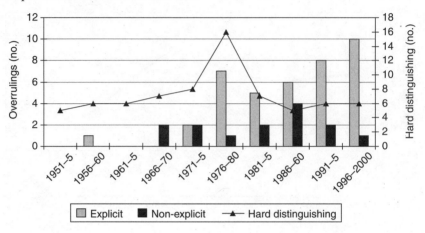

The Court has become increasingly forthright when it overrules previously binding authority. Figure 6.2 illustrates the trends in explicit and non-explicit overruling. Figure 6.3, which shows the number of explicit, non-explicit and hard distinguishing cases, provides another view of these phenomena.

Figure 6.4 shows the length of time that elapsed between the pronouncement of a precedent and its overruling by the Supreme Court of Canada. The top line ('longest') tracks the oldest precedent in each five-year period. Thus the overruled precedent that had been in force the longest during the years 1976–80 was decided 106 years prior to being overruled.[11] The term 'average' represents the average age of all precedents overruled in each five-year period. As figure 6.5 illustrates, although almost half of the Court's overrulings have taken place after the precedent had been in place for a moderate amount of time (six to twenty-four years), there has been an increase in the overruling of recently decided cases.

Differences in Fact/Law/Policy When Law Changed

Cases where the Court follows precedent differ from cases in which it overrules precedent, and in turn these cases differ from those where the Court engages in hard distinguishing. As can be seen in figure 6.6, there

Figure 6.4. Length of time between precedent and overruling, Supreme Court of Canada, 1966–2000

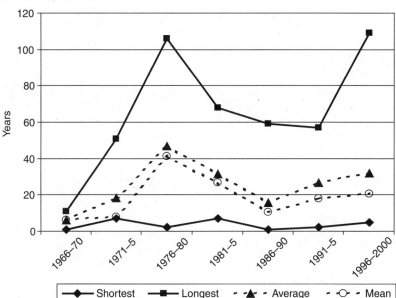

is a slight variation in the proportion of fact, law, and policy in decisions where the Court either overrules precedent or hard distinguishes it.[12] The most substantial difference is the large increase in the proportion of policy in cases featuring overruling. Paradoxically, there is a marked decrease in the proportion of law for overruling but a slight decrease for hard distinguishing.

Modes Vary When Law Changed

There are substantial variations in the modes of legal reasoning used by the Court in arriving at conventional decisions, as opposed to those where it overrules or hard distinguishes. For example, as figure 6.7 illustrates, the Court employs substantially more doctrinal reconcilia-tion, especially in overruling, than in conventional decision making. Both overruling and hard distinguishing feature more pragmatic rul-ings. Interestingly, there is less contextual analysis in cases using hard distinguishing or overruling.

Figure 6.5. Comparison of age of precedents overruled in the Supreme Court of Canada

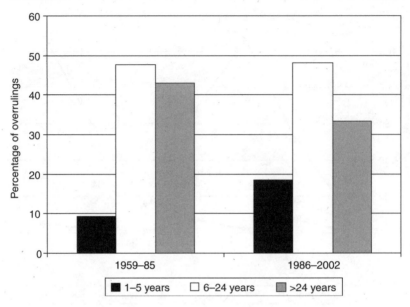

The crossover between overruling and hard distinguishing corroborates the crossovers found with respect to fact/law/policy and modes of legal reasoning. The distinctions between ordinary cases and cases wherein the Court overrules or resorts to hard distinguishing provide additional corroboration.

Figures 6.5–6.7 were generated by compiling the results of the previously discussed survey with respect to the years 1992, 1997, and 2002.[13] The cases featuring overruling or hard distinguishing were compiled from all years between and including 1992 and 2002 and were characterized as to fact/law/policy and mode of legal reasoning focusing on points relevant to the hard distinguishing or overruling.

Prior periods were not studied in as much detail, but some overall findings can be described. The general rise in contextual interpretation that commenced in 1982 was matched in cases involving overruling during that period. A sharp rise in the use of doctrinal reconciliation in cases involving overruling commenced in the 1973–82 decade – that is, it preceded the general rise by a decade. Furthermore, ever since the 1973–82 decade there has been substantially more doctrinal reconcilia-

Figure 6.6. Fact, law, and policy, by type of case, Supreme Court of Canada, 1952–2002

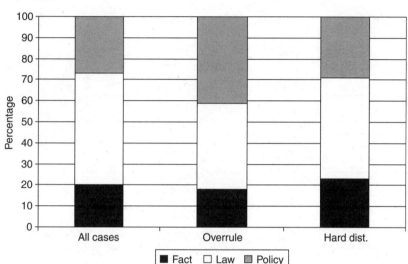

tion in overruling cases than there has been in cases that did not involve the overruling of precedent.

Examples in the Cases of Changing the Law

One of the first, if not the first, case of *explicit overruling* in the Supreme Court of Canada was *Fleming v. Atkinson* (1959), where the Court declined to follow a House of Lords case that would have exonerated a straying cow's owner of negligence. In the more recent case of *Ordon Estate v. Grail* (1998),[14] the Court expanded the heads of damages available in respect of maritime fatal accidents. In so doing, it stated:

> It follows from the foregoing discussion that this Court's decision *in Canadian National Steamships Co. v. Watson* ... is no longer good law insofar as the decision deviates from the four-step test outlined herein and directs a court to apply provincial law in maritime matters without first evaluating the applicability of the provincial law from a constitutional standpoint. Similarly, the ruling in *Stein*, ... with respect to the applicability of the British Columbia *Contributory Negligence Act* must be considered to have lost its precedential value. (¶ 94)
>
> ...

Figure 6.7. Court action by mode of legal reasoning, Supreme Court of Canada, 1952–2002

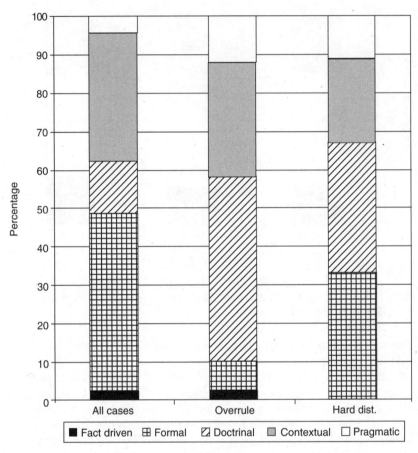

It is unfair to deny compensation to the plaintiff dependants in these actions based solely upon an anachronistic and historically contingent understanding of the harm they may have suffered. (¶ 102)

...

The anachronism and unfairness of applying the *actio personalis moritur cum persona* rule in maritime negligence actions is well illustrated by the fact that all common law jurisdictions in Canada have enacted legislation abolishing the rule, and now permit recovery by estates of deceased persons ... (¶ 115)

... [O]n an international level, [this] reform will bring Canadian maritime law into harmony with what is already the dominant practice in both civilian and common law jurisdictions around the world. On a national level, the reform will bring maritime law into conformity with the general practice in all other jurisdictions within the country. (¶ 116)

In *R. v. Salituro* (1991),[15] the Court reviewed the doctrine of *stare decisis* and set out the following criteria as to when it was appropriate for the Court to effect a change in the law:

At one time, it was accepted that it was the role of judges to discover the common law, not to change it. (¶ 26)

However, Blackstone's static model of the common law has gradually been supplanted by a more dynamic view. This Court is now willing, where there are compelling reasons for doing so, to overturn its own previous decisions. (¶ 27)

...

In keeping with these developments, this Court has signaled its willingness to adapt and develop common law rules to reflect changing circumstances in society at large. ... [W]hile complex changes to the law with uncertain ramifications should be left to the legislature, the courts can and should make incremental changes to the common law to bring legal rules into step with a changing society. However, a brief review of these cases is warranted. (¶ 29)

...

... Judges can and should adapt the common law to reflect the changing social, moral and economic fabric of the country. Judges should not be quick to perpetuate rules whose social foundation has long since disappeared. Nonetheless, there are significant constraints on the power of the judiciary to change the law. As McLachlin J. indicated in *Watkins*, ... in a constitutional democracy such as ours it is the legislature and not the courts which has the major responsibility for law reform; and for any changes to the law which may have complex ramifications, however necessary or desirable such changes may be, they should be left to the legislature. The judiciary should confine itself to those incremental changes which are necessary to keep the common law in step with the dynamic and evolving fabric of our society. (¶ 37)

Non-explicit overruling occurs when the Court is not so forthright in its modifying of the law. For example, in *R. v. Morin* (1992), the Court effectively overruled *Askov* (1990), which had mandated the almost automatic dismissal of criminal cases that had been subjected to delay, by ruling that the accused had to go to trial despite a fourteen-and-a-half-month delay and imposing an onus on the accused to show that he or she had been prejudiced by the delay.

For the purposes of my survey, academic commentary was sometimes useful in confirming that cases had been overruled where the Court was not explicit. For example, in *Thorson* (1975), the Court appeared not to follow *Smith* (1924). Peter Hogg confirms the effect of *Thorson*: 'The plaintiff was not exceptionally prejudiced by the Act [the *Smith* test], which applied to him no differently than to other Canadians. Nonetheless, the Supreme Court of Canada by a majority granted standing to the plaintiff.'[16]

Hard distinguishing involves a change to the law without overruling the prior case. Therefore *P.E.I. (Potato Marketing Board) v. H.B. Willis* (1952), which allowed the federal Parliament and a provincial legislature to both delegate authority to the same board while still prohibiting one level of government from delegating its powers to the other, is a case of distinguishing rather than overruling.[17] The earlier decision forbidding delegation directly to another legislature remained good law.

Two *Charter* cases also exemplify hard distinguishing. In *R. v. Prosper* (1994), the Court declined to dismiss charges where the province had not provided twenty-four-hour duty counsel service to those in detention. This was in the face of *R. v. Brydges* (1990), in which the Court had dismissed charges because the police had failed to advise the accused of the existence, in that province, of the twenty-four-hour duty counsel line. Even after *Prosper*, the police were obliged to notify accused of any available duty counsel service. *Prosper* itself was hard distinguished in *New Brunswick v. G. (J.)* (1999), where the Court held that the province was obliged to provide free legal aid in a child-protection proceeding.

Oldfield v. Transamerica Life (2002) distinguished *Home Insurance Co. v. Lindal* (1934) on the basis that in *Lindal* the miscreant insured would indirectly benefit from the indemnity payment while in *Oldfield*, the insured was already dead and the Court was concerned only with the rights of the innocent beneficiary. *Lindal* remained good authority on its facts.

Characteristics of Cases Which Changed the Law by Overruling

Some cases change the law by distinguishing prior cases. Sometimes the law is changed through a new interpretation of a statute that involves neither distinguishing nor overruling. Unless specifically noted, the characteristics described below relate strictly to cases of overruling.

My survey disclosed fifty-nine cases of overruling. There is some support for the notion that overruling occurs when the law is unstable. Twenty-one cases had this characteristic; in another ten it was somewhat present. However, in six cases of overruling, there was no apparent instability in the law. In twenty cases, hard distinguishing or inconsistent rulings had preceded the overruling; this dynamic was somewhat present in five further cases. However, in twenty-two cases, overruling was not preceded by hard distinguishing or inconsistent rulings by the Court.

Overall, close calls constituted just over 14 per cent of cases. Close calls occur *less* often in cases where prior case law is overruled than in cases where precedent is followed (approximately 8 per cent). Cases utilizing hard distinguishing had more close calls than average (about 32 per cent). While close calls were more prevalent in *Charter* cases (just under 20 per cent), the rate of close calls in *Charter* cases involving hard distinguishing, at 30 per cent, was also elevated and similar to close calls in cases of hard distinguishing globally. Although the small number of cases does not allow much weight to be put on it, there seemed to be a reduction in close calls with respect to cases of both hard distinguishing and overruling after 1990. At the same time, the number of unanimous overrulings and hard distinguishings also rose.

Overruling resulted in twenty-five cases where the overruled precedent would have led to a result out of step with conventional views of justice. This dynamic played somewhat of a role in a further fourteen cases. Only one case clearly did not involve this dynamic. Similarly, in twenty-five cases, the overruling was deemed necessary to bring the law into conformity with current conditions. This dynamic was involved somewhat in a further three cases. However, it was clearly *not* involved in a further fourteen cases.

Realignment with a principle or policy adumbrated in an earlier case did occur, but in only six cases and somewhat in only two further cases. This dynamic was clearly not involved in thirteen cases.

Most of the changes were minor (twenty-nine) or of intermediate consequence (twenty-five). In only five cases could the change be characterized as major.

A new interpretation of a text, of either a previous case or of a statute, played a role in twenty-two cases of overruling and played somewhat of a role in a further three cases. It played no role in six cases.

The Court often failed to properly explain its reasons for overruling.

Only fourteen cases included a detailed explanation, while seven cases had a limited explanation. This is unfavourably contrasted with thirty-eight cases where no real explanation for overruling was given. However, the Court did give detailed reasons as to the merit of the change in forty-five cases and some reasons in two further cases. In twelve cases, the Court gave no reasons, or very limited reasons, even as to the merits of the change.

Although there was some indication that changes in personnel on the bench played a role in some cases of overruling, I was unable to document this in a quantitative sense. However, Ian Bushnell has described two instances where changes in the personnel on the Court, or on the individual hearing panel, led to contradictory results.[18]

Criteria Used by the Court When Overruling

Criteria used by the Court can be divided into two categories: explicit and implicit. Implicit criteria are items cited by the Court as reasons for making the change that is the subject of the case at hand. Explicit criteria are those that the Court specifically describes as reasons for or against making changes in general. For example, when the Court refers to a House of Lords case that is subsequent and contrary to a binding Canadian precedent as a reason for questioning that precedent, the House of Lord's case would be an implicit criterion. In contrast, when the Court writes that 'any changes to the law which may have complex ramifications ... should be left to the legislature,' it is setting out an explicit criterion.[19] The implicit criteria described below were compiled in cases decided after 1992; explicit criteria were gathered at large as reflected in the footnotes.

Implicit Criteria

The two most common implicit criteria mentioned by the Court are the law in other jurisdictions and extrajudicial writing. Canadian law, statutes and caselaw also feature prominently.

The substantive *law in other jurisdictions* played a role in ten cases. Here there was usually a broad-based review of the law of numerous jurisdictions. Subsequent English authority was cited five times, down from its incidence in earlier instances of overruling, but still significant. Recent Commonwealth authority, primarily from Australia and New Zealand, was relied on three times. U.S. law and practice was referred to three times, but there was a qualitative difference here: American authority tended to be used to buttress a decision rather than as a reason for making the decision in the first place.

Academic writing, and here I am including articles by practising lawyers, was the most prominent form of *extra-judicial writing* referred to the Court. It played a role in fifteen cases. These writings comprised a variety of articles, almost always critical of the existing law. Writings from Law Reform Commissions were referred to in six cases. The Uniform Law Conference was cited once.

Canadian caselaw was also used by the Court in deciding whether to change the pre-existing rule. This ranged from cases that had been decided under a different doctrine and now seemed out of step with the rule, cases in which the rule was criticized, and dissents in prior cases. While cases higher up the judicial hierarchy carried greater weight, an occasional trial judgment was also referred to.

Other Canadian considerations were also relevant. The Quebec Civil Code was cited three times as a reason for changing the common law. In prior periods, the reverse was sometimes true: Quebec law was changed to match that in English Canada. However, on one occasion, the unique character of the Civil Code was cited as a reason to change the law in Québec at variance with the law in the rest of Canada. Concerns about federalism were cited once, as were changes to legislation in another jurisdiction.

Changed circumstances, in general, were cited three times. In addition, technological advances – the video camcorder and DNA testing – were cited twice. The need to keep the law in step with social attitudes was mentioned in two cases.

Developing the jurisprudence was a recurring theme. The need to rationalize the rule in question with other areas of the law was referred to five times. Closely similar, other developments in the law were referred to three times. The need for certainty, clarity, and simplification were mentioned four times. The Court returned to conceptual first principles three times. Also mentioned were trends in the law, problems in applying the rule, numerous exceptions to the rule, a lack of a policy basis for the rule, and the idea that tax laws should not be judge-made.

The Court is concerned with *improving the judicial system*. Respect for the jury was mentioned twice, as was the need to facilitate the functioning of the system. Procedural convenience and administrative independence were also mentioned.

Other criteria were justice and fairness, the advent of *Charter*,[20] the negative practical result of the prior case, 'commercial reality,' 'common sense,' social power relations in the context of protecting those without power, the need to facilitate organized labour relations, and concerns regarding the death penalty and the death row phenomenon.

Explicit Criteria

In many cases where the Court changes the law, few, if any, explicit criteria are mentioned. However, in some cases, the Court has set out a series of explicit criteria. According to the court, the driving force behind change is the need to keep the common law in step with the evolution of society.[21] Similar considerations include justice and fairness.[22] The Court finds it easier to change a rule of procedure than to make wholesale changes to the substantive law.[23] Procedural rules should be changed when it is necessary to bring them into accord with natural justice and modern trial practice and to reduce the length and complexity of trials.[24]

Changes should clarify a legal principle or resolve an inconsistency in the law.[25] Where the old rule is a source of more confusion than enlightenment, more uncertainty than certainty, *stare decisis* favours changing the rule.[26] Change should remedy deficient common law rules.[27] The needs of a modern society are more important than the venerability of the rule or the length of time the legislature has allowed the rule to remain in place.[28] If a rule was originally judge-made, the Court treats it as being within its purview to change.[29]

Repeatedly, the Court emphasizes that changes should be small and incremental.[30] It cautions itself to avoid any major change that would have complex and uncertain ramifications.[31] All possible consequences should be capable of assessment ahead of time; if there is a likelihood of unforeseen consequences, any change should be left to the legislature. Similarly, if the change might require the formulation of subsidiary rules or procedures, it should be left to the legislative branch.[32] There must be compelling reasons for the change.[33] *Watkins v. Olafson* (1989) contains an extensive description of the possible complexities that militated against the change being sought by the defendant.[34]

Indicia favouring change include whether the proposed change is in keeping with trends in the law, whether the rule being changed has become attenuated over time, whether the change will increase or reduce uncertainty, and whether the old doctrine can be jettisoned without prejudicing legal principle.[35] The change should be in accord with the *Charter* and should not increase the scope for criminal lia-bility.[36] Sources consulted by the Court in considering whether to change the law include its own opinions in other judgments (often in dissent), developments in provincial Courts of Appeal, developments in other countries (especially Commonwealth countries), academic commentary, and English practice.[37]

The *Friedmann* (2000) case listed several criteria with respect to over-ruling:

> A change in the common law must be necessary to keep the common law in step with the evolution of society, to clarify a legal principle, or to resolve an inconsistency. In addition, the change should be incremental, and its consequences must be capable of assessment. In the recent case of *Robinson* ... the Court ... relied on five factors to justify the reversal ... These factors were the existence of previous dissenting opinions in this Court, a trend in the provincial appellate courts to depart from the principles adopted in the original decision, criticism of the case or the adoption of a contrary rule in other jurisdictions, doctrinal criticism of the case and its foundations, and inconsistency of the case with other decisions. While they are not prerequisites for a change in the common law, these factors help to identify compelling reasons for reform. On the other hand, courts will not intervene where the proposed change will have complex and far-reaching effects, setting the law on an unknown course whose ramifica-tions cannot be accurately measured.[38]

Methodology

I surveyed every case rendered by the Court from 1951 through to 2000 and noted instances of overruling and hard distinguishing. This scan-ning commenced with a reading of each headnote and continued with a skim of the case to determine the essence of the Court's reasoning. I checked the list of cases cited in each judgment for cases the editors felt had been distinguished or overruled. I then scanned the judgment to track each move of legal reasoning employed by the judges. While conducting a subsequent literature review,[39] I made notes of cases that various authors felt constituted overruling or questionable reasoning, and I double checked those cases to see whether they constituted in-stances of overruling or hard distinguishing. My second survey (i.e., to determine fact/law/policy and modes of legal reasoning) constituted a further element of quality control, as I was vigilant to determine whether

I had missed any cases of overruling or hard distinguishing. I then tabulated these cases, combined them into five-year segments. I later reviewed all cases of overruling to summarize the characteristics that seem to have contributed to the overruling and to list the criteria considered by the Court when it did overrule.

Findings of Other Authors Respecting Changing the Law

In examining the number of cases in which the Court has overturned legislation on constitutional (including *Charter*) grounds, Charles Epp has documented a trend similar to that which I outline above: a large increase between 1975 and 1980 and a gradual rise thereafter. Requests for overturning by litigants had been on a gradually accelerating rise since 1965, but there was a very large spike in these requests after 1985.[40]

Peter McCormick has documented another aspect of the erosion of the power of caselaw precedent. He measured the persistence of precedent by the Court's citation of previous authority. Almost all cases decay and are cited less often as they age. McCormick measured this decay in terms of half-lives. The half-life of the Court's decisions is in general decline: for the Taschereau/Cartwright/Fauteux Court (1963–73) it was ten years; for the Laskin Court (1973–84) it was 8.9 years; for the Dickson Court (1984–90) it dipped to only 4 years before rebounding slightly to 5.4 years under Lamer's chief-justiceship (1990–9).[41]

Thus both Epp's and McCormick's findings are consistant with the rise in overrulings documented during my survey.

7 Other Trends: Bright Lines to Principles

Scholars of jurisprudence have sometimes described courts as using 'bright-line' or 'open-standard' tests. Debates have raged as to whether judges use foundational or non-foundational reasoning. Observers contest the extent to which the law leaves choices open to courts and the relative size of Hart's core and penumbra. Some say that courts use legal propositions as the basis for their rulings, while others proclaim principle regnant.

In order to test the claims of legal theorists as to the functioning of the Supreme Court of Canada, this chapter provides the results of my measurement of five binary poles that are reflected in the Court's reasoning. Based on my review of the jurisprudential literature, I compiled contrasting pairs for each of the five areas. These are: 1) bright-line versus open-standard tests; 2) foundational versus non-foundational reasoning; 3) clear law versus choice in the law; 4) the core of certainty versus the penumbra of uncertainty; and 5) legal propositions versus principles. Data on these items provide important insights into the court's functioning and permit comparisons with the theories postulated by scholars of jurisprudence.

Definitions and Examples

A *bright line* test is characterized by a clear division that leads to opposite results depending on which side of the line the situation falls. Once the court characterizes the underlying facts, the result is apparent and easily arrived at. Most regulatory offences specify bright lines: if the defendant committed certain acts, it is guilty. In a case governed by an *open standard*, the facts are judged on a case-by-case basis using a set of criteria. The determination as to whether certain actions constitute negligence is the most common use of an open standard test. Did the defendant fail to show the requisite care towards the plaintiff? Bright lines provide explicit directions, while open standards offer general guidelines.

Language that is open textured or capable of multiple meanings often leads to open-standard tests. Bright lines are characterized by precise lists or binary, black and white divisions. A prohibition against driving a vehicle with more than five tonnes per axle is a bright line; an enactment providing that no truck shall carry a load that is too heavy in all the prevailing circumstances propounds an open standard. *Frenette v. Metropolitan Life Insurance Co.* (1992), which holds that a policy holder's medical records must be disclosed where the policy holder has signed a waiver to that effect, propounds a bright-line test. In contrast, *R. v. Généreux* (1992) formulates an open standard in the form of a set of criteria to determine the constitutionality of Courts Martial.

Foundational rulings utilize precedents, statutes, and clearly established legal rules as their basis. Foundational reasoning arises out of, conforms to, and supports the established positivist order. Answers must be found in existing statute or precedent. Once an answer is given in one case, the same answer is to be given in subsequent cases. Judges are to apply, not make, the law.

The term *non-foundational* is best defined in Hutchinson's *It's All in the Game*.[1] Here courts make new law or use criteria other than statute or precedent. However, the court is still strongly constrained by the traditions of the legal system and any innovations it makes will be in conformity with, rather than in opposition to, prevailing trends. Non-foundational decision-making elevates the importance of arriving at the best decision in *all* the circumstances.

R. v. Milne (1992) applied clearly established property law rules to hold that no property passes where the accused knows that the payor mistakenly paid twice. On the other hand, *R. v. Clunas* (1992) illustrates non-foundational reasoning, whereby the Court overruled precedent to reform an inconvenient and illogical rule of criminal procedure. The former represents foundational reasoning, the latter non-foundational.

At the far end of this continuum is *anti-foundational* reasoning. Rulings here would be made irrespective of any legal constraint.[2] Anti-foundational 'legal reasoning' is nihilist: its only basis is the judge's individual ideology. I did not find any examples of this type of legal reasoning in the Court's jurisprudence. Given that my primary data source was the Justices' own reasons for judgment, it is possible that the Judges hid their real motivations underneath verbal obfuscations. However, I did not find any substantial indications of such a lack of judicial candour.

Sometimes the law is sufficiently unclear or the criteria provided by the relevant legal test are so open that a court has a *choice* as to which party will prevail. Here the available legal materials would support more than one outcome. In other cases, the law is sufficiently developed that the appropriate result is *clear*. There is only one really viable outcome. In *Machtinger v. HOJ Industries Ltd.* (1992), the court could have easily chosen to dismiss the appeal by either upholding the termination provisions of the contract or limiting the plaintiffs to the minimum statutory period under the *Employment Standards Act*. Instead it ordered damages for wrongful dismissal. On the other hand, because striking down the GST in *Reference re Goods and Services Tax* (1992) would have meant that almost all federal taxes would be unconstitutional, it was clear that the Court would uphold the GST. While occasionally choice resulted from open categories or definitions that were *plurisignative* or characterized by *polysemy*,[3] these cases were very rare.

The definitions for *penumbra* and *core* are taken from H.L.A. Hart's *Concept of Law*.[4] The law is said to have a solid core of settled meaning that can easily determine most controversies and a penumbra of uncertainty where the result is less clear. Hart's famous example is that of legislation prohibiting vehicles in parks. It is part of the clear core that a motor car is a vehicle; whether or not a bicycle is a vehicle is in the penumbra. A judicial ruling on bicycles would expand the core and shrink the penumbra.[5]

Barton v. Agincourt Football (1982) is a case in the penumbra. In this case the Justices had to interpret a contract that seemed, on its face, to require on-going payments to the plaintiff, a football player, by the Toronto Argonauts. However, complicating the case was the fact that, for a period, the plaintiff had signed on with an American football club, which had subsequently ceased operations. Three of the five Justices held that the plaintiff's actions in making himself unavailable to the Argonauts, despite having been cut by them, released the Argonauts from their continuing obligation. On the other hand, section 57(1) of the *Patent Act* provided the Court with a solid legal core in *Domco Industries v. Armstrong Cork* (1982), wherein a unanimous Court upheld a cause of action in infringement in favour of a licensee of the patent.

The court's preferred tool is the *legal proposition*, a rule of law, usually in the form of a concise statement found in precedent, statute, or authoritative text.[6] A *legal principle* is similar to a proposition but is much wider in scope as it may apply to a wide variety of situations. Although it is clearly supported by legal traditions, its basis is diffuse.[7] 'Offer plus acceptance equals contract' is a proposition; the principle of the sanctity of life might allow an ambulance to enter Hart's legendary park.

Extra-legal principles are those that have some support in society but are not universally recognized as having the weight of the law behind them. The primary example is political principle, such as an obligation on the part of courts to bend over backwards to find constitutional support for impugned legislation. Dworkin advocates the judicial application of extra-legal principles.[8] *Morality* sometimes enters into legal reasoning, most often as the result of the wish of judges to frustrate dishonesty and to ensure that justice is done. It occasionally has natural law overtones as well.

The Court applied the proposition that the acts of a life insured do not affect the rights of the beneficiary in *Goulet v. Transamerica Life Insurance Co. of Canada* (2002), where the insured accidentally blew himself up while attempting to deploy a bomb. In previously arriving at a different outcome, the Court used the principle that 'no one shall profit from his own wrong' to deny coverage in *Brissette v. Westbury Life* (1992), where the beneficiary had murdered his wife. The Court applied the principle that procedure should be the servant and not the master of justice in *R. v. Burke* (2002) to order a new trial where the trial judge had misunderstood the verdict of the jury. Extra-legal principles led the Court to uphold preferential hiring in favour of Canadian citizens in *Lavoie v. Canada* (2002) in the face of *Andrews v. L.S.B.C.* (1989), which compelled the Law Society to admit a non-citizen.[9]

Trends

Figure 7.1 illustrates the results of my survey measuring the five contrasting pairs discussed in this chapter. Note that the lines on the graph measure only one of the items in each of the pairs. In other words, the graph is based on the percentage of cases reflecting bright-line tests, foundational reasoning, legal propositions, clear law, and the core of established meaning. This means that the gradual overall decline in each of the items shown in figure 7.1 implies the gradual rise in the opposite pole: open-standard tests, non-foundational reasoning, principles (both legal and politicl as well as morality), choice (including

Figure 7.1. Bright-line tests, foundational reasoning, legal propositions, clear law, core of established meaning, Supreme Court of Canada, 1952–2002

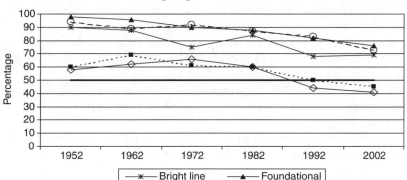

plurisignative and polysemic law), and the penumbra of uncertainty. Thus if one item in the pair was at 70 per cent, the other item in the pair would, per force, be at 30 per cent.

The slow pace of the decline in foundational reasoning has occurred despite the fact that over 50 per cent of the Court's cases now reside in the penumbra. Building blocks other than legal propositions have never comprised more than 30 per cent of the Court's reasoning; principles comprise less than 30 per cent. When legal principle does enter into the Court's reasoning, it often does so in concert with legal propositions. The number of cases in which legal propositions combined with principles was much higher in 2002 than in previous years.

Methodology

I compiled the poles above referred to based on my review of the jurisprudential literature. I had summarized each author, or set of author's views, onto an Excel spreadsheet and highlighted propositions which might be capable of empirical verification. Some propositions were tested as set out in previous chapters. This survey was designed to test the rest.

In measuring these variables, I followed the methodology outlined in section 1, reading the court's cases from the '2' years between 1952 and

2002. Based on my reading, I characterized each judgment as representing one of poles in each of the five areas. Where it was unclear how to characterize a case with regard to a given pair, that case was eliminated from the assessment of that particular area. Given the challenges of characterization, there were many cases that could not be categorized. Where the decision was of insufficient length to allow for its characterization, it also did not form part of my analysis.

I made a note of *Charter* and non-Charter cases. Where *Charter* issues were peripheral and other issues were central to the case, it was counted as non-Charter.

I then tallied the results by year using a spreadsheet computer program, which also assisted in producing figure 7.1.

8 Judicial Attitudes and Other Interesting Findings

This chapter begins with a discussion of research relating to judicial personality. At its most adamant, this research postulates that underlying judicial attitudes determine the outcome of cases; the law plays a secondary, even tertiary, role. As the summary of the research in this area discloses, judicial attitudes are somewhat correlated with the outcome of cases. But other factors, most notably the law, play much more than a mere secondary role.

Judicial Personalities: Does It Matter Who Performs the Reasoning?

It is sometimes said that judicial rulings are primarily dependent on which side of the bed the judge got up from that morning.[1] It would of course be farcical to attempt to build a theory of jurisprudence around such an idea. But a substantial body of research indicates that the background of judges may have a powerful influence on how they rule.[2] Judicial attitudes persist and are correlated with the direction judges take in their decisions. For example, one study showed that judges appointed to the Supreme Court of Canada by Liberal governments have generally been more 'progressive' than their counterparts appointed by Conservative governments.[3] A more recent study confirmed several of these findings, but found that some of the Justices' attitudes do not correlate with the political affiliation of the prime minister who appointed them. It found that the province of origin of the Justice was a more significant variable.[4]

The 'feminine' outlook has been described as less rule-bound; thus female judges may be more willing to depart from previous jurisprudence than are their male counterparts.[5] While my study was unable to document, if for no reason other than the small sample size, a greater propensity on the part of female judges to overrule precedents, there are some differences between them and their male colleagues. Candace White has shown that female Justices are stronger supporters of equality rights and that they dissent more often than do their male counterparts. They are also somewhat stronger supporters of fundamental freedoms.[6] But the correlation is not complete: for example, while female Judges have often supported positions advocated by the Women's Legal Education and Action Fund (LEAF), a feminist lobby group that targets legal cases affecting women's rights, some male Judges have been even more supportive.[7]

I attempted to measure whether Judges with academic training are more willing to overrule past decisions. Although this seemed to be the case, I was unable to quantify it with any degree of specificity. Rather, it was clear only that the trend towards appointing Judges with academic training coincided with the trend towards more overrulings.

Different judges certainly have different views as to their proper role. For example, in interviews for a current affairs television program in 1986, Justice Chouinard stated: 'I don't think it's difficult [to keep my personal opinions out of decision making] but it is an absolute must, there's no doubt about that.' Justice Lamer, interviewed for the same program, was of the opposite view: 'I'm called to make value judgments and I'm not going to make value judgments with somebody else's values. I'm going to make those judgments with my values. I think they're good. If I don't use my opinion, whose opinion am I going to use?'[8]

When most Judges advocate change, they suggest that it should be limited to the slow and incremental variety. Justice La Forest expressed a different opinion: 'I never found it necessary to limit myself to purely incremental changes and while some of my former colleagues on the Supreme Court paid lip-service to incrementalism, they frequently followed me on distant voyages of discovery. Indeed, if I may be permitted to mix metaphors, they sometimes go off on frolics of their own.'[9]

The identity of particular judges is obviously important when a judge who was in dissent on the case being overruled is part of the majority executing the overruling. For example, Justice Dickson dissented in *Bhinder v. C.N.R.* (1985) but formed part of the majority in *Central Alberta Dairy Pool* (1990), which overruled it. Justices Lamer and Cory dissented in *Kindler v. Canada* (1991) but formed part of the majority in

United States v. Burns (2001), which overruled it. By the time *Lajoie* (1974) was overruled in *Ancio* (1984), only one of the Justices from the 1974 case, Justice Ritchie, remained on the bench. He registered a plaintive dissent: 'I am unable to distinguish this case from that of *Lajoie v. The Queen*, [1974] S.C.R. 399, which is a unanimous judgment of this Court and by which I feel bound.'[10] However, the small number of cases in which there was an overlap of personnel provided an insufficient sample for analysis.

Some judges are more prone to overrule precedent.[11] Some judges are more activist than others.[12] Additionally, since the process of adjudication is dependent on human beings, it is limited by the faults and foibles of the mortal judges who staff its benches. For example, judges are not immune from errors in reasoning, including cognitive illusions.[13] To address the weaknesses stemming from such subjectivity, some investigators have explored whether judicial decisions could be made via artificial intelligence. However, computers, notwithstanding recent great strides, are not up to the task.[14]

The judicial behaviour of Justice – later Chief Justice – Dickson has recently been studied in detail.[15] In *Harrison v. Carswell* (1976), he viewed precedent as paramount and felt that the Court should exercise restraint when profoundly political issues were before it.[16] On other occasions, especially during his later years on the bench, he was willing to overrule precedent where times and attitudes had changed.[17] This anecdotal evidence shows the court making changes to the law of torts that were not based on legal principles. The $100,000 cap on damages for pain and suffering, clearly an example of judicial legislation, was the result of a pragmatic concern over high damage awards and a trade-off for complete indemnification for out-of-pocket expenses.[18]

Clearly the identity and attitudes of the particular judges deciding the case have an impact on the outcome. However, it is also clear that the law, irrespective of the individuals on the bench, also substantially influences the outcome.[19] But if close calls are just as much a matter of personality as law, should we explore alternatives? While computers can eliminate idiosyncratic personal variables, essential elements of human judgment and common sense are lost. It seems that we are still better off with judges who rail at the suggestion that they should be a 'potted plant' and occasionally inject their personal values into their decisions.[20] Justice requires a human touch as much as it requires judges to stay within the strict confines of what has gone before.

Scalogram Studies: Counting Judges' Votes

There have been several detailed jurimetric or scalogram analyses of voting patterns of the Justices of the Supreme Court of the United States, most notably by Jeffrey Segal and Harold Spaeth. These studies track judicial voting patterns against various personal characteristics of judges. Segal and Spaeth found that the votes of the Justices remained consistent with their attitudes over time. When precedents were over-ruled, conservatives voted to overturn liberal precedents and liberals voted to overturn conservative ones. Segal and Spaeth found that it was easy for judges to avoid the application of *stare decisis* to decisions they disagreed with. In short, 'the justices are rarely influenced by stare decisis.'[21] However, Youngsik Lim recently performed a quantitative analysis of the U.S. Justices' voting patterns and came to a contradictory conclusion. While he found that the American Justices would strongly follow opinions that they had rendered in prior cases (individual *stare decisis*), there was also a strong tendency to follow the Court's precedents (institutional *stare decisis*). Lim found that these tendencies varied among the several Justices.[22] Richards and Kritzer determined that 'both the justices' policy goals and legal considerations matter in [U.S.] Supreme Court decision making.'[23]

Scalogram studies of the Justices of the Supreme Court of Canada have also disclosed that judicial attitude has a significant impact on our Court's decision making. But these studies, like their American counterparts, indicate that factors other than judicial attitude also have a significant impact.[24] Philip Slayton acknowledges both the contributions and the limitations of scalogram analysis and concludes that, although judicial attitudes do play a role, 'law' is a key element in judicial decision making.[25] The early case of *Brassard v. Langevin* (1877) provides an example of a Justice (Taschereau) ruling in accord with the law and contrary to his religious attitudes.[26] More recently, Justice Iacobucci stated that he was torn between his heart and his mind when deciding the *Rodriguez* (1993) case.[27]

Several American investigators have conducted studies of lower courts with a view to determining the extent to which the ideology of judges influences the outcome of cases. Overall, their work 'corroborates the significance of ideological or partisan variables in fully understanding the lower federal courts, while also confirming that ideology explains only part of judicial behavior and is neither dominating nor pervasive in influence.'[28]

Examples of these studies include those conducted by Richard Revesz, and Cross and Tiller who identified a greater propensity on the part of judges appointed by Republican Presidents to overrule the decisions of the Environmental Protection Agency.[29] Sunstein, Schkade, and Ellman found that ideology played a substantial role in judicial outcomes but that its effect was dampened in panels where the judges had diverse ideological backgrounds.[30] Sisk and Heise determined that the religion of the judge was a significant factor in cases involving religious freedom issues. However, overall they concluded that 'the influence of political ideology upon judging on the lower federal courts [was] modest.'[31] Frank Cross found that most decisions appeared to be driven by legal and political/ideological concerns, while few seemed to be driven by strategic or litigant-specific characteristics.[32] Cross cited a study by Dan Pinello in support of the proposition that ideology accounts for only 25 per cent of judicial decision making.[33] Coupled with Cross's own conclusions, this finding supports the thesis that legal materials are the primary component of judicial decision making.[34]

Other Trends

Types of Cases and Rates of Success for Appeals

Charles Epp has documented a crossover in the Supreme Court of Canada's caseload in 1980. Prior to that time, the Court heard more tax and ordinary economic cases. After 1980, there was a shift in favour of civil liberties and rights cases.[35] In its constitutional caseload, the Court began to overturn laws at a higher rate after 1975. Requests to overturn had been steadily growing since 1970 and took a spectacular increase after 1985, with the advent of the *Charter*.[36]

Overall, the success rate for appeals has remained largely steady, ranging between just under 40 to 45 per cent.[37] However, as documented by Patrick Monahan, the success rate of *Charter* claimants has fluctuated greatly and appears to be on the rise (see figure 8.1):[38] Other differences between *Charter* and non-*Charter* are discussed in the next chapter.

Citation of Authority

By examining the trends under chief justices since 1944, when the Court was led by Thibaudeau Rinfret, until 1999, under the leadership of

Figure 8.1. Claimants' success rate in *Charter* challenges in the Supreme Court of Canada, 1991–2003

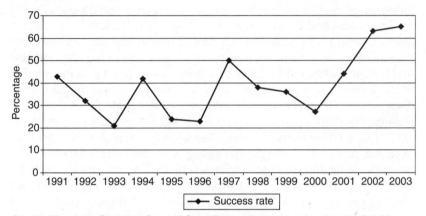

Source: Monahan, *Supreme Court of Canada, supra* note 36, as updated in P.J. Monahan, *The Supreme Court's Constitutional Decisions, 2003* (paper presented at the Seventh Annual Analysis of the Constitutional Decisions of the Supreme Court of Canada: 2003 Constitutional Cases, Osgoode Hall Law School, Toronto, 2 April 2004.

Antonio Lamer, Peter McCormick has documented a major change in the source of the authority cited by the Court over time. As can be seen in figure 8.2, the Court now prefers Canadian authority over British (including the Judicial Committee of the Privy Council) and has recently exhibited a strong preference for its own precedents. During the early *Charter* era, it began to increase its citation of cases from the United States, but these citations declined during the stewardship of Chief Justice Lamer (1990–2000).[39]

McCormick has also demonstrated that the citation of minority opinions, both concurring judgments and dissents, rose until 1990 but may now be declining somewhat. A minority opinion is one separate from the majority opinion and clearly includes an outright dissent. Separate reasons for judgment, even if they concur with the result reached by the majority reasons of the Court, are also minority opinions. A large proportion of minority opinions indicates a fractured Court. An elevated rate of the citation of minority opinions, especially dissents, indicates a less foundational Court. As illustrated in figure 8.3, minority opinions were 5 to 6 per cent of the total number of opinions prior to the Chief

Figure 8.2. Citations by the Supreme Court of Canada, 1944–1999*

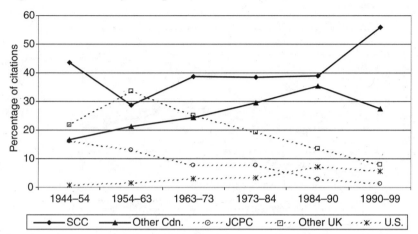

*The category 'other,' which ranged from 1 per cent to just under 2 per cent, has been omitted. The ranges of dates in figures 8.2–8.4 and 8.6 reflect chief justiceships: Thibaudeau Rinfret, 1944–54; Patrick Kerwin, 1954–63; Justices Taschereau, Cartwright, and Fauteaux, 1963–73; Bora Laskin, 1973–84; Brian Dickson, 1984–90; Antonio Lamer, 1990–9 (Lamer actually retired in 2000).
Source: P. McCormick, Supreme at Last (Toronto: Lorimer, 2000), 24, 47, 71, 96, 117, 139.

Justiceship of Bora Laskin (1973–84) and 8.5 to 10.7 per cent thereafter.[40] The top line of the graph is the total percentage of minority opinions, the bottom two lines track the citation of concurrences and dissents separately. The citation of minority opinions, especially dissenting opinions, coincides with the decline of formal legal reasoning and the rise in use of other modes of reasoning by the Court.

Unanimity and Dissent on the Court

As illustrated in figures 8.4 to 8.6, the trends in the citation of minority opinions somewhat parallels the overall level of unanimity projected by the Court.[41] McCormick has provided a useful tracking of unanimity and dissent on the Court, as summarized in figure 8.4.[42] He found that unanimity rose until 1984, but then declined.

I also tracked unanimity, but I started later and based my divisions

Figure 8.3. Citation of concurrences and dissents, Supreme Court of Canada, 1949–1999

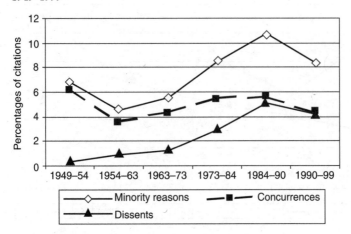

Source: P. McCormick, *Second Thoughts: Supreme Court Citation of Dissents and Separate Concurrences, 1949–1996* (2001), 81 Can. Bar Rev. 369.

on a yearly basis as opposed to on a Chief-Justiceship basis. As illustrated in figure 8.5, the Court has, since 1984, consistently decided more than half its decisions on a unanimous basis. In my study, unanimous decisions were those in which only one opinion was expressed by the Court. While a simple, 'I agree' did not render a decision non-unanimous, additional substantial reasons, even if only a paragraph long, removed the case from this category. The four-year average for 1980–3 was 77 per cent. In only two years, 1990 and 1995, when rates 49 and 43 per cent, respectively, did the rate in any given year drop below 50 per cent. It would thus appear that the decline in unanimity noted by McCormick after 1984 may now be reversing itself.

McCormick also tracked divisions within non-unanimous panels. His findings are illustrated in figure 8.6. Note that the proportion of Justices forming the plurality remained relatively constant despite the spike in unanimous decisions in 1979–84 and their decline in 1990–9. Thus the overall unanimity/division of panels on the court has remained relatively stable over time. It is interesting to note the increase in the citation of dissenting opinions since 1973 in the face of the fact that the overall proportion of dissenting opinions did not increase during that period.

Figure 8.4. Unanimous panels, Supreme Court of Canada, 1949–1999

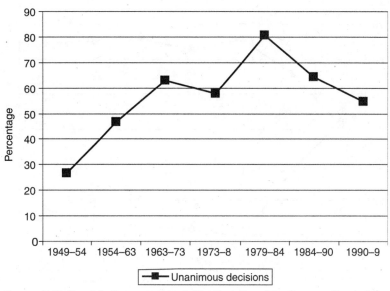

Source: P. McCormick, *Supreme at Last: The Evolution of the Supreme Court of Canada* (Toronto: Lorimer, 2000), 20, 43, 65, 90, 91, 113, 133.

Figure 8.5. Percentage of unanimous decisions, Supreme Court of Canada, 1984–2003

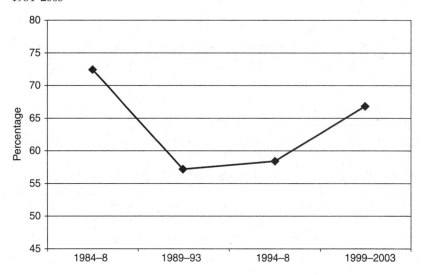

Figure 8.6. Dispersion of judges on divided panels, Supreme Court of Canada, 1949–1999

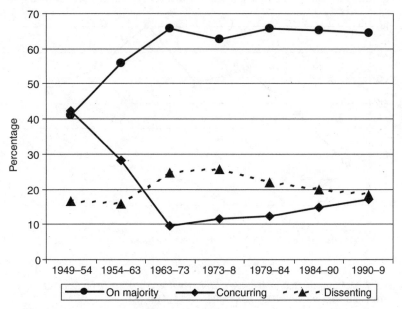

Souorce: P. McCormick, *Supreme at Last: The Evolution of the Supreme Court of Canada* (Toronto: Lorimer, 2000), 20, 43, 65, 90, 91, 113, 133.

Close Calls

I tracked cases where there was a substantial division of opinion on the Court and labelled them *close calls*. Close calls are cases that include a high proportion of dissents. A five-to-four decision is a prototypical close call: it could have gone either way. For the purposes of this monograph, the term is objective: where dissents exceed 30 per cent of the judges taking part in the decision, the case is automatically categorized as a close call. Thus, cases decided by margins of six to three, four to three, and three to two would be close calls.[42]

Panels composed of seven judges led to the possibility of five-to-two splits; in such cases 29 per cent of the presiding justices would be dissenting. Although this was close to the one-third dissent rate that occurs in six-to-three splits, five-to-two splits involved less than the 30 per cent required for a close call. I therefore required a further indica-

Figure 8.7. Close calls, Supreme Court of Canada, 1951–2000

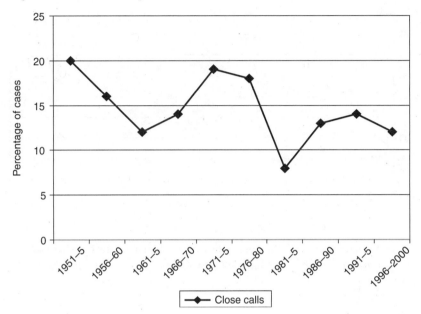

tion of closeness before labelling a five-to-two split a close call. In these cases, the Supreme Court had to overrule the decision of the Court of Appeal, and the dissenting Supreme Court Justices had to be in agree-· ment with a majority of the Court of Appeal justices. This unique reference to Court of Appeal judgments was added because five-to-two decisions are barely close calls, and the Court of Appeal decision provides a convenient tipping point. There was no such problem on panels composed of either five or nine Justices. Cases decided by margins of seven to two and four to one continue to be excluded in all circumstances, as the Supreme Court's level of dissent in these cases is 22 and 20 per cent respectively.

As can be seen in figure 8.7, the number of close calls roughly parallels the pattern of dissents tracked by McCormick. As might be expected, the trend in close calls mirrors unanimous decisions, rising in the middle period and receding when unanimity rose. The number of close calls rose gradually until 1975 and dipped sharply in the early eighties. This dip coincides with the crossovers earlier noted.

Figure 8.8. Pages per case, Supreme Court of Canada, 1972–2001

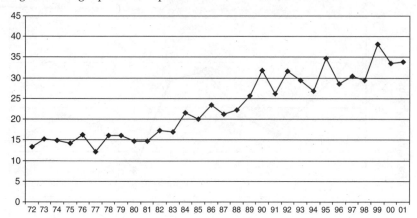

The data for close calls were collected at the same time as the survey respecting overruling and hard distinguishing as described in Chapter 6.

Number of Pages per Case

The number of pages per Supreme Court of Canada decision has risen over time, especially since the early eighties, coinciding with the cross-overs above noted. The data in figure 8.8 were calculated by noting the number of cases that I had surveyed for the purposes of tabulating the number of overrulings and hard distinguishings. I then used the Supreme Court Reports published after its bilingual format was instituted to calculate the number of pages generated by the Court on an annual basis. That number was then divided by the number of reported decisions rendered by the Court in each year.

Apparent Difficulty

The apparent difficulty[43] that the Court has encountered in deciding its cases rose between the 1960s and the 1970s but has remained constant since that time, as shown in table 8.1. This measure admittedly required a substantial component of personal judgment. It aggregates all judgments, some that I felt were fairly simple to decide, together with others that I determined to be more difficult. It should be read together

Table 8.1. Apparent difficulty* of decisions in
the Supreme Court of Canada, 1952–2002

1952	0.57
1962	0.50
1972	0.63
1982	0.65
1992	0.65
2002	0.65

*Scores range from 0.1 for the easiest case
to 0.9 for the most difficult.

with close calls when attempting to determine the Court's proportion of
'hard' and 'easy' cases under the Hartian paradigm.

An interesting sidelight respecting measuring apparent difficulty is a
recurring criticism I have received to the effect that this measure is
arbitrary or a completely subjective choice on my part. I freely acknowledge that fixing an apparent difficulty value was one of the most
difficult evaluations I undertook in this study. Yet fixing such a value
seemed important, given that the distinction between 'easy' and 'hard'
cases is central to Hart's theory. Criticism of an examiner's ability to
characterize cases as 'hard' or 'easy' is thus an intriguing comment on
Hart's theories.

9 *Charter* Cases Are Different

This chapter examines how Supreme Court of Canada cases involving the *Charter of Rights and Freedoms* are different from non-*Charter* cases. Measures for comparison include several items discussed more generally in the preceding chapters: overruling and dissents; hard distinguishing; modes of legal reasoning; apparent difficulty; the proportion of fact, law, and policy; and the five contrasting pairs analysed in chapter 7.

Definitions

A '*Charter*' case is one where the application of a provision of the *Charter* had a major impact on the outcome. For example, cases upholding an accused's right to a trial within a reasonable time or the rights of homosexuals to marry are *Charter* driven. Mere mention of the *Charter* was insufficient for a case to be categorized as a *Charter* case for the purposes of this study; rather the *Charter* had to be a substantial component of the Court's reasoning. Ordinary constitutional cases or cases decided via human rights codes are not necessarily *Charter* cases. In non-*Charter* cases, the *Charter* did not influence the outcome.

Unanimous cases and *close calls* were defined in the previous chapter.

When calculating unanimity, a *dissent* is an opinion or opinions by a minority that, had it formed the majority opinion, would have led to a different result. When calculating *dissents per case* or *dissents per judge*, I expanded the definition to include a partial dissent. A *partial dissent* is one where the dissenting Justices would have changed some but not all of the practical outcomes of the decision or where they would have provided materially different rationales for the decision.

Figure 9.1. Overruling in the Supreme Court of Canada: *Charter* and non-*Charter* cases, 1984–2003

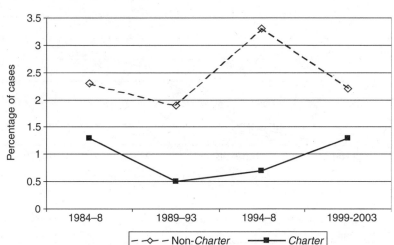

Trends

The Supreme Court overrules a substantially greater percentage of the non-*Charter* than the *Charter* cases that come before it. This persistent tendency is illustrated in figure 9.1. However, the Court used hard distinguishing proportionately much more often in *Charter* than in non-*Charter* cases (see figure 9.2). This means that it is using hard distinguishing to avoid the effect of more of its prior *Charter* decisions than the effect of its decisions relating to other issues. It should be noted that figures 9.1 and 9.2 summarize a small number of cases, which means that caution must be exercised in arriving at any conclusion based thereon.

When overruling and hard distinguishing cases are combined, the Court appears to be modifying *Charter* and non-*Charter* cases at a very similar rate. This phenomenon is illustrated in table 9.1. The similarity in the overall rate of change between *Charter* and non-*Charter* cases is also evidenced when the raw data for the period are directly combined and averaged: 3.34 per cent (non-*Charter*) and 3.1 per cent (*Charter*).

There is a sizable overlap in the modes of reasoning used by the Court in *Charter* and non-*Charter* cases. Nevertheless some interesting differences emerge, as illustrated in figure 9.3. *Charter* cases have less

Figure 9.2. Hard distinguishing in the Supreme Court of Canada: *Charter* and non-*Charter* cases, 1984–2003

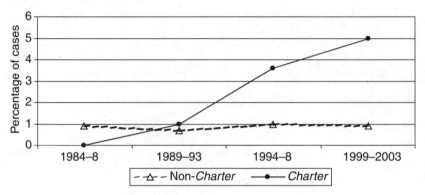

Table 9.1. Methods of changing the Law, *Charter* and non-*Charter* cases, Supreme Court of Canada, 1984–2003

	1984–8 (%)	1989–93 (%)	1994–8 (%)	1999–2003 (%)	Totals 1984–2003 (%)
Non-*Charter*					
Overruling	2.3	1.9	3.3	2.2	
Hard distin-					
guishing	0.9	0.7	10.9		
Totals	3.2	2.6	4.3	3.1	13.2
Charter					
Overruling	1.3	0.5	0.7	1.3	
Hard distin-					
guishing	0.0	1.0	3.6	5.0	
Totals	1.3	1.5	4.3	6.3	13.4

formal legal reasoning and more contextual interpretation than do non-*Charter* cases. Values-based decision-making is almost completely restricted to *Charter* cases.

There is a persistent indication that *Charter* cases are apparently more difficult to decide than non-*Charter* cases (see figure 9.4). This finding is not unexpected, given the high proportion of novel legal issues in *Charter* litigation. However, Hart's theory of an expanding core would have predicted that the gap would be closing.

Figure 9.3. Cases by mode of legal reasoning, *Charter* and non-*Charter* cases, Supreme Court of Canada, 1984–2003

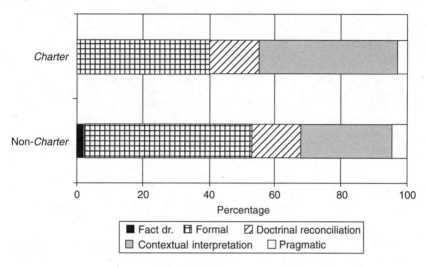

Figure 9.4. Index of apparent difficulty, *Charter* and non-*Charter* cases, Supreme Court of Canada, 1987–2002

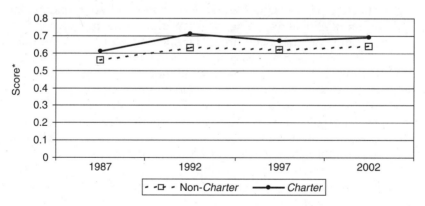

*Scores range from 0.1 for the easiest case to 0.9 for the most difficult.

Table 9.2. Fact, law, and policy in *Charter* and non-*Charter* cases, Supreme Court of Canada, 1987–2002

	Fact	Law	Policy
1987			
Non-*Charter*	17	68	15
Charter	13	64	23
1992			
Non-*Charter*	21	50	29
Charter	18	52	30
1997			
Non-*Charter*	19	60	21
Charter	18	58	24
2002			
Non-*Charter*	22	49	29
Charter	17	47	36

Table 9.2 shows the proportion of fact, law, and policy in *Charter* and non-*Charter* cases. There is almost no difference between the Court's reliance on law in *Charter* and non-*Charter* cases, but the Court relies less on fact and more on policy in *Charter* cases. This policy/fact differential is likely not unexpected given the way in which *Charter* issues tend to be brought before the Court – that is, as matters of importance to more people than just the individual litigants.

In chapter 7, I analysed the court's reasoning in five areas by measuring contrasting pairs: bright-line and open-standard tests, foundational and non-foundational reasoning, clear law and choice, proposition and principle, and core and penumbra. Here, I compare *Charter* and non-*Charter* cases in these five areas using the same pairs. It is worth noting that the sample size was relatively small; nonetheless, the differential between the two types of cases appears to be substantial.

More open-standard tests are used in *Charter* than in non-*Charter* cases. Fewer bright-line tests were used or propounded in *Charter* cases, but the gap narrowed between 1992 and 2002. The law is less clear in *Charter* cases, though more clear in 2002 than in 1992. As well *Charter* cases are more often in the penumbra than are non-*Charter* cases. Although the differential had shrunk from that in 1992, in 2002 *Charter* cases were twice as likely as non-*Charter* cases to be in the penumbra. The rise in non-foundational reasoning and in the use of principle was

Figure 9.5. Bright-line tests, foundational reasoning, legal propositions, clear·
law, core of established meaning, Supreme Court of Canada, 1992 and 2002,
Charter and non-*Charter* cases

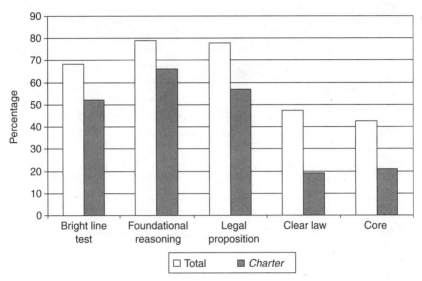

more pronounced in *Charter* cases. In 1992, the Court relied on legal
propositions slightly more often in *Charter* cases than in non-*Charter*
cases; in 2002 it relied on legal propositions less than on principle as
compared to an overall reliance on principle of more than 60 per cent.
The overall comparison is contained in figure 9.5. Overall, *Charter* decision appear to be less rule-bound than non-*Charter* decisions. In the
former the law is less clear; the Court has more manoeuvring room.

Next, we turn to a comparison of some of the items discussed in the
latter part of chapter 8, specifically number of pages per case as well
as opinions and dissents per case. As figure 9.6 illustrates, *Charter* and
non-*Charter* cases differ substantially in the number of pages they
generate. *Charter* cases generate more opinions than non-*Charter* cases
(see figure 9.7). As well, the Court is much more divided when dealing
with *Charter* issues that are measured both as a function of dissents per
case and dissents per sitting judge per case (see figures 9.8 and 9.9).
Figures 9.8 and 9.9 indicate that 1997 was a unique year. This fact has
been noted by other commentators.[1] However, as indicated by the

Figure 9.6. Pages per case, *Charter* and non-*Charter* cases, Supreme Court of Canada, 1987–2002

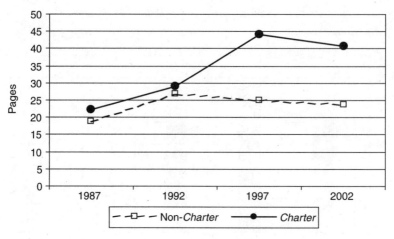

Figure 9.7. Opinions per case, *Charter* and non-*Charter*, Supreme Court of Canada, 1987–2002

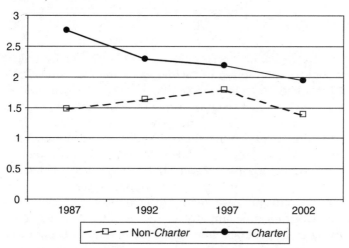

following paragraphs, even with the inclusion of data from 1997, the differences between *Charter* and non-*Charter* cases are statistically significant. The finding of statistical significance means that these differences are real phenomena, that they are not the result of chance or natural variation between cases.

Figure 9.8. Dissents per case, *Charter* and non-*Charter*, Supreme Court of Canada, 1987–2002

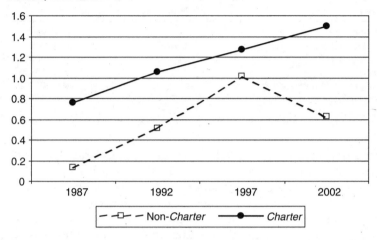

Figure 9.9. Dissents per judge, *Charter* and non-*Charter*, Supreme Court of Canada, 1987–2002

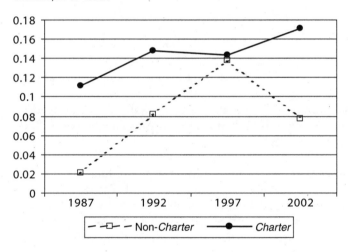

The comparisons between *Charter* and non-*Charter* cases with respect to number of pages, number of judges participating in the decision, number of opinions, number of dissents, number of opinions per participating judge, number of dissents per participating judge, and number of dissents per opinion were subjected to statistical analysis. The

Table 9.3. Statistical analysis of *Charter* and non-*Charter* cases, Supreme Court of Canada, 1987–2002

Category (no.)	Probability	Test level
Pages per case	.029	$p < .05$
Judges participating	.001	$p \leq .001$
Opinions per case	.0001	$p \leq .0001$
Dissents per case	.017	$p < .05$
Opinions per judge participating	.004	$p < .01$
Dissents per judge participating	.020	$p < .05$
Dissents per opinion	.120	

test employed was the two-tailed *t* test. The Statistical Package for the Social Sciences software was used to conduct the analysis. As shown in table 9.3, statistically significant differences between *Charter* and non-*Charter* cases were documented in all categories except in the number of dissents per opinion. The low degree of probability that obtained means that it is all but impossible that the quantitative differences between *Charter* and non-*Charter* cases described above occurred as the result of random chance. In other words, the variables (i.e., *Charter*, non-*Charter*) are clearly associated with the differences noted above.

The lack of statistically significant difference in the number of dissents per opinion is not unexpected. *Charter* cases have both more opinions and more dissents per case. Thus, with respect to *Charter* cases, there was a substantial breach of the Court's institutional discipline relating to the number of opinions rendered per case. However, the increased number of opinions was essentially evenly spread between dissenting opinions and those forming or concurring with the majority.

This greater tendency to division on the Court can also be seen by the fact that the Court is less likely to render a unanimous decision in a *Charter* case and more likely to render a close call. The data for figure 9.10 include *all* cases (i.e., *Charter* and non-*Charter*) between 1984, when the first *Charter* cases were heard by the Court, and 2003. In this respect, it contrasts with figures 9.7–9.9, which contain data from only four individual years. This data set therefore matches the data set for *Charter*/non-*Charter* overruling and hard distinguishing and was compiled at the same time. As disclosed in figure 9.10, there is a persistent difference between *Charter* and non-*Charter* cases: the former are characterized by less unanimity and more close calls. This larger sample size, when analysed statistically, showed a level of probability in excess

Figure 9.10. Comparison of Supreme Court cases with and without *Charter* issues, 1984–2003

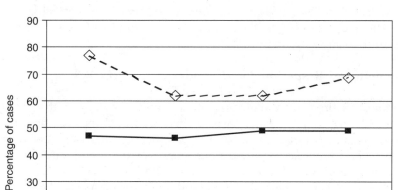

of .001, meaning that there was less than one chance in a thousand that the difference was a result of random factors.[2]

The statistical verification of difference between *Charter* and non-*Charter* cases provides corroboration of the qualitative findings of differential modes of reasoning and of differential means used by the Court in modifying its prior decisions in *Charter* as opposed to non-*Charter* cases.

Examples Respecting *Charter* and Non-*Charter* Cases

R v. Chase (1987) was a non-*Charter* case because it dealt with the definition of sexual assault without referring to the *Charter*. *Trimm v. Durham Regional Police* (1987) was a *Charter* case because the Court's determination of whether or not the relevant tribunal was impartial revolved around section 11 of the *Charter*.

R. v. Fliss (2002) was a *Charter* case because the *Charter* determined whether or not evidence obtained at the time of the wiretap would be admitted.

R. v. Hibbert (2002) was not a *Charter* case because the correctness of the trial judge's charge to the jury on the issue of identification did not depend, in any way, on the *Charter*.

Methodology Respecting *Charter* and Non-*Charter* cases

At the same time as I tabulated the other surveys, I noted whether cases were *Charter* or non-*Charter* cases. I then separated the two types to compare and contrast them with each other. Comparisons between *Charter* and non-*Charter* cases, other than overruling and hard distinguishing, used data from the years 1987, 1992, 1997, and 2002. Comparisons respecting overruling and hard distinguishing used data from all the years from 1984 through 2003. As referred to above, some of the sample sizes utilized in this chapter were small. The sample for unanimous/close calls were relatively large, at 566 cases (271 non-*Charter* unanimous, 190 *Charter* unanimous, 43 non-*Charter* close calls, and 62 *Charter* close calls). But there were only 40 cases of overruling (4 *Charter* and 36 non-*Charter*) and only 24 cases of hard distinguishing (11 *Charter* and 13 non-*Charter*). And when comparing bright lines to open standards and core to penumbra, there were only, on average, 63 non-*Charter* cases and 43 *Charter* cases per pair.

Some cases could not be characterized as being *Charter* or non-*Charter*. For example, it was not possible to characterize *Chamberlain v. Surrey School District No. 36* (2002) as being a *Charter* or non-*Charter* case because the Court could have arrived at its decision with or without the *Charter*. Both *Charter* and non-*Charter* analysis played a significant role in the Court's reasoning in that case. For this reason cases such as *Chamberlain* were not taken into consideration when contrasting *Charter* and non-*Charter* cases.

SECTION III

Testing Theories

10 How Judges Judge: Testing Legal Theory

This chapter examines the theories of H.L.A. Hart together with the contrasting theories of Ronald Dworkin, Julius Stone, Peter Goodrich, and Allan Hutchinson in light of the empirical evidence described in the previous six chapters.[1] In the first part of this chapter, I summarize the theories of H.L.A. Hart and his critics. I then examine non-foundational legal theory. This is followed by an exploration of the set of decision-making tensions in the Supreme Court of Canada propounded by Justice Bertha Wilson. Finally, I re-examine these theories and tensions in light of the Court's *Charter* jurisprudence.

Hart and His Critics

The empirical evidence, by and large, supports the thesis that the Supreme Court of Canada functions largely in accord with the tenets of foundational positivism. The Court almost always rules based on legal materials (statute, precedent) and not on moral or sociological grounds. Law is preferred over policy. Reasons for judgment almost always cite specific legal sources; they do not rely on some omnipresent divine order. The amount of foundational reasoning exceeds non-foundational reasoning by a factor of three to one.[2] The Court tends to use formal, sometimes even formalistic, legal reasoning and tends to avoid open discourse or the examination of first principles. Even in the penumbra, the Court prefers to canvass legal materials wherever possible and turns to non-legal materials only where legal materials run out. Any new rule is carefully fitted into the corpus of the law.

But there are important exceptions. Many interesting phenomena are concealed within 'by and large.' The following sections will discuss these anomalies with a view to answering the question: Do Hart's theories accurately describe the Court's behaviour?

Easy/Hard and Penumbra/Core

The two most prominent ideas associated with Hart are the dichotomy of 'easy' and 'hard' cases and the placement of legal issues in either a core of settled meaning or in a penumbra of uncertainty. Hart wrote: 'Legal rules may have a central core of undisputed meaning, and in some cases it may be difficult to imagine a dispute as to the meaning of a rule breaking out... Yet all rules have a penumbra of uncertainty where the judge must choose between alternatives.'[3] Issues at the core are 'easy,' those in the penumbra 'hard.' By way of illustration, in deciding what qualifies as a weapon, a loaded pistol is clearly a weapon. It is less clear whether a pistol without a firing mechanism also qualifies as a weapon. A cannon full of cement would likely not be a weapon unless it was used to threaten someone who was unaware that the cannon was inoperable. A child's stuffed teddy bear would never, except in the most bizarre circumstances, be a weapon. The common law records the penumbral choices made in judgments on such issues, thereby enlarging the core of certainty and shrinking the penumbra. Furthermore, because each decision clarifies the law, Hart posits that the core is constantly expanding while the penumbra is shrinking: the law 'works itself pure.'[4]

Evidence Respecting a Hard Core

The idea of a hard core of settled meaning is only partially supported by the survey evidence. Overall, the trend is towards fewer close calls, with unanimous rulings constituting more than 50 per cent of the Court's decisions. In addition, only approximately 5 per cent of cases involve overruling or hard distinguishing. Even at the Supreme Court, where cases are selected in part for their difficulty, the easy/hard index hovers just above 0.6 (maximum 'hardness' is 1).[5] Presumably this index will decline as one moves down the judicial hierarchy. All these data provide support for Hart's notion that a majority of cases will be easy to decide.

However, the evidence contradicts the idea that the core is expanding and the penumbra shrinking over time. Rather, more and more issues are penumbral. The incidence of overruling is increasing, not decreasing. As well, close calls continue to be a persistent feature of the Court's jurisprudence. Stone proposed a refinement to Hart's theory to the effect that each decision *may* limit future available meanings but may also 'work the other way to widen the range of possibilities.' This refinement is closer to the truth, given that many cases of overruling involve a new reading of a previous text.[6]

Is Legal Reasoning at the Penumbra Different?

Hart's 'soft positivism' concedes a role for a wider range of considerations when the judge leaves the core and enters the penumbra to wrestle with a hard case. Weaker precedents – precedents based on facts less analogous to the fact situation presently before the court – will need to be utilized as the court seeks to extrapolate from other law.[7] Moral considerations may have a greater role to play in judicial reasoning in the penumbra of hard cases.[8] Judges may employ different modes of reasoning where there is no clear statute or precedent.[9] Social change may transform what was once core into penumbra; the solution provided by the law may no longer accord with conventional wisdom.[10] Ultimately, it may be necessary to formulate a new rule.[11]

Although I was unable to quantify an openness to a wider range of considerations in the penumbra, this did qualitatively seem to be the case. The Court seemed to be more contextual in the penumbra. However, morality did not seem to be a major component of reasoning in the penumbra. Because overrulings occur primarily, if not exclusively, in the penumbra, reasons for judgment leading up to overrulings should have significantly different characteristics than reasons that apply clear law in easy cases. There is some indication that overrulings occur when the law is unstable – that is, in the penumbra. And overrulings are often a reaction to law that is out of step with justice, another characteristic of the penumbra. In sum, the question of whether legal reasoning differs in the penumbra remains open.

Dworkin's Chain Novel

Another popular analogy used to describe the process of judicial decision making, one first proposed by Ronald Dworkin, is that of judges as the authors of a 'chain novel.'[12] The author of the first chapter can write whatever she wants. The next author must conform his chapter 2 to her chapter 1. The authors of subsequent chapters are constrained by all of their predecessors as they contribute ongoing installments to the story. Judges in a mature legal system, just as authors in the middle of a chain novel, might be able to interpret the law, but only within well-contained parameters. The core of settled meaning becomes larger and more all-embracing as the novel proceeds. Each judicial decision fixes another brick onto an increasingly entrenched foundation. Fish maintains that even the first novelist is constrained by the shared practices, norms, and understandings of the interpretative community. No judge is ever able to 'strike out in a new direction.'[13]

If Dworkin's chain novel theory wins out over his detractors, chiefly Fish and Stone, there will be few instances of overruling, few close calls, and little hard distinguishing. New decisions will 'fit' well into existing case law. Thus, in many ways, this chain novel theory, in its basic form, is compatible with Hart's description of the common law.

Evidence in Support of Law as a Chain Novel

The chain novel theory is by and large supported by the data from my survey. Overruling and hard distinguishing are rare. Close calls occur in less than one case in five.

While there are exceptions, the analogy of judges writing a chain novel is sufficiently accurate to constitute a useful framework within which to analyse judicial behaviour. The novel is often crushingly boring, with little, if anything, changing from chapter to chapter. Each successive instalment expands the settled core of the story, which is then widely known and accepted. When the first judge writes chapter 1, almost everything is in the penumbra. This first chapter adds some settled meaning: who the protagonist is and what she wants. Chapter 2 removes the antagonist from the penumbra and adds his wants and desires to the core of settled meaning. Chapter 3 sets out the field of battle on which these competing desires are to be brought into opposition.

The changes that do occur tend to be adjectival: the furniture is rearranged, the male character buys a new car, the female protagonist masters a new cuisine. There are few plot twists or character reveals. A gothic romance does not become a high-tech sci-fi thriller. The incidents by which the novel unfolds its story may be of great interest to serious students of literature, but most people's lives go on as they did before.

Even where the Court overrules precedent, the new rule is compatible with the remaining corpus of the law. When viewed against the backdrop of a rapidly changing society, these judicial changes tend to be minor. Changes to the law of hearsay, for example, did not disturb the central premise that evidence not directly perceived by the witness requires special safeguards to ensure reliability.

Dworkin: The Rule of Principle Leads to One Right Answer

Dworkin takes his chain novel theory a step further and uses it as the basis for a principle-based theory of coherence. According to Dworkin, statutes and precedent should be interpreted in light of principles occurring elsewhere in the law. Law should be viewed as having being created by a single author who intended to express 'a coherent conception of justice and fairness.'[14] Individual judges shape their judgments to fit seamlessly into this coherent conception. This is fine as far as it goes, but Dworkin attempts to extend coherence into a platform for imposing his personal values onto the law and thus onto society as a whole.[15]

For Hart, settled propositions decide all but hard cases where the law is incomplete. In the penumbra, the law is incomplete; judges must search for the answer outside the settled law. But Dworkin maintains that the law is never incomplete, even in hard cases. For Dworkin, principles – moral and legal – always provide one correct answer.[16] And Dworkin does not limit his interpretation of integrity to hard cases: 'Law as integrity explains and justifies easy cases as well as hard ones.'[17] Furthermore, for Dworkin 'justice' is the most important principle of all.[18]

The Court's Limited Use of Principle

How accurate is this theory? As described in chapter 5, formal legal reasoning has always been, and continues to be, the dominant mode of legal reasoning in the Supreme Court of Canada. Decisions based primarily on legal principle have never constituted more than 4 per cent of the Court's decisions.

Furthermore, figure 10.1 illustrates that, even measuring principle as a constitutive part of the Court's reasoning process, this type of legal reasoning comprises only a small proportion of the Court's adjudicative process. The Court relied on propositions more than 70 per cent of the time, as against under 30 per cent for principles and moral considerations. Even when overruling precedent, the Court is unlikely to turn to principle.[19] In addition, the Court's utilization of principle is much

Figure 10.1. Percentage of decisions using proposition-based reasoning, Supreme Court of Canada, 1952–2002

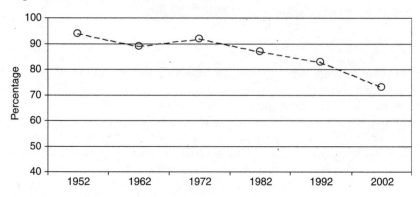

more in line with that permitted by Hart in his postscript to *Concept of Law* than with that advocated by Dworkin in *Law's Empire*. There is no short cut in the effective study of phenomena; Dworkin should have performed a wide survey before basing his universal theory on highly exceptional behaviour.

Moreover, formal legal reasoning is even more prevalent in lower courts than it is in the Supreme Court of Canada. The Ontario Court of Appeal rarely used principle as the basis for its decisions; that province's Superior Court almost never did.

More Than One Answer

As with principle, Dworkin's hope that legal reasoning would produce one right answer has not come to pass. The number of trial decisions that are regularly reversed and the number of dissents and especially close calls in the Supreme Court quickly expose the lack of foundation for this idea. Legal materials likely provide some constraint, even in hard cases, but they also provide considerable room for choice.[20] The Supreme Court's support for deference towards administrative tribunals – upholding decisions the Court believes to have been wrongly decided – is in direct opposition to Dworkin's thesis in this regard.[21] As figure 10.2 shows, the proportion of cases where the law is clear has been dropping since the mid-1960s. This means that, increasingly, several answers are supportable by legal precedent and principle. Thus it

Figure 10.2. Percentage of decisions where law is clear, Supreme Court of Canada, 1952–2002

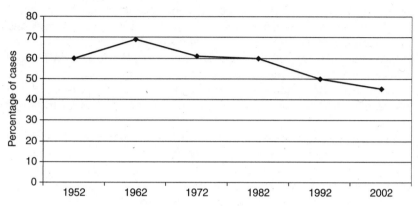

cannot be said that the model proposed by Dworkin has supplanted the one described by Hart.

Stone and Goodrich: Clear Rules or Multiple Meanings?

While Hart concedes that the 'open-textured' nature of the English language occasionally results in a minority of legal decisions being hard, Stone and Goodrich maintain that almost all legal controversies are capable of multiple outcomes. The leeways within legal linguistics – the inherent 'play' in the English language – give judges the ultimate choice. Hartian positivism operates under the presumption that judges will, in good faith, carry out the imperatives set out in the law, especially those embodied in statute or well-established precedent.[22] This good-faith analysis would allow the legislature to operate at the wholesale level and leave the retail application of incremental discretion up to the courts.[23] For Hart, judicial choice is limited to filling in gaps unforeseen by the legislature.

Julius Stone bases his critique of Hart on the proposition that almost all cases are 'hard' because judges can almost always find a way to rationalize the decision they want to make.[24] Legally speaking, almost all words are plurisignative in that they are capable of more than one meaning.[25] For Stone, the leeways of choice begin with the trial judge who can shade the facts to facilitate the decision she wants to make. Logic does not provide a certain answer; in many situations logic can be twisted to allow for a ruling in favour of either party. A significant step in legal reasoning is choosing the category under which a legal problem falls. But, here as well, the judge has considerable choice open to her. Furthermore, the practice of *ratio decidendi* allows the judge to pick and choose among the facts of earlier decisions to decide which ones do and which ones do not provide present guidance. Because each judicial choice is slightly different from the choice made in preceding cases, the new decision does not restrict judicial leeway – it increases it.[26] For Stone, the law does not 'work itself pure,' it works itself more and more obscure.

Goodrich, echoing Stone, charges that law's self-referential stance conceals the problem of polysemy, 'the necessary semantic indeterminacy of many if not all key legal terms or categories of law.'[27] Whenever legal reasoning arrives at a decision, that decision is *ipso facto* correct and therefore legal reasoning 'works.' Legal tradition and education conspire to preserve this result. Goodrich charges that lawyers and judges refuse to acknowledge the problem of meaning. The impenetrable nature of legal language means that any lay person who wants to study law first has to learn what is essentially a foreign language; but in learning legal terminology, the lay student is seduced and co-opted into the tradition of positivist law and legal reasoning.

In a similar vein, several authors contend that the open-textured nature of many statutes effectively allows judges to pick and choose among available canons of construction to frustrate legislative intent.[28] Some common law doctrines have similar choice-permitting dichotomies.[29]

Hard-line positivists resist these critiques. To the extent that legal reasoning wavers from the standard of formal adjudication, positivists advocate a return to it. Under this paradigm, legal reasoning is an almost mechanical process of connecting the dots. Foundational positivists maintain that the judges are not free to make of the law whatever they wish it to be.[30] Both the core of settled meaning and provisions constituting the penumbra of uncertainty guide the judge to a proper decision. If the decision-making method employed by the Court is purely foundational, there should be almost no cases of overruling or hard distinguishing. Close calls should be few in number.

Plurisignative and Polysemy: The Evidence

The rise in the number of cases allowing for judicial choice provides some support for Stone's thesis.[31] However, this increase may be as much the result of the Court's leave to appeal criteria, which require it to select hard cases, as the result of any overall instability in the state of the law. Close calls have declined slightly but remain above 10 per cent. Stone's theories would predict a higher level of close calls.

If Stone and Goodrich are right, hard distinguishing will be more common than overruling. Or at the very least, judges will be free to hide any overruling under a mask of distinguishing. But hard distinguishing is in decline, and the transparency of the Court's reasoning overall is increasing. Thus, on these points, the court's jurisprudence contradicts Stone and Goodrich.[32]

The more direct analysis of bright-line versus open-standard tests and of the increasing proportion of cases allowing judicial choice discloses a trend away from Hartian positivism and towards the freer judicial regime portrayed by Stone and Goodrich. The crossover in modes of legal reasoning is another indicator that the trend towards a greater attention to policy and context.[33]

However, it must be remembered that Stone's analysis utilized cases featuring formal legal reasoning. The trends postulated by Stone seem less apparent in these types of cases. The increased level of choice does not seem to be the product of linguistic looseness. Thus, while the theories proposed by Stone and Goodrich provide many useful insights, the empirical evidence indicates that their theories lack overall applicability. Overall, formal legal reasoning leads to stability, not change or adventurism.

Non-Foundational Legal Theory

Allan Hutchinson, in describing non-foundationalism, compared law to a game in which everything is always open to interpretation.[34] Jurists are to be judged on how well they play the game of adjudication; no human performance will ever be perfect, but jurists should always strive to do their best, to constantly improve. But even non-foundationalists concede that the game imposes its own restrictions as to what would possibly count as a valid move; kicking a ball out of bounds will never count as a goal. Cass Sunstein observes that human arrangements are based on incompletely theorized agreements.[35] Thus law will never speak to all eventualities with perfect clarity. Rather, its purpose is to manage the resultant uncertainties.[36]

Hutchinson characterizes *anti*-foundationalists as believing that 'anything goes' – any decision is possible. Anti-foundationalists contend, for example, that the U.S. Constitution could be read so as to mandate socialism and forbid capitalism.[37] For a foundationalist, there is only one correct answer and that is all that can 'go.' On the other hand, according to Hutchinson, *non*-foundationalists postulate that 'anything *might* go.'[38] This middle ground conceives of legal reasoning as being sufficiently fluid that the judge could go either way on any discrete issue but at the same time as being sufficiently stable to restrict the range of possible decisions. Law provides significant constraints on judicial adventurism.

Non-foundationalists contend that legal reasoning is not so determinate or value-free as once contended.[39] It is more art than science.[40] Context changes the meaning of text, both statutory and caselaw. The reader must, in the very act of reading, interpret. The reader's – that is, the judge's – perspective, her values, and her purpose change the text. But the text is not without a force of its own. Both the text and the legal system in which the text is utilized impose powerful constraints in how the text is interpreted. Even the more expansive mode of contextual interpretation provides some constraint.[41] Judge Posner describes law as 'an activity rather than a concept or a group of concepts. No bounds can be fixed *a priori* on what shall be allowed to count as an argument in law.'[42] Thus non-foundationalists occupy the middle ground between the positivists and anti-foundational critical legal scholars.

If judges are applying a fixed foundational law in good faith, there should be few cases of overruling, and those that exist will be clearly necessary and supported by cogent reasons. Hard distinguishing will be rare. These presumptions would predict that ideologically playful – non-foundational – judges will overrule more often and that, where they cannot depart in an openly radical way, they will resort to hard distinguishing.

Support for Non-Foundationalism

The most forthright means for the measurement of the presence of foundational, non-foundational, and anti-foundational legal reasoning is to survey a large number of cases and to directly characterize the type of legal reasoning being employed by the Court. As described in chapter 7, this survey yielded the result depicted in figure 10.3. The data indicate that the Court's predominant mode is foundational, but that non-foundational reasoning is gradually becoming more common (I found no instances of anti-foundational reasoning). The trend towards non-foundational reasoning is matched by similar trends that reflect an

Figure 10.3. Percentage of decisions reflecting foundational reasoning,
Supreme Court of Canada, 1952–2002

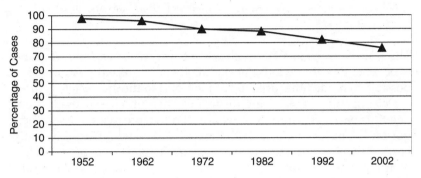

increase in judicial choice, contextual interpretation, and the use of
policy.

As outlined above, non-foundational reasoning should lead to elevated occurrences of overruling and close calls. Perhaps hard distinguishing should also be elevated. My data show that close calls persist
but not in a consistent pattern. Interestingly, overrulings *are* rising in
concert with the rise in non-foundational reasoning. However, the incidence of overruling remains very low.

Thus, similarly to other theories, it would appear that non-foundational theory provides important insights but that it fails to fully capture all the phenomena involved in legal adjudication. It may be that
'run of the mill' cases do not interest Hutchinson as much as those
where 'anything might go,' but his theory lacks inclusiveness as a result
of his not adequately incorporating these more commonplace cases.

Wilson's Deliberative Tensions

Justice Wilson has theorized that the Supreme Court copes with tensions between four sets of considerations in reaching a decision:

> The first of these is the tension between the desire to do justice in the
> individual case and the desire to rationalize the development of the juris-
> prudence in the particular area. The second is the tension between at-
> tempting to achieve certainty in the law and at the same time ensuring its
> adaptability to social conditions which are constantly changing. The third
> is the tension between the 'deciding only what is necessary for the case'

approach and the approach that views the Court in the role of overseer of the development of the jurisprudence. And the fourth is the tension between the judge as an individual member of the Court and the Court as an institution.[43]

The relative ascendancy of each set of tensions has waxed and waned over time. But, if one looks at the trends of the recent past, it may be possible to predict the direction of the Court in the immediate future.

Doing justice may lead the Justices to attempt to bend the law on a one-time basis. This approach would lead to more cases of hard distinguishing, but the trend is in the opposite direction. On a qualitative basis, the Court does seem to strive to prevent bad actors profiting from their injustice. Yet, this must be contrasted with the Court's refusal to allow those disadvantaged by a law that was later declared to be unconstitutional to reopen their cases.[44] The other pole within this tension, *rationalizing the jurisprudence*, will require the occasional overruling. These are indeed on the rise. The Court also tends, more and more, to cite its own decisions in preference to those of lower courts or courts from other jurisdictions. Facts matter less, while policy, context, and principle are ascendant. Providing clear guidance requires that overruling be used in place of hard distinguishing, which often obscures issues.[45] It thus seems that the Court is more interested in rationalizing jurisprudence than in doing justice in the individual case.

Promoting a façade of *certainty* may impel the Court towards hard distinguishing while promoting the *adaptability of the law* will engender more transparent overrulings. A Court leaning towards adaptability will explore modes of reasoning in addition to formal and foundational legal reasoning. Such a Court will also adopt more and more open standards and fewer bright-line tests, thus increasing its ability to exercise choice in the future. As the discussion in the section above dealing with Hart versus Dworkin and figure 10.4 indicate, the trend in the Court's jurisprudence is towards adaptability.

The tension between exploring *only so much of the issue as is necessary* to decide *the case* and *developing the jurisprudence* is less well defined. Certainly there are instances of both. The ascendancy of overrulings over hard distinguishing tips the balance slightly in favour of developing the jurisprudence. The increasing number of pages per judgment is also an indication in favour of developing the jurisprudence.

The decline in close calls and the steady predominance of unanimous judgments indicate a movement away from the *judge as an individual*

Figure 10.4. Measures of certainty and adaptability in the Supreme Court of Canada, 1952–200

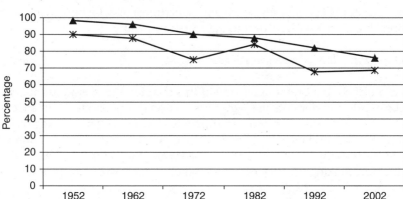

and towards the *Court as an institution*. Another indicator of the trend towards the latter is the increase of the ability of sitting Justices to influence the appointment of new members of the Court.[46]

Charter Jurisprudence: Cases in Point, or Anomalies Requiring Adjustment?

As detailed in chapter 9, there are clear differences between *Charter* and non-*Charter* cases in the Supreme Court of Canada. *Charter* cases have statistically significantly more dissents, opinions, and pages per decision. There are significantly more close calls and fewer unanimous decisions in *Charter* cases. The Court uses less formal legal reasoning and more contextual, pragmatic, principle-based, and especially more value-based reasoning in *Charter* cases. Policy plays a greater role in *Charter* cases than in non-*Charter* cases. *Charter* cases are harder to decide, a reflection of the fact that *Charter* issues have a greater tendency to reside in the penumbra. These trends coincide with a greater reliance on open-standard tests and a more pronounced trend towards non-foundational reasoning in *Charter* cases.

But the most salient distinction between *Charter* and non-*Charter* cases is the persistently different way in which the Court modifies the law. The Court overrules the law less readily in *Charter* cases but is much more prone to resort to hard distinguishing when it wishes to modify the law arising under the *Charter*. While the gap between *Charter* and non-*Charter* cases relative to overruling may be narrowing, the opposite is true with respect to hard distinguishing.

Dworkin: Still No One Right Answer

As outlined in a previous section of this chapter, the overall number of close calls and dissents in *Charter* cases casts doubt on Dworkin's view that the law leads to only one right answer. The incidence of close calls and dissents is even more elevated in the court's *Charter* jurisprudence. This refutes the 'one-right-answer' thesis and indicates that the Court's decision-making is often less 'legal' when it deals with *Charter* issues.

Wilson's Tensions Different

The relative ascendancy of the tensions described by Justice Wilson is different in *Charter* cases.[47] The elevated proportion of hard distinguishing indicates that the Court is attempting to *do justice in the individual case* while at the same time avoiding criticism for creating *uncertainty in the law*. The increasing number of open standards in *Charter* jurisprudence shows that *adaptability* also has a strong pull. The Court, by not restraining its urge to *develop the jurisprudence*, as opposed to limiting itself to *deciding the case*, may in part be the author of its own misfortune in this regard. The increased number of close calls shows how much more pull each pole of Wilson's four tensions has on the *individual justices*. There seems to be a feeling that the *Charter* must be infused with every good instinct humanity has to offer. Perhaps the Justices should relax and realize that the *Charter* is only one legal document, however important, among many.

Hart's Expanding Core Theory Not Supported

If Hart's theory of an expanding core and a shrinking penumbra is accurate, the differences between *Charter* and non-*Charter* jurisprudence would be shrinking. This does not seem to be the case. A shrinking penumbra should lead to progressively fewer close calls, especially in areas, such as the *Charter*, where a large body of caselaw has now been built up. Initially, of course, there were many open questions: a large penumbra surrounded each *Charter* issue. Consequently, one would expect that the first cases wherein the Court interpreted the *Charter* would have resulted in a large number of close calls. Yet, because the Court has now had over two decades of *Charter* litigation, the penumbra should have shrunk, the law should have become more settled, and there should now be fewer close calls in *Charter* cases. Some *Charter* issues have yet to be litigated, so there will still be some close calls, but Hart's analysis would predict an overall downward trend. Stone's analysis leads to the opposite hypothesis: lines of precedent should extend instead of restrict judicial leeway and thus judicial choice will expand.[48] The slight rise in *Charter* close calls contradicts Hart. However, the manner in which the Court arrived at those close calls fails to support Stone. The survey evidence thus supports neither Hart's nor Stone's thesis.

It may well be that the core of settled meaning is expanding but that the penumbra is expanding as well. For example, when the *Charter* was entrenched in 1982, the issue of sexual orientation was at best dimly envisioned. It was a distant comet, awaiting its first sighting. Then cases relating to homosexual rights were brought forward and these issues moved into the penumbra. Now sexual orientation is clearly established as one of the equalities protected under section 15 of the *Charter*. The continued growth of issues inside the penumbra is likely indicative of the growing numbers of issues that are becoming legalized in Canadian society.[49] The data are not conclusive in this regard.

Elevated Hard Distinguishing Supports Stone, Goodrich

If Stone and Goodrich are right, hard distinguishing will be more common than overruling. Or at the very least, judges will be free to hide any overruling under a mask of distinguishing. According to my data, the Court's overall jurisprudence contradicts Stone and Goodrich; however its *Charter* jurisprudence supports their thesis.[50] The rise of hard distinguishing in *Charter* cases indicates that issues are refusing to go quietly into the core of settled meaning. In this regard, Stone's theories are supported.

Charter *Jurisprudence: Both Cases in Point and Anomalies*

In sum, the Court's *Charter* jurisprudence represents both a case in point and an anomaly.

It is a case in point in the sense that *Charter* jurisprudence is, in many ways, a microcosm of where the quality of the Court's jurisprudence is heading. This jurisprudence is increasingly characterized by an elevated openness to new modes of reasoning and to an expanded palette of considerations. *Charter* cases are in line with the Court's gradually increasing activism.

But *Charter* jurisprudence is anomalous in that its elevated and rising rate of hard distinguishing goes against the grain of the Court's overall progression towards open and transparent reasons for judgment.

Conclusion

Although the empirical evidence has not completely supported one theory or completely disproved another, it has provided important information as to their relative accuracy in describing judicial behaviour. Clearly, the empirical evidence allows a deeper and more complete understanding of such behaviour.

It may well be that the settled core of the law as a whole is expanding while the Supreme Court's caseload is continuing to be dominated by penumbral issues. Hard issues tend to be litigated, and especially appealed, in greater proportion than do easy issues. Thus, under both the core/penumbra and chain-novel theories, once the Court rules on an issue, that issue of law should be settled, should be clearer, and should not return to the Court. However, what should be happening under these theories often does not occur. On many occasions, the law, in a broad sense, does not become clearer after the Court rules. The Court is not just confronting new issues; it is rehashing old ones, often with different results. This rehashing is evidenced by the elevated rate of hard distinguishing in *Charter* cases and the Court's increasing reliance on open standards. While the core/penumbra and chain-novel theories continue to be an excellent standards for analysing the Court, by no means are these theories invariably accurate descriptors or predictors of its behaviour.

11 Is Legal Reasoning Autonomous?

The legal profession's claim that law is an autonomous form of problem solving is central to law's legitimacy as an impartial arbiter of disputes. However, many critics question whether legal reasoning is really separate and apart from ordinary reasoning.[1] If legal reasoning is no different from that employed by non-judicial decision makers, why do we need courts, with all their ritual and expense?

One method by which law seeks to establish its neutrality and thus maintain its impartial objectivity is through an autonomous form of argumentation and reasoning.[2] Proponents of the uniqueness of legal reasoning point to *stare decisis* as the epitome of its autonomous value: legal reasoning provides the same answer each time the same question is asked.[3] Legal reasoning provides neutral answers irrespective of the power possessed by those seeking exceptions. Sometimes a change in social context effects a change to the question, but in the absence of such change, *stare decisis* mandates that the same question should always beget the same answer.

Another method used by law to appear objective is to limit the arguments that the Court may hear. If there is consensus as to which arguments are valid and which are not permissible, greater autonomy can be obtained. Neil MacCormick writes that, within legal reasoning, 'grounds and procedures of argument are more restricted and clearly defined than in general practical discourse. Hence [legal reasoning] can more frequently yield a single determinate outcome to a practical dilemma.'[4] Patrick Devlin has described the law's tendency to act as 'the gate-keeper of the status quo,' safeguarding its autonomy by assuring that new ideas are not accepted until they have been 'admitted and absorbed into the consensus.'[5]

Overruling – judicial change to the law – challenges the notion of law's autonomy. If the law changes from case to case, is it really 'law' or just something judges make up on a daily basis? In *Work in Progress*, Allan Hutchinson describes the problem as follows: 'overruling should only be permitted where there is some special or super-justification over and above the claim that the earlier decision is wrong.'[6] Otherwise, law's virtues of certainty and stability might be unduly impaired.[7] For Hutchinson, overruling ought to be permitted only where 'the application of precedent [would lead] to a conclusion that is unacceptable because, for example, it is out of step with conventional views of justice.'[8]

The formal process of discovery followed by *stare decisis* is supposed to lead to stability, but changes in society result in pressure on the law to adjust to new social realities. These pressures are comparable to the stresses along a tectonic fault line. If this stress is relieved gradually or in small spurts, the need for cataclysmic change can be avoided. Overly rigid adherence to precedent can thus result in a jurisprudential earthquake.[9] If pressures are allowed to build up, radical change, either in the form of comprehensive legislation or a major judicial overruling will be needed. If the law fails to keep pace with social change, it may leave itself open to vilification.[10] Thus a certain, likely small, amount of judicial law making is necessary to preserve the stability of the common law.

In theory, overruling should occur either when the Court has made a mistake that it wishes to correct or when social conditions have gradually changed, causing the law to fall out of step. In the case of a mistake, the length of time between the original decision and the overruling decision should be short. Where societal change is such that the rationale for the original decision has ceased to exist, the precedent will likely have been long-standing. Precedents gain weight after they have stood for a period, but then gradually decline in power.[11] Overruling should thus occur shortly after the original decision or not until some significant period of time has elapsed since the decision being overruled was made.[12] Thus overruling does not invariably constitute a breakdown in legal reasoning.

Certainly there are obvious instances where legal reasoning appears to fail. Every case in which four of the nine Justices dissent constitutes an example of the failure of legal reasoning to provide an answer. The equality test in *Law v. Canada* (1999) has failed to guide the Court away from badly divided decisions.[13] In 2000, the American presidential election was decided, in part, as the result of such a five-four split – an extremely unsatisfactory result.[14] Nevertheless, the large number of cases decided by formal legal reasoning as well as the many cases in which even the newer modes, such as contextual interpretation, result in consensus on the court show that legal reasoning remains a valuable social tool.

In this chapter, I first discuss requirements that morality imposes on any system of law, even one that seeks to ground itself in foundational positivism. I next describe the manner in which the literature describes law as constraining judges and then examine the issue in light of the findings from my survey, first generally and then from the viewpoint of whether judges make or follow the law. Examples from the Court's *Charter* jurisprudence are examined. Finally I discuss the question of whether the observed behaviour of judges imperils the common law project.

The Need to Be Moral Challenges Law's Autonomy

From the point of view of enhancing the Law's objectivity and autonomy, positivism would have preferred to totally exclude morality from the purview of 'law.'[15] But the 'perfectly legal' slaughter of six million human beings by Hitler's Nazis made this stand untenable.[16] Why a legal theorist would seek to restrict the role of morality requires a short explanation. Natural Law theory holds that law exists as an overarching universal set of moral norms often seen as emanating from a Superior Being.[17] Natural Law would thus take precedence over any statute, rule, or precedent.[18] Positivism would acknowledge the edicts of the Third Reich as law; Natural Law would not. Positivism contends that we should be ruled by what *is*, while Natural Law focuses on what *ought* to be. Positivism usually recognizes any rule that is enforced as law; Natural Law requires that these rules be moral. Positivism's virtues are certainty and stability. If all litigants were allowed to explain why they thought their position was the most moral, it would be impossible to resolve any dispute with even a modicum of autonomy or objectivity.

In light of these difficulties, positivism, now sometimes called inclusive positivism, is willing to concede that any sovereign order must have a modicum of morality to survive, yet it otherwise continues to maintain that Natural Law is for philosophers, not lawyers.[19] Ronald Dworkin is willing to go somewhat further and would empower judges to decide cases based on a wide range of principles.[20] Dworkin calls upon judges to strive to imbue their decisions with as much justice as possible by employing their integrity and morality to the best of their abilities.[21] Integrity restrains judges by requiring them to honour the will of the legislature and to recognize the need for their opinions to be coherent with existing precedent. But, for Dworkin, integrity owes a higher duty to justice than it does to precedent.[22] And 'justice' is informed by the individual values of the presiding judge.[23] Hart's disciples attack Dworkin's position for its propensity to increase indeterminacy and thus to damage law's objectivity.[24] They maintain that Dworkin fails to acknowledge that the law's autonomy sometimes requires judges to enforce laws they disagree with.[25]

As with other areas of jurisprudence, autonomy can be located along a continuum from positivism, through non-foundationalism, and into anti-foundationalism. In part, our task will be to identify the point along the continuum that best describes the extent, if any, of law's autonomy.

Do Common Law Norms Constrain Judges?

Thomas Morawetz writes that judges 'are constrained individually by a particular way of addressing and understanding interpretative questions and they are constrained collectively by the fact that [their explicitly] shared practice embraces a limited range of ways of proceeding.'[26] He uses the term 'deliberative practice' to describe the involvement of individual judges in the judicial process.[27] The judicial practice is affected by common law norms that function in three ways: first, they provide rules for justifying deliberative judgments so that judges can not do whatever they want; second, they define proper methods for solving legal problems; and third, they provide rigorous standards and methods for answering hard questions of judicial interpretation.[28] Norms – for example, 'like cases should be decided alike' – and a variety of incentives prevent major deviations from accepted judicial practice.[29]

One constraining norm is recognition by the Court of the limits to the wisdom, legitimacy, and effectiveness of judicial law reform. The Court's acceptance of these limits and its recognition of the need to justify its innovations by reference to established principles will act as a constraint.[30] Under this norm, overruling would require special reasons.[31] The Supreme Court of Canada has often acknowledged the force of this constraint.[32]

The American empirical research, as summarized in the section on scalogram studies in chapter 8, found that decisions rendered by panels composed of judges with a variety of ideological viewpoints tend to be more legal and less ideological. This finding supports the effectiveness of judicial norms. Supreme Court of Canada Justices come from a variety of ideological backgrounds; we would therefore expect norm following on the Court to enhance law's autonomy.

The overall view of jurists appears to be aptly summarized by Duncan Kennedy. He concludes that the legal environment in which judges operate allows them a certain scope within which to implement the ideological policies that they believe are most just. However, this environment also effectively constrains the scope of that freedom of action. Courts are much more constrained than are legislatures.[33]

Does Law Constrain Personal Ideology?

There is empirical evidence in support of the proposition that legal reasoning, at least in its traditional form, constitutes a special form of logic. In a groundbreaking article, Dan Hunter describes how legal reasoning uses deduction, induction, and especially analogy to provide multiple constraints. The surface level of constraint requires that there be direct similarity in the facts. Structural-level constraints require similar relationships between the parties in the cases being compared. Purpose-level constraints require that there be a logical, good faith purpose in comparing the cases.[34] Hunter's article is notable in that it describes psychological studies that support the cognitive validity and utility of reasoning by analogy.

This cognitive validity and utility may account for the ability of legal reasoning to restrain the ideology of individual judges. As summarized in chapter 8, American empirical research has found that legal factors are dominant in legal decision-making. Law restrains ideology. It does not provide complete control, but it does provide important constraints. Anecdotal evidence indicates that law plays a more predominant role in the Supreme Court of Canada than it does in the Supreme Court of the United States.

Does Law Constrain Judges? Evidence from the Survey

In broad strokes, a low proportion of precedent avoidance would favour Hart; a slightly lesser proportion would favour Dworkin; an intermediate proportion would support non-foundationalism; while a high degree of precedent-avoidance would support the *anti*-foundationalist view. Similarly, formal legal reasoning and doctrinal reconciliation are more consonant with Hart, contextual interpretation with Dworkin and Hutchinson, while pragmatic decision making is on the inner edges of anti-foundationalism.

In almost all its decision making, the Supreme Court of Canada follows precedent. But on occasion the Court does make the law. It accomplishes this both through explicit and implicit overruling as well as through distinguishing precedent. While the trend is in the direction of more and more overruling, the overall incidence remains very low (less than 2.5 per cent).

The functioning of the Supreme Court of the United States shows both avoidance and application of *stare decisis*. As an example of the latter, *Roe v. Wade* has been by and large upheld despite the success of former president Ronald Reagan in appointing Justices whose personal views were decidedly pro-life.[35] The revival of capital punishment arguably exemplifies an avoidance of *stare decisis*.[36] Anecdotal descriptions portray the U.S. Supreme Court as being fractured by ideology and personality conflicts.[37] While there are important differences between the American Court and legislative bodies, judicial attitudes appear to have an impact on that Court's adherence to precedent.[38] Although the Supreme Court of Canada has not completely escaped allegations that it functions as a legislative, as opposed to a judicial, body, the overall portrait has been of nine men and women conscientiously wrestling with the legal issues of the day.[39]

The best evidence of the extent to which *stare decisis* constrains Canadian judges would be an examination of those cases where our Court contemplated overruling but decided against doing so. Its reasoning, whether it ended up changing the law or not, would illuminate the extent of the power of this precedential doctrine. However, it was not possible to compile a sufficiently large sample of contemplated overrulings to allow this analysis to take place. Nonetheless, there were certainly instances where the Court contemplated changing the law but declined to do so.[40] The characteristics of cases involving judicial change to the law described in Chapter 6 show that many, but not all, involve extraordinary criteria justifying a departure from precedent.

In short, *stare decisis* functions like a cautionary protocol or a banner for the defenders of the status quo to rally round. It is the default procedure; those seeking to overturn precedent bear the persuasive burden.

But change is only one measure of autonomy. Modes of legal reasoning are arguably a more important indicator of whether law is an objective and neutral process of decision making. Here the survey evidence shows that formal legal reasoning remains the court's most common mode. Overall – and there are always exceptions – the Court's preferred tools of legal reasoning are specific legal propositions as opposed to overarching principles. Its default mode is still foundational. These tendencies are even more pronounced in lower courts.[41] As well, policy considerations play a much more subordinate role in the lower courts. Thus, even if the requirement to function within the strictures of formal legal reasoning is being relaxed in the Supreme Court of Canada, the same cannot be said of the lower courts.

While litigants who had, broadly speaking, behaved badly or attempted to perpetrate an injustice often fared poorly, very few cases appeared to be driven by this type of moral subtext.[42] Moreover there was no evidence of morality, in the sense of an overarching foundational order, as being a controlling factor in the court's decision-making process.

Preserving Autonomy: The Method of Change Is Important

Precedent following is undoubtedly crucial, but the manner in which the court changes the law is equally, if not more, important.[43] Are these changes and the manner in which they are being accomplished 'legal' in the sense that the Court is still practicing 'law'? Or has the Court transformed its conference room into a miniature legislature?

Deference can be shown towards a precedent even when overruling it. When the Court carefully explains the need for the change, it is showing respect to *stare decisis*. The level of deference towards precedent following, even when other considerations impel precedent departure, will be an important indicator of the level of law's autonomy.

There are four primary means by which judges change the law: overruling, hard distinguishing, the manipulation of open standards, and incremental change. Ordinary distinguishing, where there is a valid difference between the case at bar and the precedent, does not involve a change to the law. The Court can also strike down statutes on constitutional grounds, but this is not the primary subject of the current analysis. Specific instances of changing the law, including excerpts from the Court's reasons for modifying, or declining to modify precedent, are described in chapter 6.

Does the Manner in Which the Court Overrules Precedent
Support Autonomy?

Anecdotal evidence of the Justices' attitudes towards *stare decisis* discloses that the Canadian Supreme Court places less emphasis on *stare decisis* than do provincial Courts of Appeal and more emphasis on reasonableness and 'getting it right' (in an overall doctrinal sense). The Justices tend to believe that their role includes both making and interpreting the law. It appears that, for some justices, making law is more important; for others interpretation is key.[44] While overruling, by its very nature, calls law's autonomy into question, this tendency can be counteracted by the extent to which legal reasoning demonstrates a clear necessity for change.

Do overrulings in the Supreme Court of Canada include such demonstrations? The evidence compiled during this survey is mixed.

The trend in the jurisprudence of the Supreme Court is towards ever more explicit overruling accompanied by clearer and better-reasoned justifications. However, in many cases the Court provides no specific justification for overturning precedent, and in some cases the Justices appear unaware that they are changing the law. Modes of legal reasoning are different where the Court departs from precedent, but Dworkinian principle is certainly not the primary driving force behind the Court's overrulings.[45]

The theory that overruled precedents would either be very recent or quite old is not well supported. While some of these precedents had been decided within a few years of being overruled and some had been on the books for well over half a century, the largest group of overruled precedents occupied the middle range.[46]

The Court almost always advances eminently defensible reasons to change the law.[47] In the vast majority of cases involving overruling, the Court writes detailed reasons as to the defective state of the law that it is modifying.[48] These reasons reflect the need to restore stability to the law or to avoid a decision that would, in present-day circumstances, be widely viewed as erroneous.

As well, more and more of these changes are being effected in a transparent fashion, showing that they are being achieved within the bounds of legal rationality: changed circumstances require new interpretations. The legal rationality of this overruling is reinforced by the fact that there are fewer close calls in cases of overruling than in other cases.

The writings of former Chief Justice Dickson, whose tenure (1973–90) spanned the crossover period, and a recent biography of his time at the Court, provide interesting anecdotal insights into the functioning of the Court.[49] In 1980, he wrote: 'The authority to enact legislation is assigned to the legislative bodies. Judicial focus is of necessity directed to the application of laws and judges are confined in their role of adjudication.' Even though 'a state of affairs may cry out for statutory reform, the judicial arm cannot evaluate and select among policy alternatives. That function is essentially political.' He recited several of the virtues embodied in the doctrine of *stare decisis*.[50] Later, he forthrightly acknowledged the utility of making 'clever if unconvincing distinctions' as a means of avoiding the effect of a precedent 'unsuited to modern circumstances.'[51] In 1983, he cited Weiler's *In the Last Resort* for the proposition that 'judges should make law but not too much' and mentioned Professor Jaffee's advice that law making be done 'surreptitiously.'[52] The biography by Sharpe and Roach relates that early on in his time at the Court, Dickson, in a hotly contested case, applied a precedent he disagreed with.[53] Later on, Dickson's attitude towards precedent relaxed and he took a more flexible approach, overruling precedent where an old rule had 'lost sight of the justice it sought to achieve.'[54] Towards the end of his tenure, he was prepared to place his faith in general and flexible principles and to reform those parts of the common law that placed arbitrary restrictions in the way of the application of those principles.[55] Thus Chief Justice Dickson's attitudes paralleled that of the Court in general as it moved from a clearly foundational (positivist) stance towards a more non-foundational one.

Hard Distinguishing

Hard distinguishing is a direct challenge to the notion of law's autonomy. Overruling can be viewed as a necessary self-correcting mechanism. But hard distinguishing's questionable reasoning has no such cachet.[56]

While the meaning of most legal rules is determinate at any given time, a change in the context in which the rule operates may require a new interpretation of the rule.[57] Hard distinguishing attempts to change the meaning of the rule without there being a change in its underlying rationale. The first tenet of hermeneutics is that the text does not, unaided, speak for itself. Each reader brings her or his individual point of view to the text. This individuality informs the text, sometimes

infusing it with new and different meanings. The second tenet of hermeneutics constrains and balances the first. It holds that the individual
reading must be grounded in tradition and that the reader must cooperate with the originator of the text to facilitate the originator's intended
interpretation. Hard distinguishing occurs when the Court has apparently failed to ground its interpretation of the previous decision in
tradition or to cooperate with the originator (the judges who wrote the
previous decision) but has instead engaged in a reasoning unsupported by the original decision. Hard distinguishing is less transparent than overruling. Cases of hard distinguishing therefore constitute
instances of the partial inefficacy of legal reasoning as a constraining
mechanism.

This inefficacy is evidenced by the doubling of the rate of close calls
in cases of hard distinguishing (approximately 32 per cent) when compared with the Court's overall average (15 per cent). Hard distinguishing further compares unfavourably with overruling, where close calls
occur in only 8 per cent of cases. Thus it appears that the Court recognizes the wisdom of obtaining consensus prior to change but that this
consensus is difficult when it uses hard distinguishing to make its
decision.

In cases of hard distinguishing, the Court often seems to be like
a swinging pendulum, repeatedly going back and forth over issues.
Charter cases in general, especially cases dealing with the exclusion
of evidence, feature many instances of this behaviour.[58] For example,
Collins (1987) required that almost all improperly obtained evidence be
excluded, *Belnavis* (1997) held that the police could search bags belong-
ing to a passenger in a car, while *Law* (2002) excluded evidence that
police found in the taxpayer's stolen safe. The pendulum sometimes
swings back and forth on the same day when the Court deals with
administrative law. In *Allen v. Alberta* (2003) the Court restricted the
plaintiff to the extra-judicial procedures set out in her collective agreement, but in *Goudie v. Ottawa* (2003) it allowed access to the Courts. The
standard for review of an administrative decision appears particularly
changeable.[59] Income tax cases furnish another example of the Court's
changing its direction.[60]

The low incidence of hard distinguishing indicates that, overall,
law does provide constraint. Furthermore, hard distinguishing is on
the decline, a clear indication of law's autonomy overall. Nevertheless, hard distinguishing remains a troubling anomaly for the Hartian
paradigm.

Open Standards

Another reason for the Court going back and forth on issues is its increasing promulgation of open-standard tests in place of hard-and-fast rules.[61] For example, the *Charter* concept of 'human dignity' is much more malleable that a bright-line test such as 'not less than three parts per million.'[62] This enables, perhaps requires, courts to decide each case much more on its own merits as opposed to deciding it in accordance with a bright-line rule. Open standards allow the Court to provide justice in the individual case without unduly disrupting the apparent rationalization of the law.[63] Principles can sometimes function in similar ways.[64]

While open standards are increasingly being used by the Supreme Court of Canada as a major component in its adjudication, they are applied in only a minority of cases. Over the past decade they have been used in just over 30 per cent of the Court's decisions.

Incremental Change

Some legal doctrines, like slow-moving glaciers, move so slowly that they appear to be completely static. However, if they are observed over a long period, change is clearly visible. A prime example is the law of hearsay. Successive judgments over several decades have rationalized hearsay's many rules and exceptions and taken technological advances into account.[65] Another example, albeit one changing at a somewhat faster pace, is family law.[66]

Incremental change resembles the prototypical common law process: any reform is well grounded in hermeneutic tradition. There is no jarring effort to defy logic, as often occurs in hard distinguishing. Incremental change supports law's autonomy.

The Charter: *Case in Point or Anomaly?*

It appears to be more difficult for the Court to preserve its objectivity and neutrality in *Charter* cases.[67] The Court plainly has a very high degree of autonomy in the sense that it is above the day-to-day control of litigants, whether those litigants are lowly paupers or the government of Canada and its Parliament. On the other hand, the grounds and arguments that it is willing to acknowledge under the rubric of 'law' are being expanded. Many more journal articles, especially outside the discipline of law narrowly defined, are considered in *Charter* cases than in non-*Charter* ones. Philosophical values play a greater role in *Charter* cases. The Court reacts to criticism: in *Morin* (1992) it responded to public concerns arising from the widespread staying of criminal charges by retreating from its efforts to compel the government to honour its obligation to ensure that accused received their trials within a reasonable time.

The Court's increased resort to hard distinguishing in *Charter* cases exposes deep and unresolved tensions. This is accompanied by an increased number of close calls and decreased incidents of unanimity. Thirty per cent of *Charter* cases that feature hard distinguishing result in close calls, as compared to under 20 per cent of *Charter* cases overall. These unresolved tensions are increasingly Canadian: in the first years of the Court's *Charter* jurisprudence, it consulted a substantial number of decisions from foreign courts, especially those of the United States. This tendency is now beginning to recede.[68]

A greater proportion of *Charter* cases than non-*Charter* ones are decided by open standards. The *Charter* provides more judicial choice than do ordinary legal materials. There is less formal legal reasoning and more contextual interpretation in *Charter* cases.

In short, the law is less autonomous when the *Charter* is employed.

Discussion

It appears, until lately, that judges were uncomfortable with the notion that part of their function might be to change the law. In the past, the Court behaved like an ancient Mediterranean mariner, hugging the coast, afraid to venture out of sight of the shore.[69] The Court may have proclaimed its ability to change the law, but it much preferred to hold close to the shelter of *stare decisis*. As Joseph Raz has noted, courts often 'minimize the extent to which a decision is innovative in order to avoid the need to bear full responsibility for it or to avoid having to justify it by long and explicit arguments.'[70] More recently, our judicial mariners have boldly taken to the open ocean. For example, in *Ryan v. Victoria* (1999), the Court set aside the special rule in favour of railways, which had limited their exposure to negligence to cases where they had failed to comply with the applicable regulations.

Under the Hartian paradigm, we would expect to see the core of settled meaning expand over time.[71] More and more cases should be easy to decide, fewer harder to resolve. Overruling and hard distinguishing should be on the decline. Any change would proceed gradually – evolution not revolution – and would occur either immediately after the rendering of the decision to be overruled (where the precedent was decided through mistake) or much later (as a result of changed social conditions).[72] Stone predicts a contrary trend on the basis that all precedential statements are plurisignative, leaving judges with wide leeways of choice to decide for either appellant or respondent. The low incidence of overruling supports Hart, but the increase in overruling supports Stone. The finding that less than 4 per cent of cases effect a clear change in the law and that most overrulings effect minor, not major, changes supports Hart.

There are qualitative indications of *stare decisis* acting as a constraining factor in the Supreme Court of Canada. Often *stare decisis* seems to tip the balance – and we can only say 'seems' because mention of *stare decisis* could merely be a rationale for a decision to stand pat. Overrulings are of course made in spite of the strictures of *stare decisis*. However, the low level of overruling may result just as much from in-built judicial unwillingness to innovate as it does from the impact of *stare decisis*.[73] Nevertheless, this unwillingness preserves law's autonomy.

The low levels of overruling and of hard distinguishing are more supportive of Hartian positivism than of non-foundational legal reasoning. However, cases involving overruling or hard distinguishing have an elevated non-foundational flavour.

As Morawetz has noted, norms as to what constitute proper reasons may constrain judges. The norm in favour of judicial restraint will be strengthened to the extent that the Court formulates and abides by a general theory and standard with respect to overruling and changing the law. Such a standard would require limiting the process of distinguishing to those cases where there is a *genuine and principled* difference between the cases.[74] Implicit overruling and hard distinguishing diminish the Court's reputation for intellectual honesty and needlessly confuse those who turn to the law for guidance as to how to order their affairs. The Court should overrule only where it can identify benefits arising from the new rule that will outweigh the costs of the change. Any overruling should be solidly underpinned by widely accepted policies.

The low frequency of judicial changes to the law is an indication that *stare decisis*, or at least some shared judicial norm, does constrain the judiciary. Since the rise in overrulings is matched by a decline in hard distinguishing, the *overall* rate of change has remained essentially con-

Figure 11.1. Selected trends in the Supreme Court of Canada, 1952–2002

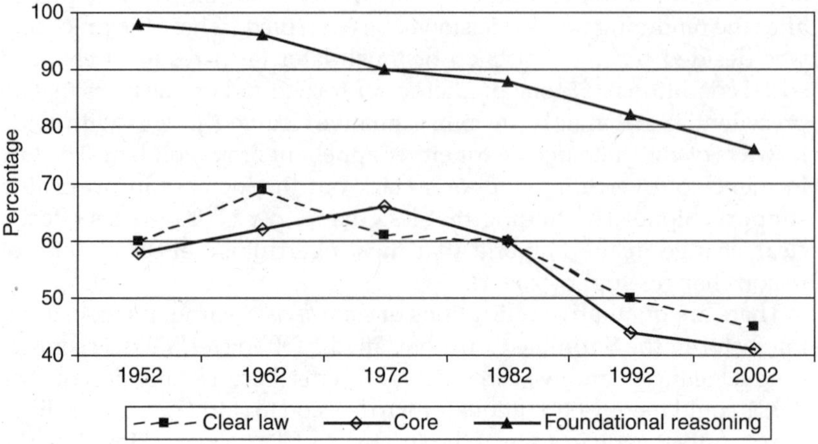

stant, subject only to fluctuations within a narrow range. The potency of this constraint is buttressed by the fact that this overall rate of change in the law has not increased in concert with other changes such as the rise in the proportion of policy in the Court's judgments, the rise of new modes of legal reasoning, and evolutions in the qualities of the Court's reasoning.

Policy considerations play an enhanced role in cases of overruling, but not in hard distinguishing. Doctrinal and pragmatic concerns feature prominently in both overruling and hard distinguishing.[75] These differences show that legal reasoning is correlated with changes to precedent.

As shown in figure 11.1, the trend is towards more legal issues residing in the penumbra and fewer capable of being decided by the solid core of the law. However, these phenomena are amplified by the Court's mandate to decide issues of importance, which by their nature tend to be difficult.

Non-foundationalist theories would predict a high level of change in the law to match the accelerated changes in society. While the rate of overruling is increasing, it is doing so at a slow rate and the actual numbers remain quite low. Furthermore, even cases that overrule precedent can be supported, to some extent, by existing legal materials.[76] Often the caselaw foreshadowed a change to the law. Thus both an analysis of the Court's overruling and the more direct measurement of its legal reasoning illustrated in figure 11.1, indicate that our Court seems to be behaving in a generally foundationalist manner. The trends depicted in figure 11.1 would seem to predict a higher rate of overruling than was found in the survey.

The Court's move towards more contextual interpretation and less formal legal reasoning indicates that it may be moving away from the foundational Hartian model. This move is matched by the rise in open standards, the application of which largely resembles ordinary, as opposed to legal, reasoning. Open standards allow many cases to be decided on individual bases, thus effecting a 'change' in the law in every case while maintaining that there has in fact been no change. Clearly these changes are less dramatic, and harder to detect, than changes effected by overruling or hard distinguishing.

But bright-line tests are more than twice as common as open standards. Almost all the authorities cited by the Court are from recognized legal sources. These findings indicate that legal reasoning has a large degree of autonomy. Even when the Court uses non-foundational legal reasoning or open-standard tests, it is still striving mightily to reach decisions that are, as far as possible, legal as opposed to political.

In theory, a bright-line test has the virtue of certainty and ease of application via formal legal reasoning. However, in *The Supreme Court and the Economy*, Patrick Monahan notes that formalistic bright-line tests may not best serve legislative goals.[77] John Braithwaite has shown that judicial rules best carry out simple legislative objectives, but that more open-ended principles are more effective in enabling the courts to facilitate complex legislative objectives.[78] Inflexible rules sometimes lead to injustice. Bright-line tests tend to lead to inconsistent rulings, hard distinguishing, and more instrumentally inconvenient rulings as the Court wrestles with the resultant doctrinal straightjacket. Unsatisfactory bright-line tests will, on occasion, require the Court to overrule its precedents to bring the law into accord with societal needs.

On the other hand, open-textured and open-standard 'tests' are often not tests at all, in that they do not determine the outcome. For example, in *Sauvé* (2002) the *Oakes* test failed to prevent a five-four split. The Court's equality jurisprudence provides another example of the dysfunctioning of an open-standard test. As Christopher Bredt and Adam Dodek recently lamented, 'The unanimity of *Law* (1999) proved to be ... short-lived. By 2002, *Law* was beginning to rupture at the seams, so that in 2003 we are back to where we were less than eight years ago:

section 15 jurisprudence is entangled in an overly-complicated analysis which produces a high degree of uncertainty.'[79]

The increasing presence of open standards will continue to put pressure on the Court to rule in a consistent manner (assuming that is its intent). It will be under particular pressure to carefully articulate the bases on which its rulings are founded. Certainly there will be an abundance of material for the Court's critics.

Conclusion: Hart in Peril?

Courts are different from legislatures. Judges, especially those lower in the judicial hierarchy, use different decision-making procedures than do legislators. The scope of legal indeterminacy is narrow when compared to the wide ranges of the law's determinacy. Foundational and proposition-based reasoning remain the norm, the default approach. The practice of law, while not perfectly autonomous, does have a high degree of autonomy. Legal reasoning provides more constraint than does non-legal reasoning.

But countervailing forces are also present. The growing number of cases where the decision is left up to judicial choice indicates that in many instances law imposes few constraints on the Supreme Court. The existence of overruling, hard distinguishing, open standards, and non-foundational reasoning challenges traditional models of legal reasoning. Changes without transparent bases are particularly worrisome.

On the other hand, not all changes to precedent are necessarily inconsistent with rational legal reasoning. Some change is necessary to keep law in sync with changing social conditions. The broad functioning of the Court is well within the bounds of *stare decisis*: the rate of precedent modification and the means by which it is effected do not currently imperil the common law project. However, many more *Charter* than non-*Charter* cases appear to be outside the bounds of traditional legal reasoning. The continuing presence of hard distinguishing and the persistence of non-explicit overrulings – together with the above observations, which do not fit neatly within Hart's descriptions of jurisprudence – indicate that, in some instances, Hart's theories do not adequately describe the Court's behaviour.

Hart's theories are not in mortal peril, but they *are* in need of modification.

12 Is the Supreme Court of Canada 'Too' Activist?

Activism is a matter of degree. At one hypothetical extreme, a Court that struck down each and every taxation statute passed by the federal government would be too activist. At the other hypothetical extreme, a Court that allowed a province to raise an army and declare war against a foreign state would not be nearly activist enough. Where is the happy medium, and how close, or how far, is the Supreme Court of Canada from its appropriate place?

The trends tracked in chapters 4 through 9 indicate that the Supreme Court of Canada is gradually becoming more activist. Overrulings, policy-based decisions, and contextual interpretation are all on the rise. Non-foundational reasoning and judicial choice have increased, especially in *Charter* cases.

Because 'activism' has a strong normative component, I will first set out my definition and then outline the debate. I will then summarize the debate as it plays out in academe, in the media, and among the judiciary. Benchmarks are necessary before 'too much/too little' questions can be answered. Quantitative measures and trends relevant to the Court's level of activism will be described. This discussion will be followed by a qualitative study of activism in the Court's 2003 cases. These analyses will then be summarized and discussed.

Activism Defined

In my opinion, the gravamen of activism is judicial usurpation of the proper functions of the legislative branch. Short of a constitutional violation, or other extraordinary circumstances, making or changing the law is usually the province of legislatures, not courts. Procedural decisions that enlarge the ability of courts to determine the issues of the day are similarly activist.

In discussing this issue, 'activism' is almost always used in a pejorative sense. Yet no one expects judges to be completely passive. As we have seen above, there is great social utility in allowing judges to change outmoded laws. The common law project is the stronger for this, provided that it is done in ways that are perceived as consistent and principled and provided that there is broad consensus in favour of the change. Judicial activism resembles fluoride. A little in the water or toothpaste strengthens teeth. Excess fluoridation may result in disease, or even death. A little activism prevents the decay of formally mechanistic jurisprudence. An excess may impair the integrity and effectiveness of the courts. The cases of *Donoghue v. Stevenson, Brown v. Board of Education*, and *Roncarelli v. Duplessis* illustrate the point.[1] These cases are all monuments to the ability of the common law to perform good and valuable work. But like all change, good or bad, they stressed the system. *Brown* dominated large portions of the American agenda for more than a decade. If a court renders too many such monumental decisions in a short period of time, its legitimacy will be strained to, or beyond, the point of rupture. This is so whether or not *Brown, Donoghue*, and *Roncarelli* were correctly decided. They all dealt with matters that could have been the subject of legislation. I believe that these three cases were correctly decided, but this does not change the fact that too much of a good thing is bad for the system. Nor does the correctness or utility of the decisions change the fact that all three were activist.

A court is activist when it chooses an outcome that is not compelled by the law but rather one that is primarily a function of the court's own values. This is doubly so when the court's choice is contrary to the choice of the elected legislature. Several commentators, with Allan Hutchinson at the fore, maintain that 'law is inevitably and inescapably political in operation and outcome.'[2] According to Hutchinson, 'law' and the 'court's own values' are inseparable, often one and the same. But even Hutchinson concedes that adjudication combines judicial freedom with legal and normative constraint.[3] Viewed as a continuum, formal legal reasoning provides more constraint than does the model of 'law *is* politics,' but even 'law *as* politics' is not completely unconstrained. In my definition of activism, the emphasis must be on the idea of compulsion: rulings that are effectively compelled by the state of the law cannot reasonably be characterized as activist. However, in cases where the Court considers whether or not to impose an activist result, it almost always has a choice.[4] For example, in *Doucet-Boudreau v. Nova Scotia* (2003), the majority of the Court could have adopted the minority's position that the doctrine of *functus officio* prevented ongoing supervision by the trial judge. The minority favoured restraint, yet the majority chose an activist stance. Whatever the advantages of allowing the trial judge to supervise the implementation of French-language instruction, the Court's choice was activist.

An effective lack of choice does not always protect the Court from charges of activism. Perceptions of activism can accumulate the same way as toxins accumulate in fish. Gay marriage is a good example. In *Vriend* (1998), the Court inserted 'sexual orientation' into the *Charter*. In doing so, it made an activist choice – the *Charter* did not, at that point, *compel* inclusion. In 2004, *Vriend* all but compelled the sanctification of homosexual marriage.[5] Under my definition of activism, present rulings in favour of gay marriage would not be particularly activist; *Vriend* leaves little scope for a restrictive ruling. But the overall trend may be too much, too far, too fast for a country that, in 1967, imposed indeterminate custody on a man for consensual homosexual acts conducted in private.[6] Less than half a century later the Court's jurisprudence has resulted in two men kissing passionately on the evening news broadcast. Critics argue that past (activist) decisions continue to haunt the Court: cumulative change impairs its present legitimacy. I submit that the legislature is better positioned to determine how much change (fluoride) is beneficial and how much change the populace can tolerate without impairing its health.

In *Charter* litigation, the issue of activism boils down to whether the Court is using the *Charter* as a legal resource or as a means to impose its ideology upon Canadian society. The Court clearly has a role in the interpretation of the constitution in general and the *Charter* in particular. As the Justices are fond of reminding us, the *Charter* was the government's idea, not theirs. Furthermore the Court itself was created by a democratically elected Parliament. From the moment the *British North America Act* was passed, it was plain that courts were expected to strike down legislation from time to time as part of their 'supervisory function.'[7] It is a matter of degree. If the Court refuses to strike legislation that contravenes the law, such as an act that purports to allow police officers to enter dwelling houses at any time for any reason, the Court is clearly abdicating its responsibilities. Section 8 of the *Charter* directs the Court to impose restrictions on the state's ability to search. When the Court requires judicial supervision of search warrants, it is merely applying the law. On the other hand, a Court that refused to allow the police to search a house despite cogent evidence that it contains evidence of a serious crime would clearly be activist.

Another way to understand the different points from which the balance can swing is to compare the level of activism in different jurisdictions. Worldwide, judicial activism is on the rise.[8] In North America, the level of judicial activism in Canada is perceived to be less than that in the United States.[9] Statistics support this perception: between 1986 and 1996, the U.S. Supreme Court overturned 2.5 per cent of its cases in which an opinion was delivered as compared to approximately 2.0 per cent for the Supreme Court of Canada. While the rate of unanimity in cases of overruling was similar (33 per cent of the American and 35 per cent of the Canadian cases), more than 36 per cent of American overruling cases had four dissenting opinions as opposed to only 4 per cent in Canada.[10] Only 20 per cent of the Canadian cases of overruling in this period were close calls. Thus in Canada, there appears to be more agreement on the Court when it comes to overruling. In short, the Canadian Court overrules less often and with more of a consensus than its American counterpart. Not surprisingly, both Americans and Canadians feel that the American Court is more ideological than the Canadian.[11]

In sum, charges of activism have an element of fire and an element of smoke, an element of lightning and an element of thunder. Fire and lightning represent the essence of improper activism: the assumption of legislative function by the Court and changes to the law that are not mandated by the legislature or social change supported by a broad consensus. For a decision to be activist, it must be open to the judge to rule in a less interventionist fashion. This is my definition. Other critics, distracted by smoke and thunder, often add unprincipled or non-transparent change or rulings based on the personal values of the Justices under the guise of applying the constitution.[12] As set forth in previous chapters, I am critical of unprincipled rulings resulting in incoherence in the law and of non-transparent reasoning, but these critiques are separate from the issue of activism. The issue is further obscured when charges of activism become confused with criticism of the merits of individual decisions. And it bears stressing: a completely inactive Court could be just as bad as an overly activist one. Activist decisions thus occupy a continuum between propriety and impropriety.

The Judicial Perspective

As often as not, Supreme Court Justices deny that there is any problem.[13] Or they confound the issue with other critiques, such as when Justice L'Heureux-Dubé alleged that 'the charge of judicial activism more frequently masks disagreement with the substantive merits of a case and the values underlying judges' decisions, rather than truly representing a dispute over the legitimacy of the judicial role.'[14] She may have a point; it is the job of academics to be critical. But criticism of the Justices is not synonymous with criticism of activism. Criticism of the Court for standing pat in *Murdoch* (1975) was so vociferous that the Court later referred to it as 'the notorious case of *Murdoch v. Murdoch.*'[15] If the critics sometimes obscure the issue of what constitutes activism, so too do the Justices. For example, Justice Bastarache mixed activism in with the need to achieve fairness: 'Considering the present debate about judicial activism, I think it is only fair that I add a word or two about the necessity for lawyers to realize that we all have a responsibility for achieving a just and fair result in all cases.'[16]

Chief Justice McLachlin engaged the issue more fully in an article published in the June 1999 issue of *Policy Options* magazine. She cited a study by Patrick Monahan to the effect that the Court was more deferential than activist with respect to the legislature.[17] But her discussion ultimately failed to come to any firm conclusion. The best that she could essay was that the Court's duty required it to balance 'appropriate' respect for the legislature with its duty to uphold the constitution. She concluded that it was 'a rather delicate task of accommodating conflicting interests and rights.'[18] Five years later, Justice McLachlin continues to be concerned about the criticism of activism being levelled against the Court.[19] Justice Iacobucci also recently admitted to having been distressed by the criticism that some of his decisions received.[20] While there is no clear evidence that charges of activism have influenced the decisions of the Canadian Court, it is certainly possible that this is the case. There is some indication that criticism contributed to the Australian High Court's pulling back from its activist stance.[21]

If the Court can avoid the criticism from lay quarters, it may have more difficulty denying its import when it is advanced by fellow judges. In *Newfoundland (Treasury Board) v. N.A.P.E.* (2002), the Newfoundland Court of Appeal charged that the Supreme Court's jurisprudence under section 1 of the *Charter* fuels criticism that the judiciary is 'actively entering the field of policy-making in its *Charter* applications beyond any tolerable levels sustainable under the Separation of Powers Doctrine.'[22] The Court of Appeal continued:

> While it would overly dramatize the importance to democratic society of advertence to the Separation of Powers to hold up the spectre of the bloodshed in which the Doctrine evolved, it is no histrionic foresight to draw real potential for heightening unease over undue incursions by the judiciary into the policy domain of the elected branches of government, going beyond those contemplated by s. 1 justifications in unintended disharmony and conflict with the Doctrine.
>
> The seeds of this potential are already evident in the unease that has frequently been expressed over undue incursions into the public policy field in *Charter* applications. Despite protestations to the contrary, *it has to be acknowledged there is an air of legitimacy to many of these complaints.*[23]

This is a remarkable, even startling, departure of the usual deference that lower courts display to the highest Court in the land. It indicates that the activism critique is reaching crisis proportions. To the extent that 'there is an air of legitimacy' to complaints of activism, an air of illegitimacy is starting to surround the Court.

The Court is not ignorant of the limits to its constitutional role. For example, in *Doucet-Boudreau* (2003), it stated:

> In carrying out their duties, courts are not to second-guess legislatures and the executives; they are not to make value judgments on what they regard as the proper policy choice; this is for the other branches. Rather, the courts are to uphold the Constitution and have been expressly invited to perform that role by the Constitution itself. But respect by the courts for the legislature and executive role is as important as ensuring that the other branches respect each others' role and the role of the courts.[24]

Is the Supreme Court 'Too' Activist? Summarizing the Debate

Clearly the court should be activist to a degree. Some change is necessary, some check on governmental abuse is desirable. The question is: What is the optimal degree of activism? In the 'Persons case,' Viscount Sankey of the Judicial Committee of the Privy Council decreed that our constitution was a 'living tree' and amended it to allow women to participate more fully in the civic affairs of the Dominion.[25] This act of judicial activism ultimately increased, not decreased, the legitimacy of the courts. There is some truth to the complaint that charges of activism are really displaced criticism of the merits of decisions made by the Court, but here we will be examining the extent to which the Court has exceeded its proper boundaries, whatever the merits of individual decisions. The fact that our constitution is a living tree does not confer power on judges to change a maple tree into an olive tree. And they must take care not to over-trim its branches, not to over- or under-water or fertilize it, and, most of all, not to graft so many new branches onto it that it collapses under its own weight.

Writing before the enactment of the *Charter*, Justice Brian Dickson (as he then was) said:

> The authority to enact legislation is assigned to the legislative bodies. Judicial focus is of necessity directed to the application of laws and judges are confined in their role of adjudication to precisely the issues that are revealed in the course of litigation. Inasmuch as a state of affairs may cry out for statutory reform, the judicial arm cannot evaluate and select among policy alternatives.[26]

Patrick Monahan, writing after the *Charter* came into force, notes that the proper judicial role is enlarged by the constitutional requirement of judicial review which necessarily

> involves unelected judges overruling the will of a democratically-accountable legislature on the basis of open-ended and abstract constitutional guarantees. The interpretation and application of these guarantees necessarily requires the exercise of wide discretion on the part of the judiciary. A continuing puzzle...has been how to account for this apparent derogation from democratic principles.

But Monahan notes that the Court views its role as being limited to simply interpreting and applying 'the objective and neutral standards contained in the constitution.'[27] Wholesale social change is beyond the mandate of the Court.

With respect to the meanings to be ascribed to the constitution, the Court has consistently refused to give great weight to the views of those who drafted its provisions.[28] As a matter of traditional statutory interpretation, this position is likely correct in law, but it *does* have the effect of giving a freer rein to the Court. In any event, when the Court has attempted to delve into the origin of constitutional documents, it often makes mistakes.[29]

Many believe that courts should leave contested political issues in the hands of legislatures.[30] But the exigencies and priorities of day-to-day politics result in legislatures' avoiding issues instead of confronting them. The legislatures would have happily evaded the issue of homosexual rights had not court action mandated its placement onto the agenda. Parliament has been avoiding the issue of the decriminalization of marijuana for more than a quarter century. A divided Court ultimately declined to strike down criminal sanctions respecting marijuana in *R. v. Malmo-Levine* (2003). But sometimes frustration impels judicial action: when Parliament failed to amend outdated legislation that favoured railroads, despite calls for reform from the Court twenty-four years earlier, the Court effected the change itself.[31] The Court was restrained in the case of marijuana, but activist in the case of railway liability.

On the other hand, the Court's more vociferous critics believe that the Justices should leave well enough alone. In the public press, it is not uncommon to see headlines such as 'Top Court Pursuing Activism, Experts Say,' 'Supreme Court Says Judges Can Ride Herd on Politicians,' and 'Guess What, All Judges are Activists.'[32] Writing in *Next City* magazine, Rory Leishman railed:

> Regardless of what legislators intended in enacting the *Charter*, the Supreme Court of Canada has renounced judicial restraint and now routinely usurps the constitutional authority of the legislative branch of government. In the process, the Supreme Court undermines freedom and the rule of law ... No one can be free in a state ruled by a dictator who flouts the rule of law, even if that dictator masquerades as a judge.
>
> Policy-making judge-politicians have no regard for rules fixed and announced beforehand; instead, they lurch from one inconsistent ruling to another. ... At a conference of leading Canadian lawyers convened last April by York University's Osgoode Hall Law School to mark the *Charter*'s 16th anniversary, ... Professor Jamie Cameron [stated] 'There is a lack of any principle to explain patterns of activism or deference in the past year,' she said, 'I can't make heads nor tails of them from one case to another.'[33]

Academic critics, such as Morton and Knopff, concur: 'In a dazzling exercise of self-empowerment, the Supreme Court has transformed itself from an adjudicator of disputes to a constitutional oracle that is able and willing to pronounce on the validity of a broad range of public policies.' Indeed, Morton and Knopff claim that, 'more often than not, [judges] make up the law as they go along.' They conclude:

> [The] Charter Revolution is ... deeply and fundamentally undemocratic, not just in the simple and obvious sense of being anti-majoritarian, but also in the more serious sense of eroding the habits and temperament of representative democracy. The growth of courtroom rights talk undermines perhaps the fundamental prerequisite of decent liberal democratic politics: the willingness to engage those with whom one disagrees in the ongoing attempt to combine diverse interests into temporarily visible governing majorities. Liberal democracy works only when majorities rather than minorities rule, and when it is obvious to all that ruling majorities are themselves coalitions of minorities in a pluralistic society.[34]

On the surface, Morton and Knopff's argument is the usurpation critique combined with a call for more democracy. The charge that judges make up the law as they go along echoes Leishman's quote of Professor Cameron. But a complete reading of Morton and Knopff leads to the conclusion that they are at least as critical of the contents of the Court's decisions as of the means by which these decisions are reached. Without putting too fine a point on it, Morton and Knopff would prefer a shift to the right.[35] Allegations of activism must always be tested to ensure that the real criticism does not stem from the critic's political agenda.[36] When commentators mix criticism of the merits of a decision with criticism of judicial activism, it provides the Court with an easy answer to its critics. Regrettably, this answer obscures the importance and urgency of the activism critique.

Janet Hiebert prefers a middle ground between those who advocate strong intervention by the judiciary in support of fundamental rights (a position she refers to as judicial hegemony) and *Charter* sceptics who view judicial review as contrary to democratic principles. She suggests that we may be relying excessively on judicial wisdom to resolve the issues of the day and that we should view Parliament and the courts as having a relationship of shared responsibility for the implementation of the rights described in the *Charter*.[37]

Whatever view one takes, others will express contrary views, sometimes supportive, but more often critical of the Court.

Is the Court's Legitimacy Being Impaired?

The result of these critiques has been a continued questioning of the legitimacy of the Court.[38] Monahan uses 'legitimacy' to describe the proper role of Court.[39] The word has two other meanings: that which causes the Court's authority to be recognized and the practical limits of its decision making.[40] These varied meanings fit along a continuum, one end being occupied by Monahan's academic theory that courts should only interpret and apply the objective standards in the constitution, and the other occupied by the point at which the Court's rulings will be met by explicit and obstinate defiance. There are numerous checks and balances to prevent the Court from getting too close to the far ends of the continuum: popular and academic theory provides feedback, the legislature can indicate its displeasure by enacting statutes designed to overturn or avoid the Court's rulings, and lower courts can raise contrary arguments. The Court must conserve its judicial energy in maintaining its legitimacy; if it tries to decide too many divisive issues, public confidence in the rationality of the Court's decision making may be over-taxed.[41]

In all likelihood, the Court is far too wise to permit matters to get so far out of hand as to foster armed insurrection against its office.[42] But less subtle erosions of its power are not beyond the realm of possibility: funding may not keep pace with inflation, surreptitious disobedience and passive resistance may greet its rulings, and restrictions may be placed on its independence.[43] The Court may lose the power to control its docket. A broader range of actors will likely attempt to influence judicial appointments.

Opposition to the Court's rulings is a useful barometer of perceptions of activism. In the United States, the Supreme Court's imposition of school desegregation in *Brown v. Board of Education* (1954) was met with a mixture of partial compliance and active resistance.[44] There was even less compliance with rulings purporting to outlaw school prayer.[45] In Canada, there was widespread defiance of Sunday closing laws despite the Court's having upheld their constitutionality in *Edwards Books* (1986).[46] And when the Court ruled that schools could not ban books that featured same-sex parents because children cannot learn tolerance unless they are exposed to views that differ from those they are taught at home, the school board's reaction was not to permit the books but to find a new basis on which to ban them.[47] Although the vagueness of the Court's ruling in *Marshall*

(1999) may have left the matter in doubt, there was certainly not full compliance with the spirit of the Court's ruling by the Department of Fisheries.[48]

Other, more subtle, indications as to the limitations of the effective power of the Court are also visible. Governments utilize indirect means to accomplish objectives that the Court had earlier ruled unconstitutional. Some commentators believe that belligerent legislative amendment of its *O'Connor* (1995) ruling obliged the Court to back off its proper role as custodian of the constitution in *Mills* (1999). Questions as to its legitimacy may have led the Court to retreat from firmer interpretations of the *Charter*.[49] Moreover, the Court has delayed hearing some controversial cases, which may be an indication of its unwillingness to risk further accusation of activism.[50]

Political scientists have studied public attitudes to judicial interventions. In Canada, Joseph Fletcher and Paul Howe have summarized a national survey of more than one thousand Canadians commissioned by the Institute for Research on Public Policy (IRPP). Overall, they concluded that 'reports of plummeting esteem for the judicial branch have been greatly exaggerated.'[51] Most Canadians, by a two-to-one margin, believe that Courts, and not legislatures, should have the final say in interpreting the *Charter of Rights and Freedoms*.[52] Canadians report a high level of satisfaction with their national high Court and trust it to make decisions that are right for the country as a whole.[53]

On the other hand, Canadians strongly disagree with some of the Court's rulings, most notably relating to the exclusion of evidence. While this disagreement has yet to undermine support for the Court,[54] half of respondents with an opinion believe that the right of the Supreme Court to decide certain controversial issues should be reduced.[55] In addition, a sizeable minority (36 per cent) believes that if the Court were to start 'making a lot of decisions that most people disagreed with, it might be better to do away with the Supreme Court altogether.'[56] While the U.S. Supreme Court has been subjected to more widespread and virulent criticism, there is less support in the United States for the idea of doing away with that country's highest court than there is in Canada for doing away with our Supreme Court. Fletcher and Howe attribute this finding to the more long-standing entrenchment of the U.S. Court in the American constitutional framework and to underlying federal–provincial tensions in Canada.[57]

Overall, there is some support for the proposition that doubts as to its legitimacy have the potential to weaken the Court.

Possible Indicators of Rising Activism

The paradigm of legal theory under which the Court is operating also impinges on its legitimacy. If law is mere political activity and not a special objective form of reasoning, judges will, on many occasions, be making decisions solely in accord with their own political beliefs and attitudes. If this anti-foundational paradigm is in operation, the need for a legal decision-making body, separate from the forthrightly political one, will be called into question. If legal cases are decided on political as opposed to legal bases, there will be an ever-increasing number of overrulings as the new decisions reflect the changing viewpoints of the judiciary.

The Court received a substantial increase in its power when Parliament handed it control of its docket in 1975.[58] If the Court is actively using this power, its cases and rulings should have an ever-increasing effect on society. If the Court is conscientiously selecting difficult cases of national importance, Hart's core/penumbra analysis would predict an increase in close calls and overrulings.

If the Court is attempting to increase its power, it will rule so as to enlarge its jurisdiction and to maintain as much flexibility to decide individual cases, especially future cases, however it may choose. If the Court has more power, it will be able to overrule more often. Overrulings based on power will effect the result sought by the Court, not necessarily the needs of justice in the case. To determine whether the Court's rulings are power-based, it will be necessary to analyse the effect of its rulings both instrumentally and doctrinally. If it is attempting to increase its power but feels that other forces oppose such an increase, the Court will likely not do so in a brazen fashion: its judges will likely be careful to hide the effect and the intent of their rulings; thus hard distinguishing can be expected to increase. Dissents will be avoided because they make the Court's decisions appear unprincipled and therefore illegitimate.

If the Court is increasing its exercise of power, the length of time between the original decision and the one overruling it should be steadily decreasing. However, the trend is moderately in the opposite direction. If the Court is overruling precedents that are clearly out of step with current conditions without disturbing the legislature's rightful place, it is unlikely that either the body politic or the legal community will be disturbed.[59] If, when overruling, the Court shows due consideration for the reliance ordinary citizens place on the law when ordering their affairs, doctrinal uncertainty will be kept within manageable bounds.[60]

Because the *Charter of Rights and Freedoms* significantly enlarged the issues the Court was called upon to resolve, *Charter* litigation is a useful subject for analysis. If the Court is arrogating power to itself, the Court and not the *Charter* will be driving the decision. The Court will use the *Charter* to mask its power. *Dolphin Delivery* (1986) restricted *Charter* review to government actions, but a backdoor now allows *Charter* values to be applied to almost every issue coming before the Court.[61] If the Court is intent on expanding its powers, it will infuse '*Charter* values' into all its decisions. Alternately, it might interpret the *Charter* so as to uphold democracy and promote democratic values. In this case, its rulings will confirm the Court's subsidiary place in the Canadian power structure and there will be fewer overrulings. Judges will show restraint in their rulings and will confirm that they are restraining themselves. The Court will engage in careful discourse if it feels the need to expand the scope of its rulings. Any overrulings will be carefully explained, and the Court will decline to rule in areas where legislative intervention is possible.

One method judges might use to increase their power is to propound open standards in broadly textured language, which increase their flexibility in individual cases. An example of such a standard is 'human dignity,' which can be employed to justify a wide variety of outcomes.[62] Open standards allow for more judicial discretion and are therefore invitations to activism. If 'human dignity'[63] is what the Court views as an 'objective and neutral standard', the Court's discretion is only minimally restrained. Sometimes standards and principles, not precise rules, may better position the Court to loyally carry out the legislature's intent.[64] But some of these principles are so open-ended that the Court, despite its best intentions, may be left open to charges of activism. Rulings that no single *Charter* right trumps another leads to an infinite number of permutations/combinations, thereby expanding the Court's range of decision-making freedom.[65]

How often the Court strikes legislation down is another important indicator of its attitude. If the Court wants the other levels of government to work out the division of powers by way of political negotiation, it will usually decline to interfere with the resulting legislation. However this goal will often result in reasons bereft of rational basis and rife with inconsistency. Where impugned legislation is upheld, hard distinguishing may be an indicator of judicial humility.

Quantitative Analyses of Activism

Charles Epp documented that, after 1975, the Court increased its over-turning of legislation on constitutional grounds.[66] In 1998 Patrick Monahan, in the 1998 study to which the Chief Justice above referred, attempted the first post-*Charter* quantitative study of the incidence of judicial activism.[67] He found that the claimant obtained a *Charter* remedy about one-third of the time (the *Charter* 'success rate'). As a more direct study of activism, Monahan examined the ninety-eight constitutional decisions of the Court in the preceding three years. He found that in only thirteen of these cases had the Court struck down part of a statute as being unconstitutional. In several of these thirteen cases, the Court's ruling required only modest changes to the legislation. While Monahan does not offer an opinion as to whether 13 per cent is high or low, Chief Justice McLachlin felt that the numbers showed that the Court 'is rather inclined to be judicially conservative and deferential to the elected arms of government.'[68]

At the 2002 and 2003 Constitutional Cases Conferences, Monahan updated his data, which are set out in figure 12.1. The success rates for 2002 and 2003 were 63 and 65 per cent, respectively; in 2000 and 2001 the rates had been 27 and 44 per cent, respectively.[69] It is of course possible to uphold a *Charter* claim without being activist. For example, not all findings that a search contravened section 8 of the *Charter* are 'activist.' However, starting in 2001 the Court increased both the number of *Charter* challenges on its docket and their rate of success.

Morton and Knopff criticized Monahan's 1998 study on the ground that the denominator for the rate of statute nullification should be restricted to those cases that sought nullification and should not include cases where no nullification was sought. Changing the denominator, and expanding the number of years covered, would cause the rate to almost triple to 32 per cent. Furthermore, Monahan's figures do not include all elements of judicial activism. Morton and Knopff expanded the definition to include opposition to the policies and actions of all branches of government. Additionally, Monahan's figures do not account for judicial policy making in the areas of criminal law enforcement, obscenity, or sexual orientation. But for Morton and Knopff, even if it is involved in only a small proportion of the Court's cases, judicial activism has effected the unwelcome change of transforming 'the courtroom into an attractive political arena.'[70]

Sujit Choudhry and Claire Hunter built on two earlier studies to

Figure 12.1. *Charter* challenges in the Supreme Court of Canada, 1991–2003

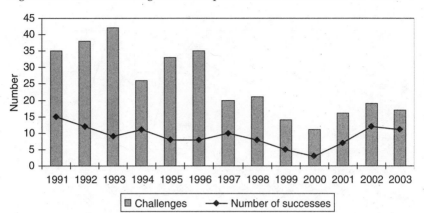

Source: Sixth Annual Analysis of the Constitutional Decisions of the Supreme Court of Canada: 2002 Constitutional Cases, Osgoode Hall Law School, Toronto, 4 April 2003; Seventh Annual Analysis of the Constitutional Decisions of the Supreme Court of Canada: 2003 Constitutional Cases, Osgoode Hall Law School, Toronto, 2 April 2004; *The Supreme Court's 1998 Constitutional Cases: The Debate over Judicial Activism Heats Up*, Canada Watch (September–October 1999), available online at http://www.robarts.yorku.ca/canadawatch/vol_7_4-5/default.htm (accessed 4 March 2004).

analyse judicial activism from 1984 to 2002.[71] Their data set was more restrictive than Monahan's: here the *Charter* claimant had to be seeking the nullification of a statutory provision. They studied three measurements: overall government win rates in *Charter* cases, win rates on cases turning on the interpretation of section 1 of the *Charter*, and win rates on statutes that could have been protected by section 33 of the *Charter*. In their model, the more often the government won, the less activist was the Court. Statute nullification, particularly when restricted to *Charter* jurisprudence, hardly comprises the entire universe of judicial activism; nevertheless it is a very useful proxy. Choudhry and Hunter found that the overall government win rate varied between a high of 83 per cent and a low of 25 per cent. Overall, the success rate was approximately 64 per cent. The rates fluctuated widely from year to year, with no discernable trend emerging. A figure from Choudhry and Hunter summarizes this finding (see figure 12.2).

Choudhry and Hunter also demonstrated that the government's win rate under section 1 of the *Charter* varied substantially from year to year, averaging approximately 25 per cent.[72] This means that section 1

Figure 12.2. Absolute government win rates in the Supreme Court of Canada, 1984–2002

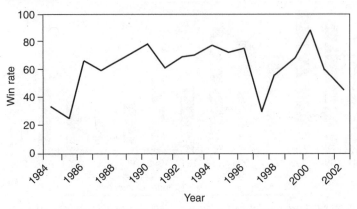

Source: S. Choudhry and C.E. Hunter, *Measuring Judicial Activism on the Supreme Court of Canada* (2003), 48 McGill L.J.

saved only one-quarter of the statutes that the Court found to contravene the *Charter*. They graphed their findings regarding section 1 as set out in figure 12.3. Choudhry and Hunter concluded that there were no discernable trends in either the overall government win rate or its win rate once section 1 had been engaged.

Choudhry and Hunter's study has methodological shortcomings, both quantitative and qualitative. Although their study seems to have met most of Morton and Knopff's quantitative criticisms of Monahan's study, thus accounting for their figure being higher than Monahan's, they failed to answer the other qualitative criticisms advanced by Morton and Knopff. These unsolved methodological problems will be addressed below when I offer my own qualitative analysis of the Court's activism. Additionally, there are quantitative problems with the Choudhry and Hunter study. In a study done by myself and Andrew Halteh, additional analysis of the figures compiled by Choudhry and Hunter demonstrated a clear downward trend in the government's rate of success once section 1 of the *Charter* had been engaged.

Halteh and I added data from 2003 to the database compiled by Choudhry and Hunter.[73] This step yielded a database comprising a full twenty years, which would allow data to be combined into four five-year groups. The data thus combined supported Choudhry and Hunter's conclusion that there was no discernable trend in the government's

Figure 12.3. Government win rates in the Supreme Court of Canada, using section 1, 1984–2002

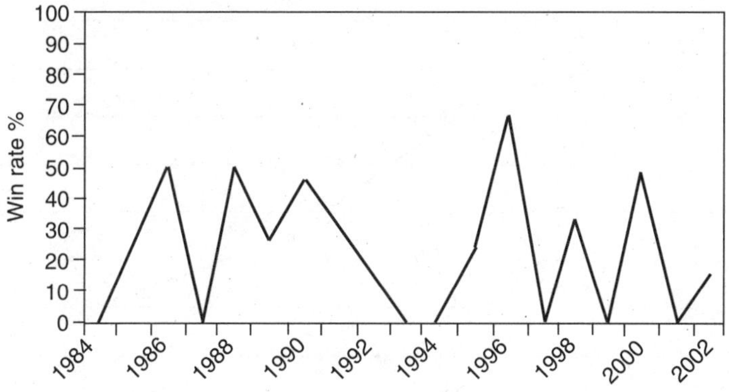

Source: S. Choudhry and C.E. Hunter, *Measuring Judicial Activism on the Supreme Court of Canada* (2003), 48 McGill L.J.

overall win rate. The combined data showed fluctuations in the government win rate within a narrow band ranging from 58 to 70 per cent. This narrow band was the same whether the data were compiled using the number of statutory sections in issue (Choudhry and Hunter's preferred method) or the number of cases. During the 1994–8 period, the ten sections involved in the *Manitoba Judges' Reference* (1997) skewed the data such that using the number of sections produced a rate at the low end of the range (59.6 per cent) while using the number of cases produced a rate at the high end of the range (70 per cent).

Based on the wild oscillations of their annual charting of the government's win rate when section 1 of the *Charter* was engaged, Choudhry and Hunter concluded that there was no discernable trend in the section 1 jurisprudence as well. However, when the data are combined into five-year groupings, there is a clear and persistent downward trend. Figure 12.4 shows the result with the 2003 data[74] added in. This trend means that once it was determined that the *Charter* had been breached, the Court became less and less willing to give the government the benefit of the doubt under section 1. In 1999–2003 the Court was willing to accept the government's view as to what is a 'reasonable limit' less than 20 per cent of the time. This trend is indicative of increasing activism on the part of the Court. Choudhry and Hunter felt that their data supported Kent Roach's conclusion that *RJR-Macdonald*

Figure 12.4. Government win rates in the Supreme Court of Canada, using section 1, five-year groupings, 1984–8 to 1999–2003

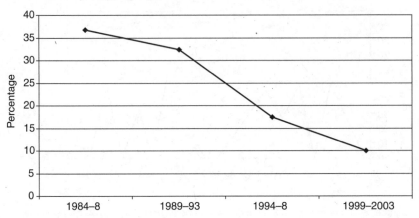

v. Canada (1995) 'did not mark the abandonment of the more deferential approach.'[75] With respect, the evidence appears to support the opposite conclusion. The concerns which Marshall, J.A. expressed in *Newfoundland v. N.A.P.E.*[76] appear to have a solid basis in the jurisprudence of the Supreme Court.

The third interesting analysis performed by Choudhry and Hunter dealt with the issue of whether the Court struck down legislation that could have been protected by a section 33 *Charter* override at a different rate than for legislation that was not eligible for protection under section 33. They found a high rate of congruence, even year to year, in the rates of striking legislation that could, and legislation that could not, be protected by section 33. Choudhry and Hunter theorized that this finding might mean that the possible re-enactment of legislation under the protection of section 33 is irrelevant to constitutional litigation. If so, it is an indication that the Court is ruling on the basis of the *Charter*'s provisions and not on the basis of possible government reaction. The congruence is thus indicative of judicial integrity.

Qualitative Analysis

Quantitative analyses often attempt to remove as many qualitative factors as possible from their data pool. This culling allows quantitative investigators to say that no human judgments – judgments that may be open to question – have tainted the results. For example, my category of close calls is entirely mathematical and thus constitutes a neutral and objective measure. By contrast, the measurement of the proportion of fact, law, and policy requires at least a modicum of judgment, while differentiating between foundational and non-foundational legal reasoning requires a substantial application of human judgment.

But removing the possibility that human judgment could contaminate the results reduces the comprehensiveness of the database, likely also reducing its accuracy. Choudhry and Hunter used the striking down of legislation on *Charter* grounds as a proxy for judicial activism. However, there is a lack of identity between striking down legislation and judicial activism. This variance introduces error into the database. In addition, their proxy excludes many cases from the database, thus increasing the possibility that their results fail to reflect the Court's behaviour. I do not wish to be overly critical: the efforts of Monahan, Choudhry, Hunter, and others to study jurisprudence in a systematic way is a great improvement over the limited and haphazard sampling of other jurists. But the limitations of any one study need to be understood. A clear picture will emerge only when these and other studies are multiplied and replicated.

I offer table 12.1 as a further study of the level of the Court's activism. It lists all of the Court's reported decisions rendered in 2003 wherein it was open to the Court to be activist. Duplicate decisions on the same issue have been eliminated. For example, both *Malmo-Levine* and *Clay* dealt with marijuana, so only *Malmo-Levine* is included. It was open to the Court to strike down the prohibition against the use of marijuana, therefore the case was included. The Court declined to strike down the prohibition and therefore the case is placed in the 'restrained' category. In *CUPE v. Ontario*, it was open to the Court to allow the government to maintain control of the choice of arbitrator, but it refused to do so and set aside the subject legislation. The case is therefore an example of activism.

Many of the decisions included in the table did not deal with whether or not a statutory provision should be struck down. All raise the issue of whether the Court is trampling on the policy-making prerogatives of the legislative and executive branches of government and whether it is attempting to abandon its proper position as supporting actor and to install itself in the leading role.[77] As the table illustrates, the Court adopted an activist stance in just over half the opportunities presented

Table 12.1. Activism and restraint in the Supreme Court of Canada, 2003

Case	Restrained	Active	Subject Matter
Allen v. Alberta	X		Administrative review
Goudie v. Ottawa		X	Administrative review
Dr. Q. v. College of Physicians	X		Administrative review
Law Society v. Ryan	X		Administrative review
Miglin v. Miglin		X	Court can review 'final' separation agreement
CUPE v. Ontario		X	Government not allowed to control choice of arbitrator
Trociuk v. B.C.		X	Mother cannot exclude father from vital statistics record
Bell v. Employees Canadian Telephone	X		Human Rights Commission guidelines power upheld
Figueroa v. Canada		X	Rights of small political parties expanded
Authorson v. Canada	X		Upheld federal legislation restricting interest entitlement
R. v. Malmo-Levine	X		Upheld criminalization of marijuana
Beals v. Saldhana		X	Upheld exorbitant Florida jury award
B.C. v. Okanagan Indian Band		X	Extended court's ability to award interim costs in public interest litigation
National Trust v. H & R Block		X	Applied justice instead of clear wording of *Bulk Sales Act*
Doucet-Boudreau v. Nova Scotia Trust		X	Upheld continuous court supervision of *Charter* judgment
N.S. Workers' Compensation Bd v. Martin		X	Compelled government to compensate victims of chronic pain syndrome
R. v. Blais	X		Declined to designate Métis as 'Indians'
R. v. Powley		X	Extended Aboriginal rights to Métis

to it in 2003.[78] But it must be noted that the level of activism was not the same in each case. *National Trust* was much more activist than was *Powley*.

I have not tracked activism over a period of time because activism is not merely a trend. Any single case is capable of severely damaging the Court's legitimacy. In any event, the quantitative studies above show the trends. A detailed qualitative examination of one year of the Court's jurisprudence is the best way to add to the knowledge in this area.

The four cases of *Allen v. Alberta, Goudie v. Ottawa, Dr. Q. v. College of Physicians* and *Law Society v. Ryan* represent the Court's ongoing struggle over whether or not to interfere with administrative tribunals. *Allen* and *Goudie* both involved the issue of whether unionized workers were restricted to contractual grievance procedures or whether they could resort to the courts. In one decision employees were allowed to resort to ordinary litigation, in the other they were not. It is hard to escape the conclusion that the Court was imposing its own view as to which result should obtain in the individual cases as opposed to consistently following a legal rule. Thus the Court's activism impaired its central obligation to provide overall guidance as to the law. These two cases are thus apparently unprincipled and opaque, as opposed to being principled and transparent. In *Dr. Q. v. College of Physicians* and *Law Society v. Ryan*, the Court held that courts are wrong to second-guess the subject administrative tribunals.

In *Miglin v. Miglin*, the Court determined that it could review and modify the provisions of separation agreements freely entered into by the parties. This decision was in the face of the contract's clear intention that it be final and not subject to review. The only way the contract could have been any clearer would have been to insert a curse against any tribunal that might attempt to vary it. The Court's activist stance in *Miglin* enlarges the jurisdiction of courts to intervene in the affairs of separated individuals. On the other hand, in *Miglin* itself, the Court determined that the spousal support provisions in the separation agreement should not be interfered with. Furthermore, the democratically enacted statute appears to support the jurisdiction of courts to vary 'final' agreements in appropriate circumstances. On a grey scale running from black to white, the Court's activism in this case is a very light shade of grey, which would be hard to translate into a binary statistic, as would be required for a quantitative study.

In *CUPE v. Ontario*, the Court struck down a legislative scheme that varied the procedure for the selection of labour arbitrators. The previous regime had established a pool of arbitrators satisfactory to both sides. Arbitrators were chosen from this pool. Now the government wanted to establish a new pool of arbitrators based on its own choice. The Court upheld labour's submissions that the new scheme produced arbitrators who might be biased in favour of the employer, especially where that employer was the subject government. I believe that this decision is eminently correct and reasonable. If courts are to decline to intervene in the individual decisions of administrative tribunals, they must be able to ensure that these tribunals are properly constituted. Thus, undue interference by one side in the appointment process should not be allowed. However, my approval of the decision on its merits does not prevent the decision from being classified as activist. Activism and correctness are different. The decision was a close call; the three-judge dissent clearly illustrates that the Court had the option to decline to strike down the legislation. The decision is activist because the Court intervened to substitute its regime in place of the one promulgated by the legislature.

Trociuk v. British Columbia struck down provisions in the *Vital Statistics Act* that allowed a mother to exclude her child's father from the child's birth record. All nine Judges felt the provisions infringed the father's section 15 equality rights. It also ruled that, where the mother and father cannot agree on the child's surname, someone must choose. Given the newborn's closer connection to the mother (males can neither give birth nor suckle), allowing the mother to make this decision is not unreasonable. The decision is activist because the Court substituted its view in place of the legislature's and because courts will now have a greater role in determining the contents of birth records.

A unanimous Court declined to intervene to prevent administrative tribunals setting up guidelines for future cases in *Bell Canada v. Canadian Telephone Employees*. It also refused to interfere with an extension of a member's term to allow completion of an ongoing inquiry. The Court upheld the Federal Court of Appeal, which had reversed a trial judgment that had ruled in favour of the employer on both issues.

Figueroa v. Canada struck down the requirement that a party field at least fifty candidates in a federal election in order to obtain official party status during the election. The Court reasoned that the requirement would hamper the development of new parties and thus impede democratic choice. The government was concerned that a limited number of national parties might better facilitate voter choice. I do not know which view is best, but in preferring its own view, the Court was clearly being activist.

In *Authorson v. Canada*, the Court unanimously upheld legislation barring veterans from claiming interest on money that the government had mismanaged in contravention of its fiduciary obligations. On its face, the legislation was blatantly unfair. The Court showed great restraint in not interfering with the impugned legislation.

R. v. Malmo-Levine, R. v. Caine was a six-to-three close call that upheld the current prohibition against the possession of marijuana. This deference to Parliament was exercised in the face of the quarter-century-old LeDain Royal Commission Report and evidence indicating that the threats posed by marijuana are similar to those posed by alcohol. The Court delayed hearing the case when it appeared that Parliament might introduce legislation.[79] The opposition from the United States to any relaxation in Canada's marijuana laws was described in the popular press.[80] Further highlighting its restraint in this matter, the Court refused to apply the harm principle enunciated by John Stuart Mill, its favourite philosopher.[81]

In *British Columbia v. Okanagan Indian Band*, the Court extended judicial power to award interim costs, particularly in public interest litigation. This decision is activist because it facilitates access to the courts, especially by parties contesting government action. As such, the decision furthers the spectre of the Court Party as described by Morton and Knopff. The decision was a six-to-three close call.

National Trust v. H & R Block is one of the Court's most activist cases of the year. Here the Court relieved against the provisions of the *Bulk Sales Act* despite the lack of statutory permission to do so. Notwithstanding that its vendor was insolvent, H & R Block did not comply with the filing requirements of the act. In this situation, the act provides that the purchaser (H & R Block) must account to the creditors (here including National Trust) for the purchase price. The Court felt that since the purchase price had been paid to the highest-ranking secured creditor of the vendor, it would be unfair to, in effect, saddle H & R with double the agreed purchase price. However, this is exactly the draconian result the act mandates as an incentive for both purchaser and vendor to comply with its provisions. Furthermore, *someone* was going to be stuck with an unwarranted loss, and it was only a matter of choosing between two innocent parties. The decision amends the *Bulk Sales Act*. The Court usurped the role of the legislature. The Court overruled the

Ontario Court of Appeal in a five-to-two decision, making it a close call.

Doucet-Boudreau v. Nova Scotia Trust garnered much more attention in the press[82] than did *National Trust*, despite having a much lower level of activism than the debtor-creditor case. The decision upheld the ruling of the trial judge, which allowed him to monitor compliance with one of his orders. No issue was raised as to the propriety of the order itself; only the supervision was appealed. While the doctrine of *functus officio* would have allowed the trial judge to 'fire and forget,' past experience had indicated that the remedy he ordered would be more effective if continued supervision were mandated. However, *functus officio* meant that it was open to the Court to strike down the continued supervision; therefore its upholding of the supervision makes the decision activist. The decision was a five-to-four close call. However, the degree of activism in this case was not great: all the supervision did was to ensure compliance with a perfectly proper order. Surely we want our courts to be more than toothless tigers. If we want to rein in the power of our courts, we should restrict their rulings, not the enforcement of their rulings. Surely our democracy deserves transparency, not passive aggression, on the part of legislatures and executives.

Nova Scotia Workers' Compensation Board v. Martin constitutes an incursion by the Court into the legislature's spending power. The Court found that a provision denying compensation to victims of chronic pain infringed their section 15 equality rights. This was in face of the legislature's concerns respecting difficulties with causality, proof, and administration. If I remember anything from high school history, it is the central role that the power of the purse played in the establishment of the sovereignty of an elected Parliament over an autocratic monarchy. The unanimous decision in *Martin* is thus highly activist. The Court fails to explain how it might deal with differential compensation schemes for the same injury depending whether it resulted from a motor vehicle accident, a slip and fall incident, or a workplace injury. Because the vagaries of adjudication, as well as the limitations of its institutional resources, deny the Court the ability to regulate the entire area of personal injury damages, it should hesitate before second-guessing the legislature.[83] These institutional limitations make principled and coherent decision making difficult if not impossible. In addition, *Martin* illustrates the cumulative power of activism: *Tétreault-Gadoury v. Canada* (1991) unlocked the door to the government's spending power, *Eldridge v. British Columbia* (1997) opened it, and *Martin* indicates that the Court has stepped all the way inside. It is interesting to note that *Doucet-Boudreau* garnered more press interest than did *Martin*.

The Aboriginal rights cases of *R. v. Blais* and *R. v. Powley* show a balance between restraint and activism respecting Métis rights. In *Blais*, the Court held, based on historical evidence and documentary interpretation, that a Métis was not an Indian for the purposes of the Manitoba *Natural Resources Transfer Agreement*. In *Powley*, the Court fleshed out the rights of Métis under section 35 of the *Constitution Act*. As Métis are specifically described in the section, the Court had to grant them *some* rights. Therefore the decision to uphold the respondent's hunting rights was only somewhat activist. Both decisions were unanimous.

The eighteen decisions described above are divided into seven restrained and eleven activist cases. Of these eighteen, only four would have been included in the quantitative database used by Choudhry et al. (*Trociuk, Figueroa, Malmo-Levine*, and *Martin*). Several cases where activism was a substantial component would have been excluded altogether. The database compiled by Choudhry et al. would have failed to include issues such as administrative review and guidelines, variation of separation agreements, the constitution of arbitration boards, public interest litigation, debtor/creditor priorities, supervision of *Charter* remedies, and Aboriginal rights. The qualitative analysis I performed excluded three cases that would have been included in Choudhry's database as instances where the government's legislation was upheld (*Siemens v. Manitoba, Ell v. Alberta*, and *R. v. S.A.B.*). These three cases are arguably instances of judicial restraint, but I did not include them because I did not feel that the arguments in favour of striking the legislation were strong enough to warrant considering whether to strike the subject legislation. The 1997 *Eldridge* case, wherein the Court compelled British Columbia to spend money to provide sign language interpretation, was also not included in Choudhry and Hunter's database.[84] I therefore respectfully suggest that in this instance, the more inclusive qualitative measure of activism yields a more accurate description than does the quantitative analysis utilizing the proxy favoured by Choudhry et al. Notwithstanding this limitation, Choudhry and Hunter's systematic study, and the further analysis of same above, is extremely useful in understanding the issue of activism in the Court's jurisprudence.

The cases where activism is an issue comprised approximately one-third of the Court's docket in 2003. By the qualitative measure above, it was activist in approximately 20 per cent of its cases. I would describe only two cases – *National Trust* and *Martin* – as being very activist. Only a further two or three cases would rise to the level of being somewhat activist: I would put *CUPE*, *Figueroa*, and perhaps *Trociuk* in this category.

Postscript

A case decided at the beginning of 2004, *Canadian Foundation for Children, Youth and the Law v. Canada*, dealt with the contentious issue of corporal punishment. The case is interesting for the present purpose because of the detailed code prescribed by the Court. Detailed codes are usually the product of legislatures. Six of the nine Justices found that the provision did not contravene the *Charter* but wrote in upper and lower age limits and proscribed the use of instruments in the corporal disciplining of children. The case mirrors the spanking behaviour of Canadians, which varies along a continuum from highly restrained to completely unrestrained. The Court showed restraint in not striking down the legislation but on balance the decision is best characterized as activist because it prescribes a detailed code.

Discussion and Conclusion: Is the Court Too Activist?

This question is like answering whether two vehicles in motion almost collided. Automobiles regularly pass within *feet* of each other. Yet, when airplanes come within a few hundred *yards* of each other, it is matter of grave concern. Some proximity, some activism, is acceptable. It is difficult to say how close the Court is operating to the danger zone. Certainly it is close enough to raise concerns regarding whether it is showing appropriate deference to other governmental bodies and to raise the issue of its legitimacy. But how close is difficult to measure. Nevertheless, a few comments may be of use.

Quantitative Findings

Overall, the quantitative data point to a trend of increasing activism on the part of the Supreme Court of Canada.

Choudhry and Hunter documented a relatively constant level of legislation being struck down. But Monahan's data point to a recent upsurge in the rate success for *Charter* claimants. As discussed above, Kent Roach's conclusion that *RJR-Macdonald* (1995) did not signal a

Figure 12.5. Percentage of cases featuring overruling in the Supreme Court of Canada, 1951–2000

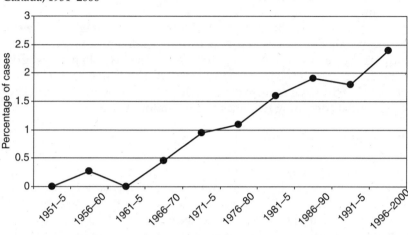

decreased level of deference by the Court to other branches of government when interpreting the *Charter*[85] is at odds with the quantitative trend in the jurisprudence. Muttart and Halteh demonstrated declining deference in the Court's section 1 jurisprudence. It appears that Roach's conclusion is based on his impression from reading at least some of the Court's decisions in the area.[86] However, the systematic analysis conducted herein provides strong indications that Roach's impression was incorrect.

The rise in the rate of overruling points to a sustained upwards trend in the Court's activism (see figure 12.5). The fact that more and more of these are explicit suggests both that the Court is confident and that it is showing consideration for those who must rely on its judgments. The large number of overruled precedents that either were more than a generation old or had been on the books for less than five years indicates respectively, that the Court is adjusting its jurisprudence to current conditions or rectifying its mistakes. Conversely, the sustained levels of overruling of precedents falling between these two extremes are indicative of judicial activism.

Additional findings support the conclusion of a gradual, but sustained, rise in activism in the Supreme Court of Canada. The rise in policy combined with the decrease in law in the proportion of fact, law, and policy utilized by the Court points to an increase in activism. The rise in contextual interpretation combined with the decrease in formal legal reasoning is part of the same trend, as is the increase in the proportion of non-foundational reasoning. On the other hand, close calls are moderating.

The gradual move away from bright-line tests together with the rise in the number of issues residing in the penumbra and/or open to judicial choice also indicate that the Court is actively shaping its jurisprudence to give it broader scope for action. This Court-centric view is reflected in the Court's increasing tendency to rely on its own jurisprudence and its declining tendency to consult foreign sources.

Qualitative Analysis

The qualitative analysis of 2003 cases portrays activism ebbing and flowing. Two cases of restraint, *Authorson* and *Malmo-Levine*, are very high profile. Had the Court not exercised restraint in these cases, 2003 would have marked a very activist year for the Court. None of the activist cases are of such high profile, and the activism in *CUPE* likely raised, instead of lowered, the Court's perceived legitimacy. But the Court's willingness to supplant the judgment of the legislature for its own in *National Trust* is very troubling. Similarly, its ongoing willingness to arrogate the power of the purse in *Nova Scotia v. Martin* indicates a lack of humility in the execution of its constitutionally limited role. Overall, 2003 did not see any major change in the Court's proximity to the danger zone. At the beginning of 2004, the Court's willingness to allow parents some leeway in spanking children likely represents an eminently acceptable compromise.

Some cases, for example *Sauvé* (2002), require the application of political values and are therefore inescapably political. In such instances, the Court cannot be faulted for applying its values. But the Court also applies its values, for example, in *National Trust* (2003) even where it is under no such democratically inspired imperative. Furthermore, even in *Sauvé*, the Court could have adopted the value of deferential humility: the state of the law did not compel the result the Court arrived at.

The Charter

Charter litigation represents the most obvious locus for court activism. The *Charter* is a powerful instrument that requires the Court to actively decide many controversial issues. On its face, the *Charter*'s scope is limited to governmental legislation and action. However, early on, in

Dolphin Delivery (1986) and subsequently, the Court has asserted the right to apply *'Charter* values' to non-*Charter* areas of the law.[87] This assertion is already fulfilling its promise to be an important basis for judicial activism in the future: as of 19 July 2004, sixty-eight Supreme Court cases mention *'Charter* values.'[88] Thus there is a basis for the proposition that the Court is using the *Charter* to increase its power.

Similarly, the elevated levels of close calls, policy and contextual interpretation, judicial choice and hard distinguishing all point to a lower level of constraint with respect to *Charter* cases. *Charter* law appears to be less objective and neutral than non-*Charter* law.

Hard Distinguishing, Humility, and Open Standards

Earlier, I theorized that hard distinguishing might, in certain circumstances, be indicative of humility on the part of the Court. If so, the *Charter* cases involving hard distinguishing point towards humility. Only one of the nine *Charter* cases characterized by hard distinguishing involved a ruling against the government. The other eight upheld the government action (or inaction) in question. The one exception, *New Brunswick v. J.G.* (1999), compelled the government to provide legal aid to parents of a child who had been apprehended by the Children's Aid Society. The use of hard distinguishing to arrive at pro-government results indicates constraint, but it must be remembered that this conclusion is based on a small number of cases.

On the other hand, the rise in open standards will increasingly invite more hard distinguishing. Because propositions are more specific – more hard and fast than open standards – outright overruling will generally be necessary to effect any change. Principles and especially open standards tend to be pliable: it will be possible to use the same standard to justify inconsistent results. The Court will foster change with less doctrinal drama where the rules are based on plastic principles. But this plasticity will lead to more close calls. Hard distinguishing may also indicate that the Court is uncomfortable with its level of activism in these cases.

How the Court Overrules

The manner in which the Court arrives at and explains its ruling may be as important as the ruling itself. It should be transparent in analysing the advantages and disadvantages of any potentially activist steps it might take. *Friedmann Equity* (2000) is an example of the Court at its most transparent. In that case the Court carefully weighed the costs and benefits of any activism.[89] Cases such as *Friedmann* indicate that legal reasoning has an important role in shielding the Court from perceptions of activism.

Commentators such as Allan Hutchinson have argued that overruling should be permitted only when the Court can point to 'some special or super-justification over and above the claim that the earlier decision is wrong.'[90] *Vetrovec* (1982) is a good example of a case where the old rule, which dealt with the evidence of accomplices, had 'lost sight of the justice it sought to achieve.'[91] In *R v. Paquette* (1977), the idea that duress was irrelevant to intent was out of step with conventional views of justice. In *Brown v. L.A. Brown & Gentleman* (1971), justice required that the prerequisites for the admission of new evidence be relaxed. While overruling may, on occasion, be a radical departure from the Court's proper role, it is more likely to be the result of a conscientious effort to develop the law in accordance with the needs of society. Such efforts appear to be the rule, but, as with other aspects of activism, there are exceptions.

The Court's Mandate within a Democracy

The Court's docket unavoidably mandates a certain level of activism. Its leave procedure and criteria, as enacted by Parliament, require it to decide cases where the Court must choose whether or not to be activist. New issues are always percolating up to controversy.[92] For example, pending cases deal with funding for autistic children, same-sex marriage, parliamentary privilege, provincial court judges' salaries, and political advertising by non-party coalitions.[93] It is not the Court's fault that cases of 'public importance' tend to be controversial. If it selected only non-controversial cases, the Court would not be complying with section 40 of the *Supreme Court Act*. Nevertheless, its selection criteria will keep the issue of activism in the forefront of critical commentary.

Apologists for judicial activism point to inaction on the part of the legislative branch.[94] Surely, they say, given the length of time it takes to get a case before the Supreme Court of Canada, any legislature which felt that it should deal with the matter itself would have had plenty of time to act before the case was heard by the Court. There is much to be said for this view. Six of the nineteen 'qualitative' cases of activism could have been resolved by legislation. Five cases of restraint (two involving attacks on legislation) could have been short-circuited by legislative action. Only four cases involved the Court's striking or ignoring legislation already passed by the legislature. On the other hand, one of the rationales for a strong version of the rule of *stare decisis* is the notion that if the rule embodied in the precedent were wrong, the legislature would have changed the rule via statutory enactment.[95] In this view, legislative inaction represents support for the impugned precedent. However, repeated instances of legislative inaction and Parliamentary avoidance reveal that this notion lacks empirical basis. In short, if judges are activist, a significant amount of the criticism for such activism must be visited upon our democratically elected politicians. Legislative inaction is a significant factor in Court activism, but it does not control all cases.

Apologists for activism also often point to the need to have the courts protect minorities from the tyranny of the majority. Frank Roncarelli would never have been able to stand up to Duplessis without the backing of the courts. While it is indisputable that there are occasions where courts have protected civil rights, Patrick Monahan points out that the 'empirical evidence suggests that the elimination of popular control in favour of an elite institution like the Supreme Court does *not* actually promote the long-term cause of justice and equality.'[96]

The Court views its actions as upholding democracy and promoting democratic values.[97] Its critics charge that the Justices, and not the *Charter,* are driving constitutional litigation.[98] They say that the Justices are arrogating more and more power to themselves. In 2003, seven cases appeared to support the democractic process while nine supported the judicial power thesis. There is thus a fairly even balance here. The Court is supporting democratic institutions, but at the same time it is usurping some of their functions.

The U.S. Supreme Court is a useful comparator when assessing the balance between activism and deference to democratically elected legislatures. The American Court is widely perceived as being much more overtly political than the Canadian Court. It much more often subordinates *stare decisis* to its own vision of what is right than does the Canadian Court. Politically highly charged issues, such as the *Roe v. Wade* abortion decision, are regularly revisited.[99] And yet, no one is advocating any serious hobbling of the U.S. Supreme Court.

In short, the Canadian Supreme Court's margin of safety for collision avoidance is not as slim as it is for automobiles, but neither is it as large as that required for safe aeronautics. The Court sometimes veers into activism but is currently operating within the margin of safety. However, one high-profile case could well move the Court into the danger zone. The best indicator of whether it is encroaching on the margin of safety is the extent to which its Justices are perceived to be acting like politicians. As discussed in chapter 11, if judges become politicians, the autonomy of legal reasoning, and especially its perceived objectivity, is put in peril.

13 Conclusion: The Gap Has Been Narrowed

In this final chapter I will summarize the major findings resulting from this study of Supreme Court of Canada jurisprudence within the context of legal theory. This summary will document several significant narrowings of the empirical gap. The second section outlines the overall efficacy of the empirical method for the study of adjudication. The third section details the modifications that need to be made to the existing paradigm of legal reasoning.

General Theoretical Findings

Several important findings, of general relevance to jurisprudence, have emerged from this study. First, the ways and means by which judges decide cases have changed over time. What counts as legal reasoning has evolved. Since adjudication is a dynamic, not static, activity, there is every reason to believe that it will change during the next fifty years just as it has changed over the past fifty. Jurists must keep vigilant watch over these shifting sands.

Second, the nihilist description of a chaotic 'anything goes' does not appear to be accurate. The outcome of most cases is, to a substantial degree, predictable. And when the outcome is unpredictable, it is not because the judges have changed overnight but because the issue has slowly evolved and has come forward in a different context. When social change results in the formation of a new reef, the law must change course. Present-day adjudication continues to have adequate legal determinants, and its non-legal determinants enjoy sufficient consensus for the satisfactory functioning of our courts. Law is multifaceted: the Critical Legal Studies movement failed to generate a workable legal theory principally because it was insufficiently comprehensive to explain many extant phenomena and behaviours.

Third, sometimes law is politics, but most of the time it is law. Law is a constellation of decision-making practices. Law, like a renovation contractor, uses a full tool box; it cannot be explained by reference only to wood, hammers, and nails. But neither would any description of law be complete if it omitted any of wood, hammer, or nails. Law employs formal and contextual reasoning, foundational and non-foundational thought. Judicial behaviour is only occasionally instrumental.

Fourth, in many ways legal reasoning is objective and neutral. Law's special form of logic is sufficiently distinct for law to be characterized as a unique discipline, capable of constraining ideology. However, legal decisions are often contestable. Sometimes this is because decision makers consciously failed to abide by law's constraints, sometimes because the issue resided in the penumbra, where there was no law to clearly guide judicial choice, and sometimes due to the unsuitability of law to resolve the issue. Law will always be a human endeavour, limited and fallible.

Fifth, these four observations must be balanced against contrary trends. The Court's jurisprudence is trending to more non-foundational reasoning and judicial choice. The rate of overruling is rising. The increasing focus on its own precedents indicates a growing confidence in the Court's own powers.

In short, Law can be described as a pyramid: at its broad base, clear statute or caselaw provides determinate answers. Most of the remaining cases are of intermediate difficulty and can be satisfactorily resolved through legal reasoning. Even in the Supreme Court of Canada, there are only a small number of cases at the apex that require extraordinary judicial effort.

Specific Findings Relative to the Supreme Court of Canada

The Supreme Court's legal reasoning has been gradually evolving in several important areas over the past fifty years. The most dramatic evidence of this change is the crossover that took place in the early 1980s when overruling surpassed hard distinguishing, when policy overtook fact, and when formal legal reasoning began to decrease in favour of contextual interpretation. The evolution in the Court's reasoning can also be seen in the increase in open-standard tests, a greater willingness to rely on principle, and a willingness to engage in non-foundational analysis. Thus, theories of jurisprudence that fail to distinguish between older and newer cases cannot describe legal reasoning accurately or in detail. This latter observation applies especially to attempted descriptions of current legal reasoning and predictions relating to future judicial behaviour. Many descriptions of the Court's functioning that were valid before the crossover would be inaccurate thereafter. Moreover, there may be other and different crossovers in the future.

Overruling is gradually, but persistently, increasing, both as a function of incidences and as a proportion of the Court's docket. Hard distinguishing, the less transparent and more ad hoc version, is overall on the decline.

Since 1950, and especially after the mid-1970s, the facts have determined fewer and fewer of the Court's decisions. The importance of policy implications rose during the same period and have continued to rise to date. Concomitant with the continued increase in the importance of policy, the prevalence of law as a determining force began to decline proportionally after the early 1980s.

In concert with the above, the Court began to move away from its almost exclusive reliance on formal legal reasoning. Commencing in the early 1980s, significant percentages of the Court's decisions began to be characterized by contextual interpretation and doctrinal reconciliation.

The move to policy and rise of contextual interpretation were matched by increases in the adoption and utilization of open standards as opposed to bright-line tests and by more non-foundational reasoning. More and more of its cases called upon the Court to make novel choices; the number of cases where the law dictated the result declined. While the Court continues to strongly prefer legal propositions as its primary tools, its utilization of subsidiary tools, especially principles, started gradually increasing beginning in the early 1980s.

The trend towards less hard distinguishing is reversed in the Court's *Charter* jurisprudence. This finding may be a reflection of the Court's ambivalence or uncertainty as to how it should decide these issues. The elevated levels of close calls and the lower levels of unanimity in *Charter* cases supports this hypothesis. The Court may be concerned with negative criticism of its rulings. A not insignificant number of *Charter* cases are decided by the values held and employed by the Justices.

Do the Findings Verify or Refute Judicial Theories?

Most legal theories have elements that receive support from and elements that are contradicted by the data and analysis of my survey of the legal reasoning of the Supreme Court of Canada.

Hart's idea of a solid core of settled meaning was supported in the sense that the law gives a determinate answer to most legal questions. However, it was refuted by the Court's tendency to revisit, and sometimes change, what had been thought to reside in the presumably immutable 'solid core.' The number of 'hard cases,' the persistent presence of close calls, and the increase in judicial choice were all somewhat in excess of what I would have predicted in light of Hart's theories.

Dworkin's notion that judges decide based on legal principle is contradicted by the limited role principle plays in the Court's reasons for judgment. The Court is guided much more by law than by Dworkin's individualistic notion of judicial 'integrity.' His chain-novel theory seems much closer to the mark. His theory that principle is the primary mode of judicial decision-making is refuted by the survey evidence.

Stone's view that plurisignative judgments will render the common law increasingly uncertain is contradicted by the Court's continued reliance on legal propositions that accord with, instead of deviating from, past caselaw. However, the increasing number of cases decided on the basis of judicial choice as opposed to legal direction provides some support for Stone's central thesis.

Hutchinson is correct in asserting that the influence of the exceptional cases where 'anything might go' extends beyond their number. Because it is extremely difficult to predict, in advance, those cases that might change precedent, these extraordinary cases increase overall uncertainty. They thereby encroach on the core of settled meaning and expand the penumbra. But Hutchinson places too much reliance on these exceptional cases, resulting in errors similar to those caused by Dworkin's single-minded focus on principle. Cases where 'anything might go' are very much in the minority. Hutchinson therefore overestimates the number of instances of non-foundational reasoning and exaggerates their overall importance with respect to the prediction of general trends. The incidence of cases where 'anything might go' remains small and therefore constitutes an insufficient primary basis for a jurisprudential theory. However, the increase in instances of non-foundational reasoning and judicial choice indicates a trend in the direction of Hutchinson's formulations; any broad-based theory must take this general trend into account. Hutchinson's observations in this regard therefore provide a

Figure 13.1. Percentage of Supreme Court of Canada cases involving overruling and hard distinguishing, 1951–2000

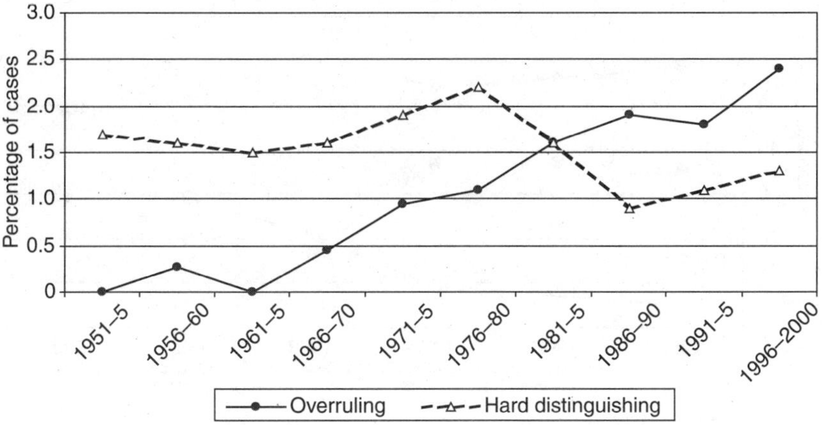

good first-stage theory to employ when studying the increasing diffi-culty in the prediction of the outcome of any individual case.

In 1950, the Court functioned in a manner largely in accord with Hart's descriptions. In 2003, some of its behaviours are beginning to resemble those described by Hutchinson. Perhaps another crossover is looming.

Refining Historical Descriptions

Paul Weiler, writing in the early 1970s, believed he detected an evolu-tion in the Court towards a grander style of reasoning commencing in the 1960s.[1] As was described in section 2 above, there was a significant crossover in the early 1980s relative to overruling and hard distinguish-ing, the proportions of fact/law/policy, and the modes of reasoning employed by the Court. To refresh the reader's memory, figures 13.1 and 13.2 highlight these crossovers. These crossover phenomena would indicate that the grander style of reasoning noted by Weiler did not reach its tipping point until a decade after his observations: it was not until the early eighties that policy surpassed fact and began to gain on law.

On the cusp of the millennium, Patrick Monahan described a Court consistently adopting a policy orientation.[2] The data in figures 13.1 and 13.2, the decline of formal reasoning, and the rise of more contextualist discourse in the Court's decisions are consistent with the direction

Figure 13.2. Decade-to-decade changes in fact, law, and policy considerations, Supreme Court of Canada, 1952–2002

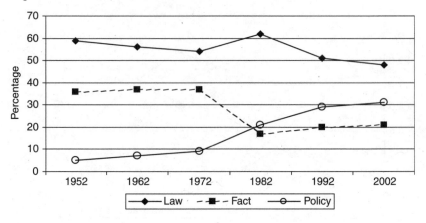

described by Monahan. However, as discussed in the next section, this contextualist discourse is not the only, or even the predominant, discourse in the Court.

Practical Jurisprudence as Applied to the
Supreme Court of Canada

The survey evidence indicates that when judges are faced with an issue, they first consult the legal materials in search of a clear answer. If such an answer is found and if it leads to a result in accord with justice, it is applied. These cases comprise the overwhelming majority at all court levels. Even in the Supreme Court, these cases form the largest block.

If the answer does not accord with justice, consideration is given, especially at the Supreme Court level, to changing the rule that provided the answer. If the rule needs minor revision, it may be modified through distinguishing or incremental development. If major revision is necessary, the rule may be supplanted by another rule through overruling. If there is no clear answer, a wider ranging inquiry and analysis may be undertaken, often resulting in contextual interpretation, policy analysis, doctrinal reconciliation, and the like. Where the legal materials fail to provide guidance, a new rule, often in the form of an open standard, may be formulated. As part of this rule formation, a wide range of approaches and sources, including the Justices' own values, may be consulted. In situations where the legal materials fail to provide a clear answer, legal reasoning becomes more diluted, less unique, and more similar to politics and philosophy. Here judges have more choice, but they often refuse to acknowledge this choice.

Jurisprudence should not claim to say that judges confine their deliberations to the consideration of legal rules, nor should it blithely conclude that law is politics or solely the result of the pre-existing attitudes of judges. But jurisprudence can predict which end of the continuum judges are tending towards. Given the large number of variables at play, any prediction can only be approximate. And prediction is further complicated by the fact that the Justices are aware that they are being watched and may, on occasion and however subtly and unconsciously, change their behaviour as the result of those studying, criticizing, and attempting to predict it. Notwithstanding these difficulties, analyses of overruling, hard distinguishing, fact/law/policy, and modes of legal reasoning are valuable analytical aids.

At the mid-point of the first decade of the twenty-first century, the Supreme Court of Canada is moving towards an increasingly multidimensional process for the determination of the issues it decides to adjudicate. Its expanded modes of legal reasoning will often result in superior reasons for judgment. However, this same trend will increase temptations to render decisions that will increase perceptions of activism and decisions that conceal, instead of reveal, the Court's true reasons. The judiciary will be under increasing pressures to be more forthright in acknowledging that they often have choices that are almost totally unconstrained by legal materials. This same pressure will push judges towards developing standards for the exercise of, and the refusal to exercise, those choices.

Law, in the sense of the doctrinal analysis of statutes and precedential cases, will continue to be the best predictor of the outcome of cases. But the expanded range of sources that the Court now consults, and will continue to consult, must also be considered by those attempting to predict the specific outcome of cases. Policy, context, and law will each play a role.

Activism and Its Implications

As described in chapter 12, there are times when the Court extends itself beyond the proper limits of its constitutional role. However, charges of activism are often little more than thinly veiled criticisms of the substance of the individual decision under discussion. There are indications that these criticisms may occasionally cause the court to shy away from fulfilling its proper role.

Perceptions of improper activism have the potential to impair the Court's efficacious functioning. It therefore behooves the Court to take care when overruling precedent, basing its decisions on values, or fashioning open standards that force more and more choice onto the judiciary. The unique constitutional and institutional nature of the Court requires it to constantly nurture its political legitimacy and justify its legal validity. Activism remains an issue on the cusp; one ill-considered opinion could lead to serious repercussions in the current hypersensitive environment.

If the Court is to successfully avoid the perception that it is behaving in an inappropriately activist fashion, its justifications for its decisions will have to be widely accepted. Legal reasoning remains the Court's primary tool in this regard. Changes in legal reasoning may expand its potential, but changing this primary tool makes it more difficult to manipulate, master, and manage. The Court's health as a legal, as well as a political, institution will depend on its ability to propound its views with incremental, yet vigorous, humility and with step-by-step clarity.

Overruling is a valuable method for correcting disconnects between the law and an evolving society. Evaluation of the criteria used by the Court when overruling constitutes a valuable barometer with respect to how secure the Court feels in this activist role. A bold Court feels more secure. Transparency and explicitly stated criteria are indicia of the maturity of the Court. Hard distinguishing indicates an immature Court or one unsure of the propriety of what it is seeking to accomplish.

All the foregoing, especially the ongoing criticism, leads me to predict that the Court will oscillate between activist and passive behaviour. Its rulings in *N.A.P.E.* (2004) and *Chaoulli v. Quebec* (2005) represent opposite poles of this oscillation. If the differences between the Court's *Charter* and non-*Charter* jurisprudence recede, the Court will have absorbed the *Charter* into its prevailing operational paradigm. If these differences, especially the Court's tendency to employ more robust modes of legal discourse in *Charter* cases, do not recede, the *Charter* will have become established as a primary source of the Court's power within the Canadian polity.

The Value and Limits of Empiricism

Overall, I submit that the approach outlined in this monograph improves on the typical approach of jurists who recite the breadth of work required for an empirical study (e.g., Raz) or the difficulty of characterizing judicial behaviour (e.g., Kennedy) and then decline to even attempt empirical verification.[3] Often jurisprudential theorists do not refer to any empirical data at all, but content themselves with examining the internal or linguistic logic of other writers. When cases are referred to, they are few in number; they are not chosen systematically nor is any overall analysis attempted. Jurists should study what courts are doing, no matter how difficult they find the study to implement. It may be easier to look for a lost ring under the light of a street lamp, but if it was lost in an area not so illuminated, no amount of searching under the street lamp will lead to the discovery of the ring.

Unsystematic sampling often causes jurisprudence to resemble the Buddhist parable of blind men examining an elephant: The emperor had heard of a wondrous beast in a far-off land and sent five blind courtiers to investigate. Upon their return, one courtier describes the elephant as a large strong tree having a trunk so huge that his arms would not fit around it. He was contradicted by one of his fellows who maintained that the elephant was like a large hose, pliable and flexible. The third courtier contradicted both, insisting that the elephant was like a pointed lance. 'No, no,' asserted the fourth. 'The elephant is a bird, with wings on either side of its head.' The fifth maintained that the elephant was like a boat, with a long keel on its underside. Unsystematic sampling is at its worse when it becomes self-selecting and designed to prove that elephants can fly. Systematic sampling examines the whole elephant.

This study of the Supreme Court's entire reasons for judgment over five decades, almost 5,000 cases, demonstrates that it is possible to systematically examine the reasons for judgment rendered by the Court and to employ this data, in concert with other materials, to make empirical evaluations of judicial behaviour. Unsystematic sampling allows jurisprudes to focus on exceptions while ignoring dominant phenomena. Regrettably, unsystematic samples appear more often than do systematic ones.

There are reasons for the dearth of empirical studies of jurisprudence. First, such studies are time consuming. Second, it is difficult to quantify judicial behaviour. Quantification requires human judgments both in setting up the study and in classifying the behaviours. Each of these judgments is open to criticism. Investigators contemplating an empirical project might well question whether the up-front costs are worth the uncertain future benefits. Third, not all questions can be answered definitively. Fourth, many jurisprudes are unfamiliar with this type of research. Lee Epstein and Gary King have recently charged that legal scholars often proceed with little awareness of, much less compliance with, the rules of inference that guide empirical research within the social and natural sciences.[4] Richard Revesz believes that law needs its own, unique methodology.[5] Michael Heise agrees and points to the rise of several methods for the study of judicial decision making, including behaviourism, attitudinalism, institutionalism, and the theory of legal reasoning.[6] I have attempted to employ, or refer to, studies utilizing all of these methods in this study.

The methodological and analytical approaches I have adopted in this book stand in contrast to those of earlier studies. My approaches have added new data and analysis to the body of jurisprudential knowledge. Nevertheless, this is an appropriate time to anticipate and counter several possible criticisms while acknowledging the limits of empirical study.

The first criticism is at the level of methodology. But this is a pioneering work; there are no other studies that have attempted a similar verification of jurisprudential theory. The jurisprudence of the Supreme Court of Canada has never been studied in such a systematic manner. I respectfully suggest that this study is a credible first effort, that it provides important insights, and that it has established a foundation upon which further efforts can be constructed.

A second potential criticism relates to the limitations inherent in statistics. Jurisprudential statistics, like sports statistics, will never tell the whole story. A pitcher's earned run average will never describe his years of training and sacrifice. It will never describe the pain and exhilaration of throwing a ninety-mile-per-hour fastball. Statistics capture neither the anguish of a grand-slam home-run ball soaring overhead nor the exultation of the game-winning strikeout. What judges are trying to do cannot be fully captured by statistics. But statistics provide many valuable insights. Qualitative analysis, the other branch of empiricism, provides an effective test of the reliability of statistics. Each empirical measure, especially those that support and solidify each other, forms part of a superstructure on which to construct a viable theory. Each datum provides support or refutation of the theory.

A third criticism would dismiss the relevance of empirical jurisprudence based on the proposition that 'it is not possible to resolve a theoretical debate.' The obvious response is that theory is only a first step in the acquisition of knowledge. Theories exist to be tested. It is the results of these tests that lead to knowledge. Where would medicine be today if it had never tested the theory that the purpose of the lungs was to cool the heart, in much the same way as a radiator cools an automobile engine? Theories do not exist to be juxtaposed in endless debate. The categories of theoretical and empirical should not be hermetically sealed off from one another, but should ebb and flow as naturally as day follows night. In short, empirical investigation may provide answers while theory will never be able to offer more than opinions. Theory and test together are stronger than either is by itself.

Although many criticisms of this study can be deflected, several important limitations should be acknowledged. First, this study is based largely on the Justices' own reasons for judgment. Some judicial reasoning may be taken at face value, but certain theorists postulate that some reasons for judgment hide as much as they reveal. For example, it is possible that the Justices were concealing the policy bases underlying their decisions in the 1950s. Judges may think different thoughts than those they are comfortable with revealing. The exploration of anecdotal accounts should detect whether dissembling is common. The analysis of broad trends should be a safeguard against judicial dissembling in reasons for judgment. Second, several important components rely, to a greater or lesser degree, on my judgment. Finally, jurisprudence is a social science. Its predictions will never be as regular as those for chemical reactions.

To reduce the impact of these problems, this study has tracked as many measurements as possible. After all, it is not possible to tell how well an automobile is functioning merely by viewing its oil gauge. I have therefore attempted to measure as many variables as possible, and, where other investigators have compiled data, I have taken advantage of their work. Additionally, my analysis has relied largely on trends as opposed to absolute levels; since my judgment is a constant over the whole period studied, the effects of any errors in judgment will be reduced.

Empiricism's Contribution to Jurisprudential Theory Formulation

Empiricism's first contribution is its acknowledgment that observation is the initial step in the study of any subject. Hart claimed that his work was a descriptive sociology. With all due respect, it is not possible to describe a phenomenon without having first observed it in a systematic fashion. Hart should have performed a full survey of judicial behaviour before attempting to describe it. Scholars who attempt to skip this first step cheat both their theories and their readers.

Empiricism's second contribution is its regular integration of observation with theory. The effect of failure to organize observations around theory is illustrated by the rise and fall of the Critical Legal Studies Movement. When the movement began, jurisprudence was overrun by forests of articles that were merely descriptive of the author's unsupported opinion at the moment of writing.[7] Critical legal scholars attacked these forests with reckless abandon but failed to plant anything in place of the trees they hacked down. The Crits' failure to propound their own theory resulted in a movement long on critical bombast but short on alternative suggestions. When positivist forest rangers returned to desolation where once majestic timbers had flourished, they viewed the Crits as destructive vandals and proceeded to replant each tree without properly considering alternate arboreal configurations.

A theory should describe phenomena and predict answers to questions. The answers may be general or specific. The more verifiable answers a theory provides, the better the theory. The anti-foundationalist theory promulgated by critical legal scholars was good at exposing what phenomena were being misdescribed – at cutting down trees – but it failed to offer a useful alternative. A partially correct theory is better than no theory at all. A chef possessed of a partial theory of herbs will cook better-tasting meals than one who merely includes a dash of 'green-coloured spices' in his dishes. Newtonian mechanics continued to be useful even in the face of evidence refuting it.[8]

The value of empiricism's use of theory to organize observations is best described by Thomas Kuhn.[9] Contrary to Kuhn's paradigm, neither the Critical Legal Scholars nor the orthodox positivists were willing to unite behind a new disciplinary matrix for the formulation of new questions and theories to be subjected to empirical testing. Jurisprudence thus continued to be primarily a clash of ideologies instead of becoming a more mature ('mature' in the Kuhnian sense) scholarly discipline. Positivism would have improved itself had it done a thorough job of verifying or refuting the anomalies described by Critical Legal Scholars and then incorporating these new findings into its paradigm. At the same time, if non-foundationalists are unwilling to be absorbed into the positivist paradigm, they will have to formulate and test their own comprehensive theory.

The work of quantitative jurists suffers for the lack of a paradigm wherein their work would be placed in context. Scalogram studies are marginalized instead of being integrated. A widely accepted jurisprudential paradigm would direct researchers towards research priorities, the same way that atomic theory prioritized the work of the Manhattan Project. The lack of a meta-theory restricts the brilliant studies undertaken by the likes of Peck, Monahan, McCormick, Morton, Russell, Withey, Kelly, Choudhry, Hunter, and others to being candles in a sea of darkness. A meta-theory has the potential to assemble these various studies into an effulgent chandelier.

Empirical knowledge of some matters can be gained by mere observation. Thus if I want to know how long my grass is, I need merely look outside my window. But if I want to know how high my grass will be next year, I will need to catalogue as many causative factors as possible and test their respective contribution to the growth of my grass. A first-level theory, such as 'sunlight affects growth,' is necessary at this stage. Without such a theoretical hypothesis, there would be no point in testing the effects of sunlight. I discover that sunlight increases the growth of my grass. But too much sunlight burns it. Perhaps I should have added more water? I quickly discover that I need a meta-analysis of how and why *each* factor affects growth and how each factor interacts with the others. This meta-analysis will be a necessary first step in the formulation of global tests. Myriad factors interact in most human activities; judicial decision making is a prime example.

This meta-analysis is empiricism's third contribution. Few jurists stand back from the day-to-day behaviour of judges in society and attempt to analyse what they are doing in a global sense. Hart contented himself with description based on partial observation of the relevant phenomena. Dworkin added wishful thinking. Those who do attempt a meta-analysis, such as Hutchinson, content themselves with formulating important questions. Mainstream jurisprudence has thus far failed to properly incorporate the myriad components and dynamics that would go into a unified paradigm of judicial decision making.

But empiricism's primary contribution is its ongoing requirement of verification. Had the learned jurisprudes whose theories were the focus of the analysis in this monograph attempted to verify their theories, they would have discovered that almost all theories are improved by incorporating explanations for anomalous data. The theory that sun-light improved grass growth was improved by the addition of the new element water. Both Hart and Hutchinson would have improved their theories if they had incorporated findings related to the rise in judicial choice and the prevalence of foundational reasoning, respectively.

Empiricism's focus on verification impels ongoing methodological refinement. Dworkin's effort, despite his limited and self-serving sample of fifty-one cases, was arguably a first step. Shalin Sugunasiri's article on the rise of contextualism in the Supreme Court was superior because its larger sample led to a greater likelihood of accuracy. However, the present study's larger and more systematic sample was necessary to verify the accuracy of her findings. By contrast, another self-selected sample could just as easily have supported doctrinal reconciliation as the Court's foremost emerging mode.[10]

The investigations undertaken during the course of this study have engendered several methodological refinements. For example, through trial and error, I discovered that five-year blocks of data disclose trends sometimes obscured by annual blocks. As described in chapter 12, such groupings enhanced the evaluation of the data compiled by Choudhry and Hunter. In addition, this study disclosed the cumulative and syner-gistic advantages of analysing trends across several indicators. The relative incidence of judicial behaviour may indicate the proper focus for jurisprudence: for example, the data respecting the Court's modes of legal reasoning suggest that jurisprudes should spend ten to twenty times as much energy studying formal legal reasoning as they do on studying the application of legal principle.

Modifying the Prevailing Paradigm

This study adopted the foundational positivist paradigm as its working theory at the beginning and remains with it at the end. The two other paradigms marked for consideration – pragmatism and principle-based ruling – were not supported. The foundational positivist paradigm has staying power for two reasons. First, as outlined above, it provides powerful and unifying descriptions as well as reasonably accurate pre-dictive power. Second, it has no viable contenders. After much initial interest, the Legal Realism and Critical Legal Studies schools of thought petered out because they were essentially anti-theories.[11] These schools described what law was *not* but failed to describe what law *is*. Their lack of explanatory or predictive power rendered them virtually useless. If a theory fails to predict, it can neither be verified nor refuted. A theory that is 20 per cent accurate is better than a theory that can only criticize the 20 per cent accuracy rate. A theory that proclaims that 'law is politics' – thereby restricting itself to asserting that judges decide on the basis of power, values, and interests – excludes from its ambit much about law that is not power, values, and interests, and thus needlessly reduces its explanatory and predictive power.

In accord with the first paradigm, this study discloses that when Supreme Court Justices decide a case, they reach first for legal propositions, which they apply via formal legal reasoning. Secondary modes of legal reasoning – primarily contextual interpretation or doctrinal reconciliation – are undertaken when a problem is complicated. The Court changes the law only in the very small number of cases where precedent required an obviously unjust or otherwise unsatisfactory result. Its reasoning is usually transparent, but on occasion the Court resorts to reasons that apparently fail to reflect defensible logic. Existing precedent and legal reasoning constrain judges from ruling in accord with their own independent beliefs and desires where these are at variance with precedent.

In summary, this study has demonstrated that traditional positivism continues to be the best description of legal decision making. This paradigm presented judicial decision making as using existing legal materials to arrive at an objectively correct decision. However, this study has also disclosed instances of the other two paradigms (pragmatism and principle-based rulings).

Rulings in accord with the second paradigm, which predicted rulings based on pragmatism, occurred when the existing rule provided a highly unsatisfactory or clearly impractical result. These cases, very few in number, can be best viewed as instances where changed social facts undermined the basis on which the original decision was rendered. These changed social facts rendered the law unclear and unstable, made the case 'hard.' As such, these limited number of pragmatic cases do not constitute significant anomalies for the first paradigm.

The third paradigm, which holds that judges rule in accordance with principles, frequently morally based principles, and that they often utilize non-foundational ideas, was evident more often than the second. While propositions still outnumber principles by a factor of more than two to one, and foundational reasoning continues to be even more dominant, the clear trends showing an increase in non-foundational and principle-based reasoning constitute anomalies that must be taken into account. Although it is canvassing an increasing variety of sources and evinces a greater concern that its jurisprudence be coherent overall, the Court is, with very few exceptions, ruling in accord with principles recognized by the prevailing legal rules. It is not ruling in accordance with the moral principles of individual judges. Contrary to Dworkin's prescription, its Justices are not behaving like Hercules on Mount Olympus.

The rise in non-foundational reasoning constitutes a more important departure from the prevailing paradigm and requires that it be adjusted. If the trend towards non-foundational legal reasoning persists, a wholesale revision may become necessary. But at the current rate of change, this will not be necessary for at least twenty-five years.

Based on my findings, I would restate the prevailing paradigm as follows (adjustments are in italics or struck through):

> *Overall,* judges are constrained by existing legal precedent. Their primary adjudicative technique consists of the application of legal propositions and precedents to the facts via formal legal reasoning resulting in objectively ~~correct~~ *defensible* decisions. Secondary modes of legal reasoning, primarily involving contextual considerations or doctrinal reconciliation, are used when a problem is complicated or where the legal point to be decided is completely novel. The Court will change the law only in the very small number of cases when precedent required an ~~obviously~~ unjust or otherwise unsatisfactory result. *Where judges feel it useful to approach an issue from another perspective, they utilize policy-oriented or non-foundational reasoning, but this results only in a slightly elevated tendency to change the law.* The court's reasoning is usually transparent and representative of the means by which it arrived at its decision. Existing precedent and legal reasoning ~~constrain~~ *strongly discourage* judges from ruling in accord with their own independent beliefs and desires where these are at variance with precedent.

The word 'overall' is added to reflect the numerous exceptions, particularly in *Charter* cases, noted during the course of this study. 'Correct' is changed to 'defensible' to recognize the numerous instances where more than one choice is open to the Court and the well-documented correlation of ideology and adjudicative outcome. The latter observation also accounts for the change to 'strongly discourage' from 'constrain.' The word 'obviously' is removed to acknowledge the increasing incidence of overruling in the Court's judgments. The added sentence reflects the increase in policy and in non-foundational reasoning that I found in the Court's jurisprudence.

I submit that this modified statement is well supported, on a balance of probabilities, by the evidence recited herein.

This modified paradigm predicts that the Court will function in accord with its formulations for the foreseeable future. Its principal techniques will be dominated by Hartian positivism and formal legal reasoning but the trend towards a more non-foundational expanded contextual interpretation will continue. Expanded contextual interpretation may surpass formal legal reasoning. Policy will continue to flow into caselaw. The Court will oscillate between advancing its ideological agenda and retreating in the face of charges of activism. Activism will often be concealed within open standards. The Court's *Charter* jurisprudence will continue to generate anomalies worthy of serious study.

Courts of Appeal and trial courts will continue to function largely in accord with Hartian positivism and formal legal reasoning in accord with the rulings of the Supreme Court of Canada.

Summary

A famous philosopher once remarked that 'the proof is in the pudding.'[11] I submit that the investigations undertaken during the course of this study have documented interesting findings that can be utilized by jurists to explicate judicial behaviour. My study has documented ongoing shifts and trends in the Court's jurisprudence indicating that theories of legal reasoning require regular revision to reflect changes in judicial behaviour. Some jurisprudential contentions have been verified, others refuted. I have demonstrated that the way in which the Court proceeds with its reasoning is, to a greater or lesser degree, reflective of its functioning as an adjudicative institution and as an increasingly political body. Important insights were gained into the Court's activism. None of these findings would have surfaced without systematic and empirical investigations of the sort herein undertaken.

This monograph demonstrates not only that is it possible to conduct empirical investigations to test theories of jurisprudence but that any description of adjudication attempted in the absence of such empirical investigations will be, at best, incomplete. The data analysed herein show that the descriptions offered by Hart and his disciples must be modified to account for an increasing incidence of overruling, policy analysis, open standards, judicial choice, and non-foundational reasoning.

These findings were made possible only by the systematic selection of a large sample of cases. The survey results both tested existing theories and pointed to a modified theoretical description that better explained the observed data. Jurisprudence is overburdened with theory and philosophy; the price of admission for a new theory should be empirical verification.

Notes

Chapter 1

1 H.L.A., *The Concept of Law*, 2nd ed. (Oxford: Clarendon Press, 1994).

2 R. Dworkin, *Law's Empire* (Cambridge, MA: Belknap Press of Harvard University Press, 1986).

3 See, for example, M. Heise, *The Past, Present, and Future of Empirical Legal Scholarship: Judicial Decision Making and the New Empiricism*, (2002) U. Ill. L. Rev. 819.

4 See, for example, L. Epstein & G. King, *The Rules of Inference*, (2002) 69 U. Chi. L. Rev. 1.

5 See Bahá'u'lláh, *The Hidden Words* (Wilmette, IL: Baha'i Publishing Trust, 1982), 3–4: 'O SON OF SPIRIT! The best beloved of all things in My sight is Justice; turn not away therefrom if thou desirest Me, and neglect it not that I may confide in thee. By its aid *thou shalt see with thine own eyes and not through the eyes of others*, and shalt know of thine own knowledge and not through the knowledge of thy neighbor. Ponder this in thy heart; how it behooveth thee to be. Verily justice is My gift to thee and the sign of My loving-kindness. Set it then before thine eyes' (emphasis added).

6 R. Case, *Understanding Judicial Reasoning: Controversies, Concepts and Cases* (Toronto: Thompson Educational Publishing, 1997), 13, 31–4.

7 A. Hutchinson, *It's All in the Game: A Non-Foundational Account of Law and Adjudication* (Durham, NC: Duke University Press, 2000).

8 See, for example, J.W. Singer, *The Player and the Cards: Nihilism and Legal Theory*, (1984) 94 Yale L.J. 1.

9 See Case, *Understanding, supra* note 6, at 98–101.

10 J. Losee, *A Historical Introduction to the Philosophy of Science*, 4th ed. (Oxford: Oxford University Press, 2001). For Plato, see ibid., 16; Aristotle, 5;

Roger and Francis Bacon, 31 *et seq.*, Interestingly, Sir Frances was a lawyer. For the Roman Catholic Church's position, see ibid., 41; for Popper, 153; for Kuhn, 197, 228; for Lakatos, 203 *et seq.*

11 Epstein & King, *supra* note 4, at 69.

12 T.S. Kuhn, *The Structure of Scientific Revolutions,* 3rd ed. (Chicago: University of Chicago Press, 1996).

13 Losee, *Philosophy of Science, supra* note 10, at 202.

14 Kuhn, *Scientific Revolutions, supra* note 12.

15 Osborn defines jurisprudence it as 'the science or theory of law.' Dukelow and Nuse expand the definition to include 'the philosophy or science of law which ascertains the principles which are the basis of legal rules.' See P.G. Osborn, *A Concise Law Dictionary,* 5th ed. (London: Sweet and Maxwell, 1964), 179, and D.A. Dukelow and B. Nuse, *The Dictionary of Canadian Law,* 2nd ed. (Toronto: Carswell Thomson, 1995), 646. For Lord Lloyd's discussion of what can be included under the rubric of jurisprudence, see Lloyd & Freeman, *Lloyd's Introduction to Jurisprudence,* 5th ed. (London: Stevens and Sons, 1985), 1–23. For a discussion of historical trends in jurisprudence, see R. Posner, *The Problems of Jurisprudence* (Cambridge, MA: Harvard University Press, 1990), 4–23. Notwithstanding these extended definitions, I will, by and large, continue to use 'jurisprudence' in the more restricted sense outlined above.

16 Hart, *supra*, note 1. For a critique of Hart's methodology, see H.H. Hill, *H.L.A. Hart's Hermeneutic Positivism: On Some Methodological Difficulties in 'The Concept of Law,'* (1990) 3 Cdn. J. Law & Jur. 113.

17 *Supra* note 1, 81–118.

18 If the standard fluctuates, chaos will result: O. Phol, *Shrinking Kilogram Sows Mass Confusion in Labs,* Globe and Mail, 27 May 2003, A1.

19 For more detail on these various theories, see M.D.A. Freeman, *Lloyd's Introduction to Jurisprudence,* 7th ed. (London: Sweet and Maxwell, 2001). The theories of Hart, Dworkin, and Hutchinson were briefly described in the preceding section. Stone was referred to above, and his theory is described later in this chapter. Singer, Kairys, Unger, and Tushnet were prominent critical legal scholars whose writings are quoted throughout this book. Kennedy's best treatment of jurisprudence is contained in *A Critique of Adjudication: Fin de Siècle* (Cambridge, MA: Harvard University Press, 1997).

20 See, for example, R.M. Unger, *The Critical Legal Studies Movement,* (1983) 96 Harv. L. Rev. 561.

21 See T. Morawetz, *Law's Premises, Law's Promise: Jurisprudence after Wittgenstein* (Aldershot, UK: Ashgate/Dartmouth, 2000). For a discussion

as to whether and for how long legal rules are 'clear,' see A.C. Hutchinson, *A Postmodern's Hart: Taking Rules Sceptically*, (1995) Mod. L. Rev. 788.

22 See, for example, A. Halpin, *Reasoning with Law* (Oxford: Hart Publishing, 2001), 29–50.

23 See, for example, page 32 *infra*.

24 J. Stone, *Precedent and Law: Dynamics of Common Law Growth* (Sydney, Aust.: Butterworths, 1985).

25 P. Goodrich, *Legal Discourse: Studies in Linguistics, Rhetoric and Legal Analysis* (New York: St Martin's Press, 1987).

26 For a discussion of Natural Law theory, see Lloyds (5th) *supra* note 15, at 92 *et seq.*; R. Devlin, *Mapping Legal Theory*, (1994) 32 Alta. L. Rev. 601; and W. Morrison, *Jurisprudence: From the Greeks to Post Modernism* (London: Cavendish, 1997), 38–75.

27 See Dworkin, *supra* note 2. See also Hart, *The Concept of Law*, *supra* note 1, 241, 253, 264, 267–9, 272–6. In his postscript, Hart allows that some principles may be recognized as rules, but for the present purposes I am accepting Dworkin's formulation in this regard. In any event, at page 269, Hart wrote, 'It is therefore untrue that statements of legal rights and duties can only make sense in the real world if there is some moral ground for asserting their existence.' See also A. Hutchinson, *It's All in the Game*, *supra* note 7, 133 *et seq.*, and R.A. Posner, *The Problematics of Moral and Legal Theory* (Cambridge, MA: Belknap Press of Harvard University Press, 1999), 92.

28 See N. MacCormick, *H.L.A. Hart* (London: Edward Arnold, 1981), 26–7, 129–30.

29 See, for example, S. Fish, *Doing What Comes Naturally* (Durham, NC: Duke University Press, 1989), 37–42 *et seq.*

30 A.W.B. Simpson, 'The Common Law and Legal Theory,' in *Oxford Essays in Jurisprudence*, 2nd ser., ed. A.W.B. Simpson (Oxford: Clarendon Press, 1973), 91. Simpson expressed the idea as follows: 'The point about the common law is not that everything is always in the melting pot, but that you never quite know what will go in next.'

31 *Hard distinguishing* occurs where a court indicates that there is a difference between the case at bar and the precedent but the difference appears to be highly questionable. The reasoning in such cases is often specious.

32 A bright-line test provides clear criteria that allow the judge to place the facts on one or the other side of the test. For more detail, see chapter 7.

33 An *open standard* provides the judge with a list of considerations that he must balance when determining whether the facts do or do not meet the

standard. Open standards require the application of personal judgment, opinion, or discretion.

34 *Formal legal reasoning* applies a legal proposition to the facts to arrive at a ruling. It tends to be somewhat mechanical.

35 *Contextual interpretation* draws on a wide range of factors as the Court considers how to best interpret and apply the law in the context presented by the case at bar.

36 *Doctrinal reconciliation* is used to harmonize conflicting or discordant decisions. It usually involves a restatement of the law.

37 For more detail, see chapter 6 *infra*.

38 For a definition, see *supra* note 31. For more detail, see chapter 6.

Chapter 2

1 The general historical background in this section comes from numerous sources, including J.G. Snell and F. Vaughan, *The Supreme Court of Canada: History of the Institution* (Toronto: The Osgoode Society, 1985); F. Iacobucci, *The Supreme Court of Canada: Its History, Powers and Responsibilities*, (2002) 4 J. App. Prac. & Process 27; McCormick, *Supreme at Last: The Evolution of the Supreme Court of Canada* (Toronto: James Lorimer, 2000); B.A. Crane & H.S. Brown, *Supreme Court of Canada Practice* (Toronto: Carswell, 2002); and I. Bushnell, *The Captive Court: A Study of the Supreme Court of Canada* (Montreal and Kingston: McGill-Queen's University Press, 1992). Additional information can be obtained from the annual Performance Reports published by the Court.

2 See Snell & Vaughan, ibid., 192 and also MacGuigan, *Precedent and Policy in the Supreme Court of Canada*, (1967) 45 Can. Bar Rev. 627.

3 Canadian Bar Association, Committee on the Appointment of Judges in Canada, *Report of the Canadian Bar Association Committee on the Appointment of Judges in Canada* (Ottawa: Canadian Bar Foundation, c1985) (the report is generally referred to as *The Appointment of Judges in Canada*); F.C. DeCoste, *Political Corruption, Judicial Selection, and the Rule of Law*, (2000) 38 Alta. L. Rev. 654; R. Devlin, A.W. MacKay, & N. Kim, *Reducing the Democratic Deficit: Representation, Diversity and the Canadian Judiciary, or Towards a 'Triple P' Judiciary*, (2000) 38 Alta. L. Rev. 734

4 See R. Blackwell, *Canadian Debate Intensifies on Method of Picking Top Court*, Globe and Mail, 28 October 2005, A17; R. Blackwell, *Election Call Will Suspend Top-Court Selection Process*, ibid., 17 November 2005, A7; A. Hutchinson, *Process to Bring Judicial Politics into Public View*, Lawyers Weekly, 23 September 2005, 1; D. Driver, *SCC Appointment Applications*, ibid.,

14 October 2005, 2; L. Sossin, *Judicial Appointments: Law Professors Have Their Say*, ibid., 18 November 2005, 1. Subtle campaigning may still play a role: M. Eberts, *The Real Judicial Appointment Process ...*, ibid., 30 September 2005, 3.

5 Some of these reversed their proportions, in effect crossing over. See *infra*, especially chapter 5.

6 The *Constitution Act*, as enacted by the *Canada Act* (1982) (U.K.) c. 11, s. 1, ss. 41, 42. This continues the typically Anglo-Canadian practice of keeping part of the constitution unwritten. One could be excused for thinking that because the federal Parliament created the Supreme Court by simple statute, it could fundamentally alter, or even abolish, the Court by simple statute as well.

7 Iacobucci, *supra* note 1, at 33–4.

8 P.J. Monahan, *The Supreme Court of Canada in the 21st Century*, (2001) 80 C.B.R. 374.

9 Respectively, in *Hunter v. Southam Inc.*, [1984] 2 S.C.R. 145, at 155, and *Vriend v. Alberta*, [1998] 1 S.C.R. 493, at para. 134.

10 See, for example, F.L. Morton & R. Knopff, *The Charter Revolution and the Court Party* (Peterborough, ON: Broadview Press, 2000); K. Makin, *Judicial Activism Has Gone Too Far, Court Says*, Globe and Mail, 12 December 2002, A-1.

11 Monahan, *supra*, note 8, at 375, quoting from papers presented at the Supreme Court Centennial Symposium held in Ottawa on 27 September 1975.

12 R.S.C. 1970, c. S–19, s. 36.

13 See *An Act to Amend the Supreme Court Act (etc.)*, S.C. 1974–75–76, c. 18, ss. 3–5.

14 *Criminal Code*, R.S.C. 1985, chap. C–46, s. 691 as amended by S.C. 1997, c. 18, s. 99.

15 See also R.B. Flemming, *Tournament of Appeals: Granting Judicial Review in Canada* (Vancouver: UBC Press, 2004).

16 For information on appeal applications to the Supreme Court of Canada from 1988 to 2002, see the annual reports on leave to appeal applications by B.A. Crane, H.S. Brown, et al., in the *Supreme Court Law Review* from 1990 to 2002. Full citations for reviews after 1992 are provided in the bibliography.

17 R.B. Flemming & G.S. Krutz, *Selecting Appeals for Judicial Review in Canada: A Replication and Multivariate Test of American Hypotheses*, (2002) 64 Journal of Politics 232. For a recent summary of what the court looks for, see Kirk Makin's interview with Justice Binnie, *Supreme Court Appeal Bids as Much*

Art as Science, Globe and Mail, 5 April 2004, B14. Flemming, in *Tournament of Appeals, supra* note 15, 92 *et seq.* theorizes that negotiation among the justices, both in and between appeal panels, plays a role.

18 I. Greene et al., *Final Appeal: Decision-Making in Canadian Courts of Appeal* (Toronto: James Lorimer, 1998), 109.

19 Makin, *Supreme Court Appeal, supra* note 17.

20 In Canada, all Justices have an opportunity to see all applications for appeal and presumably have at least some input. For a description of the process, see Greene, *Final Appeal, supra* note 18, 107 *et seq.* See also Flemming, *Tournament of Appeals, supra* note 15, at 104 *et seq.*

21 See the articles collected in F.L. Morton, ed., *Law, Politics and the Judicial Process in Canada,* 3rd ed. (Calgary: University of Calgary Press, 2002), 289–361.

22 I. Brodie, *Friends of the Court: The Privileging of Interest Group Litigants in Canada* (Albany: State University of New York Press, 2002), 38–47.

23 C.R. Epp, *Do Bills of Rights Matter? The Canadian Charter of Rights and Freedoms,* (1996) 90 Am. Pol. Sci. Rev. 765, at 775.

24 P.R. Muldoon, *Law of Intervention: Status and Practice* (Aurora, ON: Canada Law Book, 1989), 17.

25 Author's notes taken during speech of I. Brodie at the 'Constitutionalism in the *Charter* Era' conference held at the University of Western Ontario, London, 12 September 2003; in 'The Supreme Court of Canada's Constitutional Decisions in 2001: An Overview' P.J. Monahan stated that the Court was influenced by elites (paper delivered at the Fifth 'Annual Analysis of the Constitutional Decisions of the Supreme Court of Canada' conference, which dealt with 2001 Constitutional Cases, Osgoode Hall Law School, Toronto, 12 April 2002. See also Morton & Knopff, *Charter Revolution, supra* note 10.

26 I. Brodie, *supra* note 22, at 124.

27 F.L. Morton & R. Knopff, *Charter Revolution, supra* note 10.

28 In this regard, the debate between Gregory Hein and Ian Brodie is instructive: See G. Hein, 'Interest Group Litigation and Canadian Democracy' and I. Brodie, 'Response to Gregory Hein,' both in Morton (ed.), *Law, Politics and the Judicial Process, supra,* note 21, 343–61.

29 This summary is culled from many sources, most notably from Greene et al., *Final Appeal, supra* note 18, at 117 *et seq.*

30 See, for example, B. Dickson, *The Role and Function of Judges,* (1980) 14 Gazette 138, 175 and I. Greene, *The Charter of Rights* (Toronto: Lorimer, 1989), 117 *et seq.*

31 See McCormick, *Supreme at Last, supra* note 1, at 63–4.

32 See Greene et al., *Final Appeal, supra* note 18, at 19, and D.M. Beatty, *Talking Heads and the Supremes* (Toronto: Carswell, 1990), 272 *et seq.* See also P.H. Russell, *The Judiciary in Canada: The Third Branch of Government* (Toronto: McGraw-Hill Ryerson, 1987), 349 *et seq.*

33 *London Tramways Co. Ltd. v. London County Council,* [1891] A.C. 375 at 379. This was reiterated in the *Earldom of Norfolk Peerage Claim,* [1907] AC 10 at 16, wherein it was stated: 'Whenever a Court of this House, acting judicially, declares the law, it is presumed to lay down what the law is and was, although it may have been misunderstood in former days, and this House is bound by its own declaration of the law in all matters within its jurisdiction.'

34 See *Woods Manufacturing Co. v. The King,* [1951] S.C.R. 504 at 515 per Rinfret, C.J.

35 *Practice Statement (Judicial Precedent),* [1966] 1 W.L.R. 1234.

36 L. Goldstein, ed., *Precedent in Law* (Oxford: Clarendon Press, 1987), 107; N. MacCormick & R.S. Summers, *Interpreting Precedents: A Comparative Study* (Aldershot, UK: Ashgate/Dartmouth, 1997), 350.

37 M.C. Miller, *A Comparison of the Judicial Role in the United States and in Canada,* (1998) 22 Suffolk Transnat. L. Rev. 1; S. Brenner & H.J. Spaeth, *Stare Indecisis: Alteration of Precedent in USSC, 1946–1992* (New York: Cambridge University Press, 1995); L. Epstein et al., *The Supreme Court Compendium: Data, Decisions and Development,* 3rd ed. (Washington, DC: CQ Press, 2003).

38 C. L'Heureux-Dubé, *By Reason of Authority or by Authority of Reason,* (1993) 27 U.B.C. Law Rev. 1; A. Mayrand, *L'autorité du précédent au Québec,* (1994) 28 R.J.T. 761; MacCormick & Summers, *Interpreting Precedents, supra* note 36; and S.D. Sugarman, *A New Approach to Tort Doctrine: Taking the Best from the Civil Law and Common Law of Canada,* (2002) 17 Sup. Ct. L. Rev. (2nd) 375.

39 J.W. Salmond, *The Theory of Judicial Precedents,* (1900) 16 L. Quarterly Rev. at 376, 381–2. See also F.A. Anglin, *Stare Decisis and Other Subjects as Viewed in the Civil Law and at Common Law* (address given to the Jeune Barreau de Québec, Ottawa, 2 February 1922), and Goodrich, *Reading the Law* (Oxford: Basil Blackwell, 1986).

40 W. Landes and R.A. Posner, *Legal Precedent: A Theoretical and Empirical Analysis,* (1976) 19 J. Law and Economics 249 at 271. If the Court were as likely to overrule as to follow precedent, some litigants would see this as a licence to proceed to trial; lawyers could not counsel almost certain defeat. Other plaintiffs, even those with just causes, might be dissuaded from asserting their rights, given to the uncertainty of success.

41 *Nova Scotia (Workers' Compensation Board) v. Martin,* [2003] 2 S.C.R. 504.

42 R.E. Keeton, *Venturing to Do Justice, Reforming Private Law* (Cambridge, MA: Harvard University Press, 1969). See also R. Posner, *The Problems of Jurisprudence* (Cambridge, MA: Harvard University Press, 1990), 95.

43 *Lawrence et al. v. Texas*, (2003) 539 U.S. 558 at 605. For further discussion of *stare decisis* in the United States Supreme Court, see J.C. Rehnquist, *The Power That Shall Be Vested in a Precedent: Stare Decisis, the Constitution and the Supreme Court*, (1986) 66 B.U.L. Rev. 345; R.H. Fallon, Jr., *Stare Decisis and the Constitution: An Essay on Constitutional Methodology*, (2001) 76 N.Y.U. Law Rev. 570; and T.R. Lee, *Stare Decisis in Historical Perspective: From the Founding Era to the Rehnquist Court*, (1999) 52 Vand. Law Rev. 647. In *Lawrence*, Justice Scalia noted in dissent that the reasoning of the majority was so careless as to call into question almost all the court's constitutional jurisprudence including the *Roe v. Wade* abortion case and the contraceptive privacy case of *Planned Parenthood v. Casey*.

44 W.F. Ehrcke, *Stare Decisis*, (1995) 53 Advocate 847, at 848. For a further discussion of hard distinguishing, see *infra*, chapter 6.

45 K. Llewellyn, 'The Bramble Bush,' in N. Sargent et al., eds., *Introduction to Legal Studies* (North York, ON; Captus Press, 1990), 84–6.

46 *Murdoch v. Murdoch*, [1975] 1 S.C.R. 423.

47 *R v. Paquette*, [1977] 2 S.C.R. 189, allowed the accused to raise the defence of duress as he was only a party and not a direct participant in the offence. Dunbar had been similarly involved, but in that case the Court held that the defence of duress was not open to him. The first case of overruling was actually *Fleming v. Atkinson* (1959), but it seems to have been an isolated instance, unlike *Peda* and *Paquette*, which seemed to indicate a shift in the Court's practice.

48 See, for example, *A.V.G. Management v. Barwell Developments*, [1979] 2 S.C.R. 43 and *R. v. B.(K.G.)*, [1993] 1 S.C.R. 740.

49 *R v. Morin*, [1992] 1 S.C.R. 771 reversed the holding in *Askov* that all accused were entitled to have their trial within six to eight months and imposed an onus on accused to show prejudice flowing from delay in their trials.

50 See T.S. Kuhn, *The Structure of Scientific Revolutions*, 3rd ed. (Chicago: University of Chicago Press, 1996).

51 This was in response to a sharp decline in close calls during this period and an article by Patrick Monahan stating that the court was unanimous in approximately three-quarters of its decisions: Monahan, *Supreme Control: Is It Jean Chrétien's Court?* Globe and Mail, 27 June 2003, A15.

52 M.E. Gold, *The Mask of Objectivity: Politics and Rhetoric in the Supreme Court of Canada*, (1985) 7 Sup. Ct. Law Rev. 455. With respect to moral defensibil-

ity, see D. Lyons, *Moral Aspects of Legal Theory: Essays on Law, Justice and Political Responsibility* (Cambridge: Cambridge University Press, 1993), 217.

53 A parallel problem infects the sports world: brilliant athletes regularly offer inarticulate explanations of their performance: see L.M. Solan, *The Language of Judges* (Chicago: Chicago University Press, 1993), 176. Solan points out that this leads to incoherent caselaw and often forces judges to be dishonest or at least to feel that they are being so. See also R. Posner, *The Problems of Jurisprudence* (Cambridge, MA: Harvard University Press, 1990), 93.

54 R.J. Sharpe & K. Roach, *Brian Dickson: A Judge's Journey* (Toronto: Osgoode Society for Canadian Legal History and University of Toronto Press, 2003). E. Lazarus paints a negative picture of the decision-making processes of the United States Supreme Court in *Closed Chambers: The Rise, Fall and Future of the Modern Supreme Court* (New York: Penguin Books, 1999).

Chapter 3

1 K. Roach, *The Supreme Court on Trial* (Toronto: Irwin Law, 2001), 162.

2 This point will be discussed in more depth in chapters 10 and 12.

3 J. Raz, *The Authority of Law: Essays on Law and Morality* (Oxford: Clarendon Press, 1979), 181 (emphasis added).

4 D. Kennedy, *A Critique of Adjudication: Fin de Siècle* (Cambridge, MA: Harvard University Press, 1997), 269, 191.

5 H.L.A. Hart, *The Concept of Law*, 2nd ed. (Oxford: Clarendon Press, 1994), v.

6 J. Raz, *The Authority of Law*, *supra* note 3, at 181 (emphasis added).

7 See Kennedy, *Critique of Adjudication*, *supra* note 4, at 269, 191.

8 Ibid.

9 A.C. Hutchinson, *Casaubon's Ghosts: The Haunting of Legal Scholarship*, (2001) 21 Legal Studies 65.

10 See, for example, Rule 4 (2) h of the *Rules of Professional Conduct* of the Law Society of Upper Canada.

11 See, for example, A.C. Hutchinson, *It's All in the Game: A Non-Foundational Account of Law and Adjudication* (Durham, NC: Duke University Press, 2000), 299–300.

12 See, for example, Weiler, *In the Last Resort: A Critical Study of the Supreme Court of Canada* (Toronto: Carswell, 1974).

13 *Law and Learning: Report to the Social Sciences and Humanities Research Council of Canada* by the Consultative Group on Research and Education in Law (H. Arthurs, chair) (Ottawa: Social Sciences and Humanities Research Council of Canada, 1983), esp. 153–63. For several articles updating the

state of legal scholarship and education in the context of the Arthurs's report, see Canadian Journal of Law and Society 18, no. 1 (2003).

14 R.N. Moles, *Definition and Rule in Legal Theory: A Reassessment of H.L.A. Hart and the Positivist Tradition* (Oxford: Basil Blackwell, 1987), 134.

15 T.S. Kuhn, *The Structure of Scientific Revolutions*, 3rd ed. (Chicago: University of Chicago Press, 1996).

16 See Kennedy, *Critique of Adjudication, supra* note 4 at 295.

17 G.K. Sisk & M. Heise, *Judges and Ideology: Public and Academic Debates about Statistical Measures*, (2005) 99 Nw. U.L. Rev. 743

18 For a description of ideal types, see L.A. Coser, 'Max Weber,' in *Masters of Sociological Thought: Ideas in Historical and Social Context*, 2nd ed. (New York: Harcourt Brace Jovanovich, 1977), 223–7. For an example in Weber's own writings, see M. Weber, *The Protestant Ethic and the Spirit of Capitalism*, trans. T. Parsons (London: Routledge, 1992), 71, 98, 200 n. 28.

19 See *supra*, chapter 1, note 34 for a definition of hard distinguishing.

20 For some reason, the Court's overruling behaviour has never previously been systematically studied: R. Haigh, *A Kindler, Gentler Supreme Court? The Case of Burns and The Need for a Principled Approach to Overruling*, (2001), 14 Sup. Ct. L. Rev. (2d) 139.

21 D.M. Beatty, *Talking Heads and the Supremes* (Toronto: Carswell, 1990), 78–9, 86, 88, 99.

22 C.P. Manfredi, *Judicial Power and the Charter: Canada and the Paradox of Liberal Constitutionalism* (Toronto: McClelland and Stewart, 1993), 212.

23 C.P. Manfredi, *Judicial Power and the Charter: Canada and the Paradox of Liberal Constitutionalism*, 2nd ed. (Don Mills, ON: Oxford University Press, 2001), 196.

24 Weiler, *Last Resort, supra* note 12 at 37, 229

25 F.L. Morton & R. Knopff, *The Charter Revolution and the Court Party* (Peterborough, ON: Broadview Press, 2000).

26 Roach, *The Supreme Court on Trial, supra* note 1.

Chapter 4

1 For a theoretical examination of law and policy, and policy as law, see R.S. Summers, *Instrumentalism and American Legal Theory* (Ithaca, NY: Cornell University Press, 1982), 153, and D. Kennedy, *A Critique of Adjudication: Fin de Siècle* (Cambridge, MA: Harvard University Press, 1997), 98, 104, 133, and 150–60.

2 Some commentators, most notably Peter Russell, feel that some of the decisions I characterized as being low in policy, such as *Johannesson v. West*

St. Paul (1952), were in fact policy based. However, any such policy bases,
if they exist, were not typically manifested in the Court's majority reasons
for judgment and thus were not reflected in my methodology.

3 *Teno v. Arnold*, [1978] 2 S.C.R. 287; *Keizer v. Hanna*, [1978] 2 S.C.R. 342; and
Andrews v. Grand & Toy, [1978] 2 S.C.R. 229.

Chapter 5

1 See, for example, McCormick, *Supreme at Last: The Evolution of the Supreme
Court of Canada* (Toronto: Lorimer, 2000), 69–70, where he contrasts
formalism with the emerging contextualist approach.

2 See, for example, S.M. Sugunasiri, *Contextualism: The Supreme Court's New
Standard of Judicial Analysis and Accountability*, (1999) 22 Dalhousie L.J. 126

3 M. Bastarache, *Supreme Advice to the Successful Litigator: Advocacy in the
Supreme Court of Canada* (address given to the County of Carleton Law
Association, Ottawa and Quebec, 6 and 7 November 1998).

4 A third sub-mode, *ipse dixit*, which sometimes plays a subsidiary role in
the Court's reasoning, was too rare to be measured quantitatively. It
involves a judge's rendering an opinion based on her personal view of
what the law should be. These portions of the Court's reasons often read
as if they were a prose version of the deeming provision of a statute. An
example of *ipse dixit* can be seen in *R. v. Z. (D.A.)* (1992), where the pro-
tections of the *Young Offenders Act* respecting extrajudicial statements were
determined not to apply to a defendant who had since passed his eigh-
teenth birthday. *Ipse dixit* also played a part in defining whether a certain
instrument was a weapon in *R. v. Lamy* (2002).

5 See, for example, R. Dworkin, *Law's Empire* (Cambridge, MA: Belknap
Press of Harvard University Press, 1986), 15–20, 130 *et seq.*, 255 *et seq.*

6 Close calls are defined in chapter 9. In essence they are decisions where
the Court had a substantial number of dissents. Five-to-four decisions are
the quintessential close call.

7 All data are for the year 2002. To compile the data for the Ontario Court of
Appeal and Superior Court, I followed the procedures outlined in note 2,
chapter 4.

8 *Harvard College v. Canada (Commissioner of Patents)*, [2002] 4 S.C.R. 45 at
para. 153

9 *Paré v. Bonin*, [1977] 2 S.C.R. 342.

10 *Sauvé v. Canada (Chief Electoral Officer)*, [2002] 3 S.C.R. 519 at para. 67
(emphasis added).

11 *Chamberlain v. Surrey School District No. 36*, [2002] 4 S.C.R. 710 at para. 132.

Chapter 6

1 D.A. Dukelow & B. Nuse, *The Dictionary of Canadian Law*, 2nd ed. (Toronto: Carswell, 1995), 854.

2 H.C. Black, *Black's Law Dictionary*, 4th ed. (St Paul, MN: West Publishing, 1968), 1257–8.

3 In *Wray*, the court had admitted improperly obtained evidence while in *Feeney* it refused to do so. In both cases, the rights of the accused had been infringed.

4 As discussed in chapter 6, *infra*, distinguishing may result in no major weakening of the precedent or may almost entirely undercut it. Incremental changes, such as have been made to the hearsay evidence rule, may over decades result in changes more significant than those caused by outright overruling.

5 See *Dictionary of Canadian Law*, *supra* note 1, at 343, and *Black's Law Dictionary*, *supra* note 2, at 561.

6 See J. Raz, *The Authority of Law: Essays on Law and Morality* (Oxford: Clarendon Press, 1979), 186–7.

7 Ibid., at 186. But occasionally distinguishing does extend rules. See, for example, *R. v. Taillefer*, [2003] S.C.R. 307, where *Palmer* (1980) was distinguished to enlarge the situations under which new evidence is admissible on appeal. See also B. McLachlin, 'The Mason Court in Context,' in C. Saunders, ed., *Courts of Final Jurisdiction: The Mason Court in Australia* (Annandale, NSW: Federation Press, 1996), 118–37; R.J. Sharpe & K. Roach, *Brian Dickson: A Judge's Journey* (Toronto: Osgoode Society for Canadian Legal History and University of Toronto Press, 2003), 160 *et seq.*, 183.

8 Raz, *supra* note 6, at 187.

9 For more detail respecting hard distinguishing, see the examples section at page 74.

10 [1990] 2 S.C.R. 489 at para 75. See also paragraph 77 of the judgment, where Justice Sopinka quotes Tarnopolsky and Pentney, who also utilize the term in Discrimination and the Law, Fifth Cumulative Supplement (September 1989). The term 'radical departure' also appears several times in I. Bushnell, *The Captive Court: A Study of the Supreme Court of Canada* (Montreal and Kingston: McGill-Queen's University Press, 1992).

11 That case was *A.V.G. Management Science Ltd. v. Barwell Developments Ltd.*, [1979] 2 S.C.R. 43.

12 The data were compiled using the averages for fact, law, and policy generated for the years 1972, 1977, 1982, 1987, 1992, 1997, and 2002. All

cases of overruling and hard distinguishing were then surveyed to obtain the same statistic. For these latter cases, the examination focused on the reasoning used by the court to overrule or distinguish the existing authority. I restricted the 'all cases' category to those decided from 1972 to date because more overruling and hard distinguishing occurred during this period and I therefore felt that this restricted period constituted a more useful comparator.

13 In determining the mode of legal reasoning, the focus was on the Court's reasoning in the course of hard distinguishing or deciding whether to overrule. I restricted myself to the limited period because there was more overruling during this period and an increasing variety of modes of legal reasoning from 1992 onwards.

14 *Ordon Estate v. Grail*, [1998] 3 S.C.R. 437.

15 *R. v. Salituro*, [1991] 3 S.C.R. 654.

16 P.W. Hogg, *Constitutional Law of Canada*, loose-leaf ed. (Toronto: Carswell Thomson, 1997), 56–6.

17 For the contrary view that the case involves overruling, see J.T. Saywell, *The Lawmakers: Judicial Power and the Shaping of Canadian Federalism* (Toronto: University of Toronto Press, 2002), 246.

18 Bushnell, *Captive Court*, *supra* note 11, at 157–8, 403–4.

19 *R. v. Salituro*, *supra* note 15, at para. 37.

20 Where the Court relies on the *Charter*, it is not overruling precedent any more than it would be if it were applying a statute that reversed an earlier common law decision. However where the precedent would almost certainly have been overruled even in the absence of the *Charter*, I have counted the decision as an instance of overruling.

21 See *Bank of Montreal v. Dynex* (2002); *Bow Valley v. Saint John* (1997); and *Salituro* (1991). See also *Bank of America v. Mutual Trust* (2002).

22 *Porto Seguro* (1997).

23 Ibid.

24 *Vetrovec* (1982); *Porto Seguro* (1997).

25 *Bank of Montreal v. Dynex* (2002); *Bow Valley v. Saint John* (1997).

26 *Canada v. Ranville* (1982).

27 *K.G.B.* (1993).

28 *A.V.G. Management v. Barwell* (1979).

29 *K.G.B.* (1993).

30 *Bank of Montreal v. Dynex* (2002); *Bow Valley v. Saint John* (1997)

31 *Canada v. Ranville* (1982).

32 *Bank of Montreal v. Dynex* (2002); *Bow Valley v. Saint John* (1997); *London Drugs v. Keuhne* (1992); *Salituro* (1991).

33 *Binus* (1967); *Robinson* (1996).
34 [1989] 2 S.C.R. 750.
35 *K.G.B.* (1993); *Canada v. Ranville* (1982).
36 *K.G.B.* (1993); *Robinson* (1996).
37 *Robinson* (1996); *Vetrovec* (1982).
38 *Friedmann Equity Developments Inc. v. Final Note Ltd.*, [2000] 1 S.C.R. 842, at paras. 42 and 43, references to other cases have been omitted.
39 The commentaries on the Court's jurisprudence published by the Canadian Bar Association to commemorate the Court's one hundred and twenty-fifth anniversary were particularly useful: see E. Veitch & P.-G. Jobin, eds., *Commemorative Edition on the 125ᵗʰ Anniversary of the Supreme Court of Canada* (Ottawa: Canadian Bar Association, 2001), reprinted as volumes 79 and 80 of the Canadian Bar Review.
40 C. Epp, 'Do Bills of Rights Matter?' in F.L. Morton, ed., *Law, Politics and the Judicial Process in Canada*, 3rd ed. (Calgary: University of Calgary Press, 2002), 523.
41 See McCormick, *Supreme at Last: The Evolution of the Supreme Court of Canada* (Toronto: Lorimer, 2000), 48, 74, 97, 120, 141.

Chapter 7

1 A. Hutchinson, *It's All in the Game: A Non-Foundational Account of Law and Adjudication* (Durham, NC: Duke University Press, 2000), 31–7, 42–53.
2 Cf. ibid., 180.
3 See J. Stone, *Precedent and Law: Dynamics of Common Law Growth* (Sydney, NSW; Butterworths, 1985), and Goodrich, *Legal Discourse: Studies in Linguistics, Rhetoric and Legal Analysis* (New York: St Martin's Press, 1987).
4 H.L.A. Hart, *The Concept of Law*, 2nd ed. (Oxford: Clarendon Press, 1994), 12–13.
5 See ibid, 126–9.
6 S.J. Burton provided another useful definition in *Judging in Good Faith* (Oakleigh, Australia: Cambridge University Press, 1992), 39–40.
7 R. Case has provided another useful definition in *Understanding Judicial Reasoning: Controversies, Concepts and Cases* (Toronto: Thompson Educational Publishing, 1997), 98, 110.
8 See, for example, R. Dworkin, *Law's Empire* (Cambridge, MA: Belknap Press of Harvard University Press, 1986), 243–50, 404–7.
9 See, for example, *Law Society of Upper Canada v. Skapinker*, [1984] 1 S.C.R. 357, and *Andrews v. Law Society of British Columbia*, [1989] 1 S.C.R. 143.

Chapter 8

1 See, for example, A. Kozinski, *What I Ate for Breakfast and Other Mysteries of Judicial Decisionmaking*, (1993) 26 Loyola of Los Angeles L. Rev. 993.

2 See, for example, G.A. Schubert, *The Judicial Mind: the Attitudes and Ideologies of Supreme Court Justices, 1946–1963* (Evanston, IL: Northwestern University Press 1965); D.E. Fouts, 'Policy-Making in the Supreme Court of Canada, 1950–1960' and S.R. Peck, 'A Scalogram Analysis of the Supreme Court of Canada, 1958–1967,' both in G. Schubert & D. Danelski, eds., *Comparative Judicial Behaviour: Cross-Cultural Decision-Making in the East and West* (Toronto: Oxford University Press, 1969); S.R. Peck, *The Supreme Court of Canada, 1958–1966: A Search for Policy through Scalogram Analysis*, (1967) 65 Can. Bar Rev. 666; L. Loevinger, 'Jurimetrics: The Next Step Forward' in Lloyd, Lord of Hampstead & M.D.A. Freeman, *Lloyd's Introduction to Jurisprudence*, 5th ed. (London: Stevens and Sons, 1985), 783 *et seq.*; S.S. Nagel, *Judicial Characteristics and Judicial Decision-Making* (PhD diss., Northwestern University, 1961); and A.D. Heard, *The Charter of Rights and the Supreme Court of Canada: The Importance of Which Judges Hear an Appeal*, (1991) 24 Can. J. Pol. Sci. 289. C. Epp compiled data on the justices' attitudes towards civil liberties and rights: *Do Bills of Rights Matter? The Canadian Charter of Rights and Freedoms*, (1996) 90 Am. Pol. Sci. Rev. 765 at 772. Thaddeus Wong is currently studying the attitudes of the court's justices relative to income tax decisions. For an overall description of behavioural and attitudinal jurimetric scholarship, see M. Heise, *The Past, Present, and Future of Empirical Legal Scholarship: Judicial Decision Making and the New Empiricism*, (2002) U. Ill. L. Rev. 819.

3 P. Sittiwong, *Canadian Supreme Court Decisions, 1949–1980* (MA thesis, North Texas University, 1985). The study was later updated and refined: C.N. Tate & Sittiwong, *Decision Making in the Canadian Supreme Court: Extending the Attributes Model across Nations*, (1989) 51 J. Politics 900.

4 D.R. Songer & S.W. Johnson, *Attitudinal Decision Making in the Supreme Court of Canada* (paper delivered at the Annual Meeting of the Midwest Political Science Association, Chicago, 25–8 April 2002).

5 R. Posner, *The Problems of Jurisprudence* (Cambridge, MA: Harvard University Press, 1990), 404–5. It is of course possible for a male to have a 'feminine' outlook, so this is only a rough approximation. And just because a judge is female does not mean that she will automatically or improperly favour the interests of her sex: B. Wilson, *Will Women Judges Really Make a Difference?* (1990) 28 O.H.L.J. 507.

6 C.C. White, 'Gender Differences on the Supreme Court,' in F.L. Morton, ed., *Law, Politics and the Judicial Process in Canada* (Calgary: University of Calgary Press, 2002), 85. The study was done in 1998; the three female justices studied were Wilson, McLachlin, and L'Heureux-Dubé.

American studies have also show male/female differences: Songer & Johnson, *supra* note 4. In Canada, Songer and Johnson found that 'female [Supreme Court of Canada] judges have significantly more liberal records than their male counterparts on civil liberties cases, but there are no substantial gender differences in either criminal or economics cases.'

7 For example, Justice Lamer supported positions advocated by LEAF on every case on which he sat: C.P. Manfredi, *Feminist Activism in the Supreme Court* (Vancouver: UBC Press, 2004), 21.

8 CTV *'A Gift of Freedom,'* W5, 8 June 1986. See also I. Greene et al., *Final Appeal: Decision-Making in Canadian Courts of Appeal* (Toronto: Lorimer, 1998), 200–2.

9 Hon. G.V. La Forest, *Judicial Lawmaking: Creativity and Constraints* (address to 'Gérard V. La Forest at the Supreme Court of Canada 1985–1997,' University of New Brunswick, 2002), 14–15. The opinion expressed by Justice LaForest coincides with Allan Hutchinson's view that 'law is politics,' a process which compels judges to choose 'between competing values or commitment to a particular normative assumption.' *It's All in the Game: A Non-Foundational Account of Law and Adjudication* (Durham, NC: Duke University Press, 2000), 252. For a description of the attitude of the justices towards *stare decisis*, see I. Greene, *Final Appeal, supra* note 8, at 104–5, 126–7.

10 *R. v. Ancio*, [1984] 1 S.C.R. 225 at 227.

11 P. McCormick and I. Greene, *Judges and Judging* (Toronto: Lorimer, 1990), 214 *et seq.* For instances where justices ruled according to law despite their own views, see *Brassard v. Langevin* (1877) and *Rodriguez* (1993).

12 P. McCormick and I. Greene, ibid., and P.J. Monahan, *The Supreme Court's 1998 Constitutional Cases: The Debate over Judicial Activism Heats Up* (1999) 7 (nos 4–5) Canada Watch, available online at http://www.robarts .yorku.ca/canadawatch/vol_7_4-5/default.htm (accessed 4 March 2004)

13 C. Guthrie, J.J. Rachlinski & A.J. Wistrich, *Inside the Judicial Mind*, (2001) 86 Cornell L. Rev. 777.

14 See C.R. Sunstein, *Of Artificial Intelligence and Legal Reasoning*, (2001) 8 U.Chi.L.Sch. Roundtable 29; and C.R. Callen, *From Theory to Practice: 'Intelligent' Procedures for Drawing Inferences in Static and Dynamic Legal*

Environments: Othello Could Not Optimize. Economics, Hearsay, and Less Adversary Systems, (2001) 22 Cardozo L. Rev. 1791.

15 R.J. Sharpe & K. Roach, *Brian Dickson: A Judge's Journey* (Toronto: Osgoode Society for Canadian Legal History and University of Toronto Press, 2003).

16 Ibid., 147, 150 et seq.

17 Ibid., 399.

18 Ibid., 194–6. For the case, see *Teno v. Arnold*, [1978] 2 S.C.R. 287. Posner, *Problems, supra* note 5, states that tort liability does not proceed from logic; perhaps the same can be said of the law of personal injury damages.

19 For an empirical study of this issue at the trial level, see C.K. Rowland & R.A. Carp, *Politics and Judgment in Federal District Courts* (Lawrence: University Press of Kansas, 1996).

20 The 'potted plant' reference is to R.A. Posner, *Overcoming Law* (Cambridge, MA: Harvard University Press, 1995), 227.

21 J.A. Segal & H.J. Spaeth, *The Supreme Court and the Attitudinal Model Revisited* (Cambridge: Cambridge University Press, 2002), 309–10; H.J. Spaeth & J.A. Segal, *Majority Rule or Minority Will: Adherence to Precedent on the U.S. Supreme Court* (Cambridge: Cambridge University Press, 1999), 288. Dworkin's conclusions in *Taking Rights Seriously* were contradicted.

22 Y. Lim, *An Empirical Analysis of Supreme Court Justices' Decision Making*, (2000) 29 J. Legal Stud. 721.

23 M.J. Richards & H.M. Kritzer, *Jurisprudential Regimes in Supreme Court Decision Making*, (2002) 96 Am. Pol. Sci. Rev. 305 at 315.

24 See the studies listed in note 2, *supra*.

25 P. Slayton, *A Critical Comment on Scalogram Analysis of Supreme Court of Canada Cases*, (1971) 21 U.T.L.J. 393 at 399, 401.

26 See I. Bushnell, *The Captive Court: A Study of the Supreme Court of Canada* (Montreal and Kingston: McGill-Queen's University Press, 1992), 77–80.

27 See T. MacCharles, *Iacobucci, a Giant of a Judge, Retires*, Toronto Star, 22 June 2004, A16.

28 G.K. Sisk & M. Heise, *Judges and Ideology: Public and Academic Debates about Statistical Measures*, (2005) 99 Nw. U.L. Rev. 743 at 759.

29 R.L. Revesz, *Environmental Regulations, Ideology, and the D.C. Circuit*, (1997) 83 Va. L. Rev. 1717; F.B. Cross & E.H. Tiller, *Judicial Partisanship and Obedience to Legal Doctrine: Whistleblowing on the Federal Courts of Appeals*, (1998) 107 Yale L.J. 2155.

30 C.R. Sunstein, D. Schkade & L.M. Ellman, *Ideological Voting on Federal Courts of Appeals: A Preliminary Investigation*, (2004) 90 Va. L. Rev. 301.

31 Sisk & Heise, *Judges, supra* note 28, at 771.

32 F.B. Cross, *Decisionmaking in the U.S. Circuit Courts of Appeals*, (2003) 91 Cal. L. Rev. 1457.
33 D.R. Pinello, *Linking Party to Judicial Ideology in American Courts: A Meta-analysis*, (1990) 20 Just. Sys. J. 219.
34 This is consonant with the overall conclusion reached by Sisk and Heise cited above (see *supra* note 28). Sisk and Heise reviewed the above studies, including Sunstein et al., before arriving at their conclusion.
35 Epp, *Do Bills of Rights Matter? supra* note 2, at 772.
36 Ibid, 772–3; P.J. Monahan, *The Supreme Court of Canada in 2002: An Overview* (paper presented at the 2002 Constitutional Cases conference, Osgoode Hall Law School, Toronto, 4 April 2003).
37 P. McCormick, *Supreme at Last: The Evolution of the Supreme Court of Canada* (Toronto: Lorimer, 2000), 41, 88, 108–9, 131. However, the Rinfret court (1949–54) had a success rate closer to 50% (McCormick, 17). The success rates for the past three years are as follows: 2000: 46%; 2001 31%; 2002 53% (*Supreme Court of Canada Statistics, 1992 to 2002*, published in 2003 by the Court as a special bulletin).
38 For further statistics in this area, see Monahan, *The Supreme Court of Canada's 1997 Constitutional Cases: A Statistical Overview*, Canada Watch 6, nos. 4–6 (October 1998) Special Issue: Supreme Court of Canada in 1997, available online at http://www.robarts.yorku.ca/projects/canada-watch/index.html (accessed 16 April 2006)
39 McCormick, *Supreme at Last, supra* note 37.
40 P. McCormick, *Second Thoughts: Supreme Court Citation of Dissents & Separate Concurrences, 1949–1996*, (2002) 81 Can. Bar Rev. 369.
41 See McCormick, *Supreme at Last, supra* note 37, at 20, 43, 65, 90, 91, 113, and 133.
42 The dissenting decision can be supported by multiple reasons: thus *RJR-Macdonald* (1995) is a close call.
43 For a definition of apparent difficulty, see chapter 5, page 53.

Chapter 9

1 See, for example, P.H. Russell, *The Supreme Court and the Charter: Quantitative Trends – Continuities and Discontinuities*, and P.J. Monahan, *The Supreme Court of Canada's 1997 Constitutional Cases: A Statistical Overview*, both in Canada Watch, October 1998. S. Choudhry and C.E. Hunter documented that the government won only 28.5% of cases in 1997; the win rate for the previous three years had consistently been above 70% and for 1998 was 60%. *Measuring Judicial Activism on the Supreme Court of Canada: A Comment*

on Newfoundland (Treasury Board) v. NAPE, (2003) 48 McGill L.J. 525 at 546.
2 I would like to thank Bryn Greer-Wootten of York University's Institute for Social Research for his assistance with the statistical calculations above.

Chapter 10

1 I presented an overview of these theories in chapter 1.
2 See figure 7.1.
3 H.L.A. Hart, *The Concept of Law,* 2nd ed. (Oxford: Clarendon Press, 1994), 129.
4 Lord Mansfield, as then he was not, in *Omychund v. Barker* (1744), 26 E.R. 15 at 23. The phrase is perhaps unnecessarily theological in tone but, at least for present purposes, can be restricted to the notion that the law is becoming gradually, even inexorably, clearer and more settled. See also S.R. Perry, *Judicial Obligation, Precedent and the Common Law* (Toronto: Centre for Research on Public Law and Public Policy, 1987), 32–3, and D. Cornell, 'From the Lighthouse: The Promise of Redemption and the Possibility of Legal Interpretation,' in G. Leyh, ed., *Legal Hermeneutics: History, Theory and Practice* (Berkeley and Los Angeles: University of California Press, 1992), 147, esp. 156.
5 See chapter 5, pages 53, 62–3. Deciding whether a case is 'easy' or 'hard' is notoriously difficult, especially after the fact.
6 As reported in chapter 6, twenty-two cases of overruling had this characteristic and three had it somewhat. See also J. Stone, *Precedent and Law: Dynamics of Common Law Growth* (Sydney, NSW: Butterworths, 1985), 57.
7 N. MacCormick, *Legal Reasoning and Legal Theory* (Oxford: Clarendon Press, 1978), 69, 246
8 W.J. Waluchow, *Inclusive Legal Positivism* (Oxford: Clarendon Press, 1994), 121; M.H. Kramer, *In Defense of Legal Positivism* (Oxford: Oxford University Press, 1999), 137.
9 Perry, *Judicial Obligation, supra* note 4 at 12.
10 See, for example, R. Posner, *The Problems of Jurisprudence* (Cambridge, MA: Harvard University Press, 1990), 456, and A.C. Hutchinson, 'Crits and Cricket: A Deconstructive Spin (Or Was It a Googly?),' in R. Devlin, ed., *Canadian Perspectives on Legal Theory* (Toronto: Emond Montgomery, 1991), 191.
11 N. MacCormick, *Legal Reasoning, supra* note 7, at 101.
12 R. Dworkin, *Law's Empire* (Cambridge, MA: Belknap Press of Harvard University Press, 1986), 228 *et seq.*
13 See S. Fish, *Doing What Comes Naturally* (Durham N.C.: Duke University

Press; 1989), 87–202, and A. Marmor, *Interpretation and Legal Theory* (Oxford: Clarendon Press, 1992), 76. For a discussion of a chain novel in a literary context, see M. Nersessian, *Writers in a Chain Gang*, Globe and Mail, 11 August 2004, R–1.

Michael McConnell prefers the analogy of referee or editor to that of author: 'The judges' task, it seems, is to ensure that the author of each chapter conforms to the rules of chain novel writing, not to write the books themselves.' This has the advantage of appearing appropriately deferential to the judiciary, but McConnell's analogy fails to deal with the fact that his referees are the players. See M.W. McConnell, *Fidelity in Constitutional Theory: Fidelity as Integrity. The Importance of Humility in Judicial Review. A Comment on Ronald Dworkin's 'Moral Reading' of the Constitution*, (1997) 65 Fordham L. Rev. 1269; quote is at page 1274. When I use the term 'chain novel theory,' I will be referring to the version of this theory restricted and limited to judges fitting their judgments into the existing legal materials in a seamless and coherent fashion.

14 Dworkin, *Law's Empire, supra*, note 12, at 9, 225. For an interesting discussion of Dworkin's ideas in this regard, see D. Kennedy, *A Critique of Adjudication: Fin de Siècle* (Cambridge, MA: Harvard University Press, 1997), 33–8. See also F. Schauer, review of *The Jurisprudence of Reasons: Law's Empire*, by Ronald Dworkin, (1987) 85 Mich. L. Rev. 847.

15 See Kennedy's analysis in this regard, ibid., 119–28.

16 See R. Dworkin, *Taking Rights Seriously* (Cambridge, MA: Harvard University Press, 1978), 81, and *Hard Cases*, (1975) 88 Harv. Law Rev. 1057. However, Dworkin fails to provide any direction as to how to arrive at this one right answer: S. Guest, *Ronald Dworkin*, 2nd ed. (Edinburgh: Edinburgh University Press, 1997), 13.

17 Dworkin, *Law's Empire, supra* note 12, at 266, 351 *et seq.*

18 Ibid., 405 *et seq.*

19 Principle did play a major role in six cases and may have played somewhat of a role in two further overrulings. In thirteen cases, the Court did not rely on principle as the basis for the reversal of the precedent. In most cases (thirty-eight) it did not appear that principle played a role. For a discussion of what to look for in legal reasons to distinguish between legal principles and legal propositions, see C. Yablon, *Are Judges Liars? A Wittgensteinian Critique of 'Law's Empire,'* (1990) 3 C.J.L.J. 123.

20 See chapter 7. See also S.J. Burton, *Judging in Good Faith* (Oakleigh, Australia: Cambridge University Press, 1992), 143, 237.

21 See M. Allars, *On Deference to Tribunals, with Deference to Dworkin*, (1994) 20 Queen's L.J. 163.

22 Burton, *Judging in Good Faith, supra* note 20, esp. 107, 143, 203–4, 237; A.C. Hutchinson, *It's All in the Game: A Non-Foundational Account of Law and Adjudication* (Durham, NC: Duke University Press, 2000), 180–215, 256; R. Siltala, *A Theory of Precedent: From Analytical Positivism to a Post-Analytical Philosophy of Law* (Oxford: Hart Publishing, 2000), 89.

23 P. Weiler, *In the Last Resort: A Critical Study of the Supreme Court of Canada,* (Toronto: Carswell, 1974), 48. See also C.R. Sunstein, *Legal Reasoning and Political Conflict* (New York: Oxford University Press, 1996), 4, where society leaves it up to the courts to apply 'on incompletely theorized agreements.' Legislatures can work more in concert with courts to reduce the open texturedness of language with a view to facilitating their legislative purpose. Sunstein (163–4) describes the U.K. Parliament as being more proactive in this regard than U.S. legislatures.

24 Stone, *Precedent and Law, supra,* note 6. Hart's work may also have methodological problems from a philosophical point of view: H. Hamner Hill, *H.L.A. Hart's Hermeneutic Positivism: On Some Methodological Difficulties in 'The Concept of Law,'* (1990) 3 Cdn. J. Law Juris. 113.

25 Stone, *supra,* note 6, at 49–60.

26 Ibid., 61–80, 123–55. See also I Bushnell, *The Captive Court: A Study of the Supreme Court of Canada* (Montreal and Kingston: McGill-Queen's University Press, 1992), 52, 55.

27 P. Goodrich, *Legal Discourse: Studies in Linguistics, Rhetoric and Legal Analysis* (New York: St Martin's Press, 1987), 60, 8 '[The] self-asserted certainty of the law in its paradigm instances is palpably more rhetorical than actual' (58).

28 See, for example, K.N. Llewellyn, *Remarks on the Theory of Appellate Decision and the Rules or Canons about How Statutes Are to Be Construed,* (1950) 3 Vand. L. Rev. 395; G.P. Miller, *Pragmatics and the Maxims of Interpretation,* (1990) Wisc. L. Rev. 1179; D. Kennedy, A *Semiotics of Legal Argument,* (1991) 42 Syracuse L. Rev. 75; and Sunstein, *Legal Reasoning, supra* note 23, at 188. For a contrary view, see R. Sullivan, *Statutory Interpretation in the Supreme Court of Canada,* (1999) 30 Ottawa L. Rev. 175.

29 See D. Kennedy, *A Critique of Adjudication, supra* note 14 at 142–7.

30 M. Freeman, 'Positivism and Statutory Construction: An Essay in the Retrieval of Democracy,' in S. Guest, ed., *Positivism Today* (Aldershot, UK: Dartmouth Publishing, 1996), 11.

31 Stone, *Precedent and Law, supra* note 6, at 140–55.

32 See chapter 6.

33 See, for example, the contextual approach in *Krangle v. Brisco,* [2002] 1 S.C.R. 205, as contrasted with *Honan v. Doman Estate,* [1975] 2 S.C.R. 866,

both of which deal with damages. The crossover is described in chapters 4, 5, and 6.

34 Hutchinson, *It's All in the Game, supra* note 22. For a direct application of game theory in the context of judges' attempting to preserve their precedents, see E. O'Hara, *Social Constraint or Implicit Collusion? Toward a Game Theoretic Analysis of Stare Decisis*, (1993) 24 Seton Hall L. Rev. 736. See also T. Morawetz, *Law's Premises, Law's Promise: Jurisprudence after Wittgenstein* (Aldershot, UK: Ashgate/Dartmouth, 2000).

35 C.R. Sunstein, *Legal Reasoning, supra* note 23, at 4, 36.

36 Informal discussion with Jean Leclair, Colloque: Osgoode Hall Law School/Université de Montréal, 9 December 2002. Note how much of a departure this is from Dworkin's one-right-answer thesis.

37 J.W. Singer, *The Player and the Cards: Nihilism and Legal Theory*, (1984) 94 Yale L.J. 1 at 22–3.

38 Hutchinson, *All in Game, supra* note 22, at 180–215.

39 See, for example, ibid.

40 Ibid., 151–79.

41 See S.M. Sugunasiri, *Contextualism: The Supreme Court's New Standard of Judicial Analysis and Accountability*, (1999) 22 Dalhousie L.J. 126.

42 This is one of nine characteristics of law he describes in *Problems, supra* note 10, at 459–60.

43 B. Wilson, *Decision-Making in the Supreme Court*, (1986) U.T.L.J. 227 at 228.

44 See for example, *R. v. Sarson*, [1996] 2 S.C.R. 223.

45 See chapter 6.

46 R.J. Sharpe & K. Roach, *Brian Dickson: A Judge's Journey* (Toronto: Osgoode Society for Canadian Legal History and University of Toronto Press, 2003), 286, 296, 298.

47 For the data in this regard, see chapter 9, pages 100–10.

48 Stone, *Precedent and Law, supra,* note 6, at 140–55.

49 See, for example, M. Mandel, *The Charter of Rights and the Legalization of Politics in Canada* (Toronto: Thompson Educational Publishing, 1992).

50 For the data in this regard, see chapter 9, pages 100–10.

Chapter 11

1 R. Posner, *The Problems of Jurisprudence* (Cambridge, MA: Harvard University Press, 1990), 53, 74, 107, 423, 430, 459 *et seq.*

2 Ibid., 10; N. MacCormick, *Legal Reasoning and Legal Theory* (Oxford: Clarendon Press, 1978), 76; A. Halpin, *Reasoning with Law* (Oxford: Hart

Publishing, 2001); and R. Case, *Understanding Judicial Reasoning* (Toronto: Thompson Educational Publishing, 1997).

3 MacCormick states: '[The] notion of formal justice requires that the justification of decisions in individual cases be always on the basis of universal propositions to which the judge is prepared to adhere as a basis for determining other like cases and deciding them in the like manner to the present one.' *Legal Reasoning, supra* note 2, at 99. On the other hand, there are good reasons for judges deciding similar cases similarly even without a doctrine of *stare decisis*. See, for example, E. O'Hara, *Social Constraint or Implicit Collusion? Toward a Game Theoretic Analysis of Stare Decisis* (1993) 24 Seton Hall L. Rev. 736. Posner maintains that the law is predictable as a result of the hesitancy of judges to change the law, not as the result of any doctrine: *Problems, supra* note 1, 51–2. See also A.C. Hutchinson, *Work in Progress: Evolution and the Common Law* (Cambridge: Cambridge University Press, forthcoming), and G.J. Postema, 'Some Roots of Our Notion of Precedent,' in L. Goldstein, ed., *Precedent in Law* (Oxford: Clarendon Press, 1987).

4 N. MacCormick, *Contemporary Legal Philosophy: The Rediscovery of Practical Reason*, (1983) 10 J. Law & Soc. 1, at 7. See also F. Schauer, 'Legal Positivism and the Contingent Autonomy of Law,' in T. Campbell and J. Goldsworthy, eds., *Judicial Power, Democracy and Legal Positivism* (Aldershot, UK: Ashgate, 2000), 215, 217; and J. Raz, 'The Problem about the Nature of Law,' in M.D.A. Freeman, ed., *Lloyd's Introduction to Jurisprudence* (7th ed.) (London: Sweet and Maxwell, 2001), 69. See also A. Altman, *Legal Realism, Critical Legal Studies, and Dworkin*, (1986) 15 Philosophy and Public Affairs 205 at 231 *et seq.*, where the issue is discussed from the opposite direction.

5 P. Devlin, *The Judge* (Oxford: Oxford University Press, 1979), 1.

6 Hutchinson, *Work in Progress, supra* note 3 at 157. It should be noted that the context of the quote indicates that it is predicated on the presumption that *stare decisis* constrains judicial behaviour.

7 See a practitioners' lament in C.L. Rotenberg & M. Lam, *Stare Decisis: Oh Where Have You Gone?* (1995) 28 Imm. L.R. (2d) 214.

8 A. Hutchinson, 'Crits and Cricket: A Deconstructive Spin (Or Was It a Googly?)' in R. Devlin, ed., *Canadian Perspectives on Legal Theory* (Toronto: Emond Montgomery, 1991), 191.

9 See R.E. Keeton, *Venturing to Do Justice, Reforming Private Law* (Cambridge, MA: Harvard University Press, 1969); and Posner, *Problems, supra* note 1, at 95. Another metaphor would be glaciers and icebergs: glaciers, once thought to be solid, regularly break off and fall into the sea as icebergs. If

218 Notes to pages 130–1

they did not decay in this incremental fashion, eventually a whole region of ice would collapse into the sea, with catastrophic consequences.

10 See, for example, the fallout from *Murdoch* (1973), which stimulated the establishment of the feminist Women's Legal Education and Action Fund: http://www.leaf.ca/about-begin.html (accessed 13 February 2004).

11 See J.W. Salmond, *The Theory of Judicial Precedents*, (1900) 16 L. Quarterly Rev. 376 at 382–3, and W. Landes and R.A. Posner, *Legal Precedent: A Theoretical and Empirical Analysis*, (1976) 19 J. of L. and Economics 249.

12 For the survey results respecting cases that resulted in a change in the law, see chapter 6.

13 See, for example, *Gosselin v. Quebec* (2002). See also *Lavoie* (*Bailey v. The Queen*), (2002) where *Law* led to three different results. A legal test that fails to decide an issue is a poor legal test, perhaps not deserving so to be called.

14 See D. Hunter, *Reason Is Too Large: Analogy and Precedent in Law*, (2001) 50 Emory L.J. 1197. In another instance, all Justices agreed as to the test to be applied, and that the law was clear, but the Court still split 5–4. L.M. Solan, *The Language of Judges* (Chicago: Chicago University Press, 1993), 101.

15 See, for example, G.J. Postema, 'Law's Autonomy and Public Practical Reason,' in R.P. George, ed., *The Autonomy of Law: Essays on Legal Positivism* (Oxford: Oxford University Press, 1996), 79.

16 See H.L.A. Hart, 'Positivism and the Separation of Law and Morals' and L.L. Fuller, 'Positivism and Fidelity to Law: A Reply to Professor Hart,' in *Lloyd's Introduction to Jurisprudence*, 5th ed. (London: Stevens and Sons, 1985), 446–53.

17 See, for example, Augustine, as quoted in W. Morrison, *Jurisprudence: From the Greeks to Postmodernism* (London: Cavendish, 1997), 62, 63.

18 See, for example, J.M. Finnis, in *Lloyd's Introduction, supra*, note 16, at 225. Natural Law theorists see positivism as merely one manifestation of the Natural Law: ibid., 213. Positive law is merely a man-made codi-fication of Natural Law. Being a man-made reflection, it is by definition imperfect and may or may not accurately capture law's full majesty. For Natural Law theorists, perfect morality is always superior to law. Law emanates from morality and cannot exist separately from it.

19 See, for example, W.J. Waluchow, *Inclusive Legal Positivism* (Oxford: Clarendon Press, 1994); A.J. Sebok, *Legal Positivism in American Jurispru-dence* (Cambridge: Cambridge University Press, 1998), esp. 39 ff. and 83 ff.; J. Coleman, 'Inclusive Legal Positivism,' in M.D.A. Freeman, ed., *Lloyd's Introduction, supra* note 4, at 430; F. Schauer, 'Legal Positivism and the Contingent Autonomy of Law,' in T. Campbell and J. Goldsworthy, eds.,

Judicial Power, Democracy and Legal Positivism (Aldershot, UK: Ashgate, 2000), 220; and J.M. Breslin, *Making Inclusive Positivism Compatible with Razian Authority*, (2001) C.J.L.J. 133.

20 See, for example, R. Dworkin, *Law's Empire* (Cambridge, MA: Belknap Press of Harvard University Press, 1986), 225.

21 See, for example ibid., 255.

22 Ibid., 405–7

23 A. Marmor, *Interpretation and Legal Theory* (Oxford: Clarendon Press, 1992), 39, 51, 56–7, 70. The contrasting views of two Supreme Court Judges in this regard are set out *supra* in chapter 8, page 88.

24 J. Allan, *Positively Fabulous: Why It Is Good to Be a Legal Positivist*, (1997) 10 Can. J.L. & Juris. 23; A. Marmor, *Interpretation and Legal Theory*, ibid., 39.

25 A.C. Hutchinson, 'The Last Emperor,' in Alan Hunt, ed., *Reading Dworkin Critically* (New York: Berg, 1992), 55–6. See also the postscript to H.L.A. Hart, *The Concept of Law*, 2nd ed. (Oxford: Clarendon Press, 1994), 269.

26 T. Morawetz, *The Epistemology of Judging: Wittgenstein and Deliberative Practices*, (1990) 3 C.J.L.J. 35, at 59.

27 Ibid., 47, 54.

28 Ibid., 55.

29 N. MacCormick, *Legal Reasoning, supra* note 2, at 76; R.A. Cass, *Judging: Norms and Incentives of Retrospective Decision-Making*, (1995) 75 B.U.L. Rev. 941; F. Schauer, *Incentives, Reputation, and the Inglorious Determinants of Judicial Behavior*, (2000) 68 U. Cin. L. Rev. 615; and G.N. Rosenberg, *Incentives, Reputation, and the Glorious Determinants of Judicial Behavior* (2000) 68 U. Cin. L. Rev. 637.

30 P. Weiler, *In the Last Resort: A Critical Study of the Supreme Court of Canada* (Toronto: Carswell, 1974), 118. See also *Friedmann Equity Developments Inc. v. Final Note Ltd.*, [2000] 1 S.C.R. 842, esp. paras 42 and 43. For a detailed examination of the Court's power and the constraining forces impinging on it, see R. Johnson, *Taxing Choices: The Intersection of Class, Gender, Parenthood and the Law* (Vancouver: UBC Press, 2002), which discusses *Symes* (1993) in detail.

31 See, for example, *Watkins v. Olafson*, [1989] 2 S.C.R. 750, esp. paras 13–16.

32 See for example *R. v. Salituro*, [1991] 3 S.C.R. 654, *Friedman Equity Developments Inc. v. Final Note Ltd.*, [2000] 1 S.C. R. 842, and other cases referred to in chapter 6.

33 D. Kennedy, *A Critique of Adjudication: Fin de Siècle* (Cambridge, MA: Harvard University Press, 1997), 115, 160–1, 182 *et seq.*, 188, 198, 212. As discussed previously, this analysis is based on the surface-level behaviour of judges.

34 Hunter, *Reason*, supra, note 14, 1215 *et seq.* Martin Golding's formulation is slightly different: If *x* and *y* both have characteristics F and G, *x* additionally has characteristic H, *and F and G are H relevant characteristics*, then *y* has characteristic H. See M.P. Golding, *Legal Reasoning* (New York: Alfred A. Knopf, 1984).

35 See E. Lazarus, *Closed Chambers: The Rise, Fall and Future of the Modern Supreme Court* (New York: Penguin Books, 1999), 360 *et seq.*, 376 *et seq.*, 404 *et seq.*, and R.A. Kahn, 'Institutional Norms and Supreme Court Decision-Making: The Rehnquist Court on Privacy and Religion,' in C.W. Clayton & H. Gillman, eds., *Supreme Court Decision-Making* (Chicago: University of Chicago Press; 1999), 175.

36 Lazarus, ibid., 6, 147 *et seq.*, 158 *et seq.*, 487, *et seq.* See also Segal & Spaeth and Lim, as discussed in chapter 8, page 90.

37 Lazarus, *Closed Chambers*, supra, note 35, and B. Woodward & S. Armstrong, *The Brethren: Inside the Supreme Court* (New York: Avon Books, 1981).

38 See chapter 8, page 90, and M.J. Richards & H.M. Kritzer, *Jurisprudential Regimes in Supreme Court Decision Making*, (2002) 96 Am. Pol. Sci. Rev. 305, at 315 in particular.

39 See, for example, R.J. Sharpe & K. Roach, *Brian Dickson: A Judge's Journey* (Toronto: Osgoode Society for Canadian Legal History and University of Toronto Press, 2003).

40 See, for example, *Friedmann Equity Developments Inc. v. Final Note Ltd.*, [2000] 1 S.C.R. 842. The case is also notable for describing several, albeit somewhat open-ended, criteria that must be present before the Court will be willing to overrule precedent.

41 See figures 4.3 and 5.7.

42 Morality played a role in four cases in 1952, 1962, and 1972. In 1982 there were two cases, and in 1992 one case, where morality appeared to play a role. There were seven cases (10%) where morality appeared to play a role in 2002.

43 See, for example, D.M. Adams, *Skepticism and the Apologetics of Law*, (1990) 3 C.J.L.J. 69.

44 I. Greene et al., *Final Appeal: Decision-Making in Canadian Courts of Appeal* (Toronto: Lorimer, 1998), 104–5, 125–7.

45 See chapters 5 and 7: While legal principles, as opposed to legal propositions, play an important part in the Court's rulings, less than 5 per cent of the court's rulings are based on the principle-based reasoning advocated by Dworkin.

46 The chronology of overruling fails to support any overall theory: While there are instances of decisions being overruled shortly after they were

delivered (the mistake thesis), such as when *Morin* (1992) overruled *Askov* (1990), and new law supplanting old and hoary precedent, such as when *Thorson* (1975) supplanted *Smith* (1924), there are also many instances of the overruling of precedents that have stood for an intermediate period. For example, *Brown* (1971) overruled *Dormuth* (1964) and *Ancio* (1984) overruled *Lajoie* (1974).

47 See chapter 6.

48 In 45 instances, detailed reasons were provided; in 2 some reasons were provided. However, in 12 instances of overruling almost no reasons were provided. As might be expected, these 12 cases coincided with cases in which the Court provided little or no 'super-justification' for overruling.

49 Sharpe & Roach, *Dickson, supra*, note 39, at p. 237.

50 B. Dickson, *The Role and Function of Judges*, (1980) 14 Gazette 138, 180.

51 Ibid., 180–3.

52 B. Dickson, *The Judiciary: Law Interpreters or Law Makers*, (1983) Man. L.J. 1, 7.

53 Sharpe & Roach, *Dickson, supra* note 39, 147–50.

54 Ibid., 198, 218, 237.

55 Ibid., 218, 198. Contrast, for example, his judgments in *Harrison v. Carswell* (1976) and *Canada (Minister of Indian Affairs) v. Ranville* (1982).

56 Distinguishing, particularly hard distinguishing, has negative effects. Such underhanded tactics have a tendency to diminish the respect for the judicial system. In some cases transparently instrumental justifications can lead to the impression that rulings are based on extra-judicial criteria, including bribery or pressure brought to bear upon the Justices. Distinguishing often leaves an area of the law in doctrinal disarray. The tactics of distinguishing lead to the ponderous and impenetrable language of the 'Philadelphia lawyer.' For a discussion on the tactics of distinguishing, see Schlag, *Cannibal Moves: An Essay on the Metamorphoses of the Legal Distinction*, (1988) 40 Stan. L. Rev. 929.

57 J.M. Balkin, *Deconstructive Practice and Legal Theory*, (1987) 96 Yale L.J. 743 at 781.

58 See Sharpe & Roach, *Dickson, supra* note 39, 343–4.

59 See, for example, *Canadian Broadcasting Corp. v. Canada (Labour Relations Board)*, [1995] 1 S.C.R. 157.

60 See L. Philipps, *The Supreme Court of Canada's Tax Jurisprudence: What's Wrong with the Rule of Law*, (2000) 79 C.B.R. 126, and S.W. Bowman, *Interpretation of Tax Legislation: The Evolution of Purposive Analysis*, (1995) 43 Cdn. Tax J. 1167.

61 See, for example, Posner, *Problems, supra*, note 1, 42–4 and chapter 7 *infra*.

62 See, for example, Posner, *Problems, supra* note 1, 42–4.

63 This is one of Justice Wilson's four tensions: see *Decision-Making in the Supreme Court*, (1986) U.T.L.J. 227.

64 See, for example, *R. v. Law*, [2002] 1 S.C.R. 227.

65 See, for example, B.P. Archibald, *The Canadian Hearsay Revolution: Is Half a Loaf Better Than No Loaf at All?* (1999), 25 Queen's L.J. 1.

66 See, for example, C. L'Heureux-Dubé, *What a Difference a Decade Makes: The Canadian Constitution and the Family since 1991*, (2001) 27 Queen's L.J. 361.

67 See, for example, *Doucet-Boudreau v. Nova Scotia*, [2003] 3 S.C.R. 3.

68 See figure 8.2.

69 For another use of this metaphor, see Lord Wright, *The Study of Law*, (1938) 54 L.Q.R. 185 at 186, as quoted in B. Dickson, *The Role and Function of Judges*, (1980) 14 Gazette 138 at 178.

70 J. Raz, *The Authority of Law: Essays on Law and Morality* (Oxford: Clarendon Press, 1979), 208. The full excerpt is as follows: 'By and large this is also true of distinguishing, though here the confusion over what counts as ratio and the limited scope for reform often tend to blur the border between following and distinguishing a precedent. Often the Courts minimize the extent to which a decision is innovative in order to avoid the need to bear full responsibility for it or to avoid having to justify it by long and explicit arguments. In cases of indeterminacy there is often no clear divide between application and innovation. Whether or not a case falls within the vague, indeterminate borderline area of a descriptive concept is often itself an indeterminate issue.'

71 H.L.A. Hart, *The Concept of Law*, 2nd ed. (Oxford: Clarendon Press, 1994), 12, 129.

72 Hutchinson, *Work in Progress, supra* note 31; J.W. Salmond, *The Theory of Judicial Precedents*, (1900) 16 Law Quarterly Rev. 376, at 382–3.

73 See, for example, Posner, *Problems, supra*, note 1, 51–2; Hutchinson's view is that *stare decisis* is a 'convenient tool which judges use when and where they want to in order to serve their social goals in cases' (personal correspondence).

74 See, for example, Weiler, *In the Last Resort: A Critical Study of the Supreme Court of Canada* (Toronto: Carswell, 1974), 117–19.

75 See chapter 6.

76 See for example, R.S. Summers, *Instrumentalism and American Legal Theory* (Ithaca, NY: Cornell University Press, 1982), 85.

77 P. Monahan, *The Supreme Court and the Economy* (prepared for the Royal Commission on the Economic Union and Development Prospects for

Canada, 1984). See also J. Braithwaite, *Rules and Principles: A Theory of Legal Certainty*, (2002) 27 Australian J. of Legal Philosophy 46.

78 Braithwaite, ibid., and Monahan, ibid.

79 C.D. Bredt & A.M. Dodek, *Breaking the Law's Grip on Equality: A New Paradigm for Section 15* (paper presented at the 2002 Constitutional Cases Conference, Osgoode Hall Law School, Toronto, 4 April 2003).

Chapter 12

1 *Donoghue v. Stevenson*, [1932] A.C. 562 (H.L.); *Brown v. Board of Education* (1953), 347 U.S. 483 (U.S.S.C.); *Roncarelli v. Duplessis*, [1959] S.C.R. 121. *Donoghue v. Stephenson* expanded liability in favour of ultimate consumers, via tort analyses, to product manufacturers despite the fact that the manufacturers had no contractual relationship with the ultimate consumer. *Brown v. Board of Education* mandated the racial desegregation of public schools. *Roncarelli v. Duplessis* awarded damages where a public official, here the premier of Quebec, had obtained the cancellation of a liquor licence to punish the plaintiff's lawful support of his co-religionists.

2 A.C. Hutchinson, *Judges and Politics: An Essay from Canada*, (2004) 24 Legal Studies 275 at 278–9, 287.

3 Ibid., 287.

4 See, for example, C.P. Manfredi, *Judicial Power and the Charter: Three Myths and a Political Analysis*, (2001) 14 Sup. Ct. L. Rev. (2d) 331, 335. For a contrary view, see K. Roach, *The Myths of Judicial Activism*, (2001) 14 Sup. Ct. L. Rev. (2d) 297.

5 Note that in *Egan* (1995) the Court used section 1 of the *Charter* to decline to implement the right. However, in *M. v. H.*, [1999] 2 S.C.R. 3, the ruling in favour of the insertion of 'sexual orientation' was made explicit. The point is now so well established that the federal government did not even bother to contest it at the reference re same-sex marriage: K. Makin, *Denying Marriage to Gays Unfair, Ottawa Tells Court*, The Globe and Mail, 1 April 2004, A4. The result of the same-sex reference can be found at *Reference re Same-Sex Marriage*, [2004] 3 S.C.R. 698. This is yet another example of change rippling out, often with unforeseen consequences. See K.J. Kress, *Legal Reasoning and Coherence Theories: Dworkin's Rights Thesis, Retroactivity, and the Linear Order of Decisions*, (1984) 72 Cal. L. Rev. 369.

6 *R. v. Klippert*, [1967] S.C.R. 822.

7 See P.J. Monahan, *The Supreme Court of Canada in the 21st Century*, (2001) 80 Can Bar Rev. 376; P.J Monahan, *Judicial Review and Democracy: A Theory of Judicial Review*, (1987) 21 U.B.C. Law Rev. 87.

8 See K. Malleson, *The New Judiciary: The Effects of Expansion and Activism* (Aldershot, UK: Ashgate/Dartmouth, 1999), 21 (pp. 7–35 focus on the situation in the United Kingdom).

9 M.C. Miller, *A Comparison of the Judicial Role in the United States and in Canada*, (1998) 22 Suffolk Transnat. L. Rev. 1. Canadian courts are generally perceived as being less activist than those in the United States but more activist than those in the United Kingdom. But even in the United Kingdom the courts seem to be becoming more active in governance: S. Sterett, *Politics and Jurisprudence in the British Courts*, (1988) 1 C.J.L.J. 173.

10 C.P. Banks, *Reversals of Precedent and Judicial Policy-Making: How Judicial Conceptions of Stare Decisis in the U.S. Supreme Court Influence Social Change*, (1999) 32 Akron L. Rev. 233.

11 D. Bricker, *Public Opinion and the Courts* address, presented at the Osgoode Hall Law School's Annual Constitutional Cases Conference, Toronto, 3 April 2003.

12 The foregoing is my formulation based on the critiques in the literature, my study of the Court during the preparation of this book, and in the judgment of the Newfoundland Court of Appeal in *Newfoundland (Treasury Board) v. N.A.P.E.* (2002), 221 D.L.R. (4th) 513 (Nfld. C.A) at paras 342, 364, 365. Leave to appeal was granted on 5 June 2003: [2003] S.C.C.A. No. 45, and the appeal was argued in late May 2004. The case and the literature are discussed below, at pages 149–53.

13 See also Hutchinson, *Judges and Politics*, supra note 2, at 286.

14 C. Schmitz, *'Activism' Critics Posing Threat to Judicial Independence: Dubé*, (1999) 19 (no. 16) Lawyer's Weekly 1.

15 *Nova Scotia v. Walsh*, [2002] 4 S.C.R. 325, para. 108. Globe and Mail editorials included *A Sterile View of Rights*, 6 September 1973, 46; *End Sexual Nepotism*, 8 October 1973, 6; *The Contributions of a Wife*, 27 July 27 1974, 6. Academic commentary included R.L. Doering, *Murdoch v. Murdoch and the Law of Constructive Trusts*, (1974) 6 Ottawa L.R. 568; Jacobson, *Murdoch v. Murdoch: Just about What the Ordinary Rancher's Wife Does*, (1974) 20 McGill L.J. 308; E. Caparros, *Le travail de la femme d'un 'rancher': Une décision renversante de la Cour Suprême*, (1974) 15 C. de D. 180. Doering's article includes references to popular opinion opposed to the decision, Jacobson's to possibilities for law reform, and Caparros's to what Mrs Murdoch's position would have been under civil law.

16 M. Bastarache, *Supreme Advice to the Successful Litigator: Advocacy in the Supreme Court of Canada* (address to the County of Carleton Law Association, Ottawa, Quebec, 6 and 7 November, 1998).

17 This is presumably the paper Professor Monahan, as he then was, pre-

sented at the 1998 Constitutional Conference, Osgoode Hall Law School, Toronto, 16 April 1999: *Constitutional Cases, 1991–1998*. For a critique of this paper, see F.L. Morton & R. Knopff, *The Charter Revolution and the Court Party* (Peterborough, ON: Broadview Press, 2000), 19–20. As will be seen below, Monahan's conclusions are open to contest.

18 B. McLachlin, *Courts, Legislatures, and Executives in the Post-Charter Era*, Policy Options (June 1999), 42 at 44.

19 See N. Martin, *A Diverse Supreme Court Reflects Nation: McLachlin*, Winnipeg Free Press, 4 June 2004, B11, and K. Makin, *Judicial Activism Debate on Decline, Top Judge Says*, Globe and Mail, 8 January 2005, A1.

20 K. Makin, *Iacobucci Reflects on His Own Supreme Court Trials*, Globe and Mail, 22 June 2004, A3.

21 See G. Williams, 'Judicial Activism and Judicial Review in the High Court of Australia,' in T. Campbell and J. Goldsworthy, eds., *Judicial Power, Democracy and Legal Positivism* (Aldershot, UK: Ashgate, 2000), 413 at 427–8.

22 *Newfoundland (Treasury Board) v. N.A.P.E.* (Nfld. C.A), *supra* note 12, para. 342. The Supreme Court dismissed the appeal, but did not comment on activism. See [2004] S.C.C. 66.

23 *Newfoundland v. N.A.P.E.* (Nfld. C.A.), ibid., paras. 342, 364, 365 (emphasis added). For me, democracy is the idea that it is possible to change the government without resort to armed rebellion. We elect parliament at least every four or five years; four years is a short enough period that risking one's own life does not make sense. But there is no such practical method for the replacement of judges.

24 *Doucet-Boudreau v. Nova Scotia (Minister of Education)*, [2003] 3 S.C.R. 3, para. 35.

25 *Edwards v. Attorney-General for Canada*, [1930] A.C. 124 at 136 (P.C.).

26 B. Dickson, *The Role and Function of Judges*, (1980) 14 Gazette 138 at 180–1.

27 Monahan, *Judicial Review, supra* note 7, at 86, 93. It is interesting to note that at least one of the framers of the *Charter* is 'not a fan of original intent.' Allan Blakeney feels that the temper of the times has now changed and that it is probably time to consider that gay rights are now implicit in the *Charter*: D. Saunders, *Would You Like Your Constitution 'Living' or 'Dead'?* Globe and Mail, 21 February 2004. Roy McMurtry is one of the authors of the Ontario Court of Appeal decision in favour of same-sex marriage rights. The poles on this issue are best illustrated by David Beatty, who notes that the rule of law requires judges to adjudicate *Charter* issues, and by Morton and Knopff, who maintain that judges are not constrained by the *Charter*. See Beatty, 'The End of Law: At Least as We Have Known It,' in R. Devlin, ed., *Canadian Perspectives on Legal Theory*

(Toronto: Emond Montgomery, 1991), 391 and Moton & Knopff, *Charter Revolution, supra* note 17.

28 Monahan, *Judicial Review, supra* note 7, at 91, 115–26.

29 P.J. Monahan, *Politics and the Constitution* (Toronto: Carswell, 1987), Monahan, *The Law and Politics of Quebec Secession*, (1995) 33 O.H.L.J. 1 at 182.

30 See, for example, A. Hutchinson, *The Court Shushes the Rich*, Globe and Mail, 19 May 2004, A21; K. Lunman & G. Galloway, *Battle Lines Drawn over Gay Marriage*, Globe and Mail, 29 April 2004, A4; and T. Tyler, *Forced Payout Called, 'Chilling,'* Toronto Star, 12 June 2004, A27.

31 *Ryan v. Victoria (City)*, [1999] 1 S.C.R. 201, para. 33

32 K. Makin, Globe and Mail, 13 November 2003, A16; K. Makin, Globe and Mail, 7 November 2003, A-1; and A. Hutchinson, Globe and Mail, 9 January 2003.

33 R. Leishman, *Legislators for Life*, Next City (Fall 1998), 34. For Professor Cameron's paper, see J. Cameron, *The Vagaries of Review at the Supreme Court of Canada*, Canada Watch (October 1998).

34 See Morton and Knopff, *Charter Revolution, supra*, note 17, at 34, 9, 149. See also D. Beatty, *Constitutional Conceits: The Coercive Authority of Courts*, (1987) 37 U.T.L.J. 183.

35 See, for example, Morton & Knopff, ibid. at 25–6, where they name the Canadian Civil Liberties Association, feminists, the Charter Committee on Poverty Issues, gay rights advocates, the Canadian Prisoners' Rights Network, and the Canadian Committee on Refugees as members of the 'Court party.'

36 See Hutchinson, *Judges and Politics, supra* note 2, at 279

37 J.L. Hiebert, *Charter Conflicts: What Is Parliament's Role?* (Montreal: McGill-Queen's University Press, 2002), 23–42, 43 *et seq.*, 218.

38 See ibid, 21 *et seq.* This questioning is not restricted to academe. Recent polls indicate that only 43 per cent of Canadians strongly disagree with the proposition that judges have too much power and a majority believe that political parties sometimes influence the courts: Ipsos-Reid polling, 3 April 2002, Sixth Annual Analysis of the Constitutional Decisions of the Supreme Court of Canada Conference, Osgoode Hall Law School, Toronto.

39 Monahan, *Judicial Review and Democracy, supra* note 7.

40 P.H. Russell, *The Judiciary in Canada: The Third Branch of Government* (Toronto: McGraw-Hill Ryerson, 1987).

41 Ibid., 26. Public scepticism may be exacerbated if the Court is perceived as facilitating wishes of elites. See Monahan's address at the Fifth Annual Analysis of the Constitutional Decisions of the Supreme Court of Canada

conference dealing with 2001 Constitutional Cases at Osgoode Hall Law School, Toronto, 12 April 2002; D.J. Pond, *The Supreme Court of Canada and the Politics of Public Law* (PhD diss., University of Toronto, 1992), 72.

42 Although the notion of armed insurrection *was* raised by the Newfoundland Court of Appeal, *supra* note 22, paragraph 342. The Supreme Court is certainly aware of the activism debate: Makin, *Judicial Activism Debate on Decline, supra* note 19, at A1.

43 It is interesting to note that the Governor-General's budget has been reduced: J. Bronskill, *Clarkson's Office Trims Spending*, Toronto Star, 26 December 2004, A23.

44 J.R. Corsi, *Judicial Politics* (Englewood Cliffs, NJ: Prentice-Hall, 1984), 306–10.

45 Ibid., 310–14.

46 See Brent, *Sunday Row Ends Quietly: Legalizing Sunday Shopping in Canada*, *Financial Post*, 7 August 1993, 6(1).

47 *Chamberlain v. Surrey School District No. 36*, [2002] 4 S.C.R. 710, para. 66; J. Armstrong, *B.C. Board Finds New Basis to Ban Books*, Globe and Mail, 14 June 2003, A 10.

48 See P. Fitzgerald, *Fishing for Stories at Burnt Church: The Media, the Marshall Decision and Aboriginal Representation*, Canadian Dimension (July–August 2002), 29.

49 See, for example, D.M. Beatty, *Talking Heads and the Supremes* (Toronto: Carswell, 1990), 88 *et seq.*; D. Stuart, *Charter Justice in Canadian Criminal Law* (Toronto: Carswell, 2001), 15–24.

50 The Court delayed the hearing of the *Clay* appeal to decriminalize marijuana.

51 The quote is from an editor's note by Peter Russell and Paul Howe in *Choices* (2000) 6 (no. 3) at 2, the issue in which Fletcher and Howe describe the results of the IRPP study.

52 J.F. Fletcher & Howe, *Canadian Attitudes towards the Charter and the Courts in Comparative Perspective*, (2000) 6 (no. 3) *Choices* 11–13. This finding was as true in 1987 as it was in 1999.

53 Ibid. 16–18. Support for the Supreme Court of Canada by Canadians is slightly higher than support for the U.S. Supreme Court by Americans. See also J.L. Gibson, G.A. Caldeira & V.A. Baird, *On the Legitimacy of National High Courts*, (1998) 92 Am. Pol. Sci. Rev. 343.

54 J. Fletcher & Howe, *Supreme Court Cases and Court Support: The State of Canadian Public Opinion*, (2000) 6 (no. 3) *Choices* 30 at 31. At page 35, the authors conclude, 'the Court's rulings on the exclusion of evidence are beyond the pale for most Canadians: the Court's reasoning is precisely the reverse of their own.'

55 Fletcher & Howe, *supra* note 52, at 18. Starting at page 15, the authors compare attitudes towards a large number of national high courts.
56 Ibid., 19.
57 Ibid., 20. Two American investigators, James Gibson and Gregory Caldeira, in *The Etiology of Public Support for the Supreme Court*, (1992) 36 Am. J. of Pol. Sci. 638, attribute earlier contrary findings to the way in which earlier polling questions were framed. Overall public support for the U.S. Supreme Court continues at high levels despite the fiasco of the 2000 presidential election: J.L. Gibson, G.A. Caldeira & L.K. Spence, *Measuring Attitudes towards the United States Supreme Court*, (2003) 47 Am. J. Pol. Sci. 354, and J.L. Gibson, G.A. Caldeira & L.K. Spence, *The Supreme Court and the U.S. Presidential Election of 2000: Wounds, Self-Inflicted or Otherwise?*, (2003) 33 B.J.Pol.S. 535. See also V.J. Hoekstra, *Public Reactions to Supreme Court Decisions* (Cambridge: Cambridge University Press, 2003), esp. 115–29.
58 H. Mellon & M. Westmacott, *Political Dispute and Judicial Review: Assessing the Work of the Supreme Court of Canada* (Scarborough, ON: Nelson Thomson Learning, 2000), 196.
59 See R.A. Posner, *The Problematics of Moral and Legal Theory* (Cambridge, MA: The Belknap Press of Harvard University Press, 1999), 142–3, where he discusses the appropriateness of judicial intervention and states that the judge's action is a 'significant datum' that the legislature ought to take into account.
    Strict precedent in the form of *stare decisis* is less important in civil law jurisdictions because the judge goes first to the code in each instance. Each case is thus decided primarily on its individual merits, with caselaw occupying a subsidiary role. Therefore there should be more overruling but fewer cases of hard distinguishing in private law cases from Quebec. Fewer cases overall should thus be cited in Civil Code cases as compared from private law cases emanating from the rest of Canada. See, for example, C. L'Heureux-Dubé, *By Reason of Authority or by Authority of Reason*, (1993) 27 U.B.C. Law Rev. 1, and A. Mayrand, *L'autorité du précédent au Québec*, (1994) 28 R.J.T. 761.
60 See, for example, R. Siltala, *A Theory of Precedent: From Analytical Positivism to a Post-Analytical Philosophy of Law* (Oxford: Hart Publishing, 2000), 111–15, and S.R. Perry, *Judicial Obligation, Precedent and the Common Law* (Toronto: Centre for Research on Public Law and Public Policy, 1987), 6–8, 15, 20, 23, 25, 31–2.
61 See *Pepsi-Cola Canada v. Retail, Wholesale and Department Store Union*, [2002] 1 S.C.R. 156, which opened the door to the general application of *Charter*

values and *Bell ExpressVu*, [2002] 2 S.C.R. 559, wherein the court held that *Charter* values could be used in the interpretation of statutes.

62 D. Stuart, *Zigzags on Rights of Accused: Brittle Majorities Manipulate Weasel Words of Dialogue, Deference and Charter Values* (paper prepared for the Sixth Annual Analysis of the Constitutional Decisions of the Supreme Court of Canada Conference, Osgoode Hall Law School, Toronto, 4 April 2003); *Gosselin v. Quebec (Attorney General)*, [2002] 4 S.C.R. 429.

63 See *Law v. Canada (Minister of Employment and Immigration)*, [1999] 1 S.C.R. 497.

64 J. Braithwaite, *Rules and Principles: A Theory of Legal Certainty*, (2002) 27 Australian J. of Legal Philosophy 46. See also Monahan, *The Supreme Court and the Economy* (prepared for the Royal Commission on the Economic Union and Development Prospects for Canada, 1984). See also Weiler, *In the Last Resort: A Critical Study of the Supreme Court of Canada* (Toronto: Carswell, 1974), 48, and M. Freeman, 'Positivism and Statutory Construction: An Essay in the Retrieval of Democracy,' in S. Guest, ed., *Positivism Today* (Aldershot, UK: Dartmouth, 1996), 11. In *Legal Reasoning and Political Conflict*, Sunstein noted that rules, by themselves, tend to be either over- or under-inclusive (New York: Oxford University Press, 1996), 4.

65 See, for example, *Chamberlain v. Surrey School District No. 36*, [2002] 4 S.C.R. 710. When the 'unwritten' constitution is used as the basis for counter-manding government action, charges can be transformed into catcalls. See Patrick Monahan's description of the Montfort Hospital case in *Doing the Rules: An Assessment of the Federal Clarity Act in Light of the Quebec Secession Reference* (Ottawa: Renouf, 2000), 10. The case in question is *Lalonde v. Commission de restructuration des services de santé* (2001), 56 O.R. (3d) 505 (C.A.), where the Court of Appeal structured its decision around the *written* constitution.

66 C. Epp, 'Do Bills of Rights Matter?' in F.L. Morton, ed., *Law, Politics and the Judicial Process in Canada*, 3rd ed. (Calgary: University of Calgary Press, 2002), 523.

67 The study was presented at the 1998 Constitutional Conference, Osgoode Hall Law School, Toronto, 16 April 1999. It has now been published as *The Supreme Court's 1998 Constitutional Cases: The Debate over Judicial Activism Heats Up*, Canada Watch (September–October 1999), and is available online at http://www.robarts.yorku.ca/canadawatch/vol_7_4-5/default.htm (accessed 4 March 2004)

68 McLachlin, *Courts, supra*, note 18, 45.

69 Sixth Annual Analysis of the Constitutional Decisions of the Supreme Court of Canada: 2002 Constitutional Cases, Osgoode Hall Law School,

Toronto, 4 April 2003; and Seventh Annual Analysis of the Constitutional
Decisions of the Supreme Court of Canada: 2003 Constitutional Cases,
Osgoode Hall Law School, Toronto, 2 April 2004. For the earlier data, see
supra note 67. Note that, due to their different perspectives, Monahan's
graph is often the mirror of Choudhry and Hunter's graphs in the sections
that follow.

70 Morton & Knopff, *Charter Revolution, supra* note 17, at 19–21.
71 S. Choudhry & C.E. Hunter, *Measuring Judicial Activism on the Supreme
    Court of Canada: A Comment on Newfoundland (Treasury Board) v. NAPE*,
    (2003) 48 McGill L.J. 525. Claire Hunter is now clerking at the Supreme
    Court of Canada. The earlier studies were by F.L. Morton, Russell & M.
    Withey and by J. Kelley. For a published summary of Kelley's work, see
    J.B. Kelley, 'The Supreme Court of Canada's Charter of Rights Decisions,
    1982–1999' in F.L. Morton, ed., *Law, Politics and the Judicial Process in
    Canada*, 3rd ed. (Calgary: University of Calgary Press, 2002), 496. See also
    F.L. Morton, P.H. Russell & T. Riddell, *The Canadian Charter of Rights and
    Freedoms: A Descriptive Analysis of the First Decade, 1982–1992*, (1996) 5
    N.J.C.L. 1, and J.B. Kelly, *The Charter of Rights and Freedoms and the Rebal-
    ancing of Liberal Constitutionalism in Canada, 1982–1997*, (1999) 37 O.H.L.J.
    625. When these figures are graphed in five-year increments, the govern-
    ment success rate ranges between 58 and 70 per cent.
72 Section 1 of the *Charter* may save legislation where it constitutes a 'reason-
    able limit' on a *Charter* right that 'can be demonstrably justified in a free
    and democratic society' despite its having contravened a substantive
    Charter right. The section 1 win rate is compiled by assembling all the
    cases that was has been a *Charter* violation (denominator) and calculating
    the proportion that was saved by section 1 (numerator).
73 Mr Halteh was an undergraduate student in a law and society course in
    which I was a teaching assistant. All the activism research we conducted
    was under my supervision. For a discussion of the 2003 cases we com-
    piled, see *infra*, pages 163–70.
74 For a discussion of the 2003 cases we compiled, see *infra*, pages 163–70.
    The downward trend was the same with or without the 2003 data.
75 Choudhry, *et al., supra* note 71, at 553. Roach's remark came from *The Supreme
    Court on Trial* (Toronto: Irwin Law, 2001), 162. For a doctrinal analysis of
    the Court's deference jurisprudence, see S. Martin, *Balancing Individual
    Rights to Equality and Social Goals*, (2001) 80 Can. Bar Rev. 299 at 348 *et seq.*
76 See *supra*, notes 22 and 23.
77 The acting metaphor is freely adapted from Hutchinson, *Judges and
    Politics, supra* note 2, at 284.

78 The phrase 'presented to it' is inaccurate to the degree that the Court controls its own docket. Some speculate that the Court sets its docket with a view to skewing its public profile: see chapter 2.

79 See K. Lunman, *Supreme Court Delays Pot Case*, Globe and Mail, 14 December 2002, A7. There was speculation that Ottawa was trying to influence the court's ultimate decision: K. Makin, *Lawyer Doubts Ottawa's Pot Talk*, Globe and Mail, 12 December 2002, A8.

80 See, for example, G. Smith, *Canada's Pot Policy under Fire from U.S.*, Globe and Mail, 13 September 2002, A-7 and T. MacCharles, *Ottawa Backs Off Pot Law Plans*, Toronto Star, 10 May 2003, A-1.

81 See D.M. Brown, '*Sauvé* and Prisoners' Voting Rights: The Death of the Good Citizen?' (paper delivered at the 2002 Constitutional Cases Converence, Osgoode Hall Law School, Toronto, 4 April 2003).

82 See, for example, J. Simpson, *Our Supreme Court Strays over the 49th Parallel*, Globe and Mail, 11 November 2003, A–25; and Hutchinson, *Judges and Politics, supra*, note 2, at 277.

83 If the Court is going to micro-manage, it might find itself deciding which model of wheelchair a disabled person might be entitled to. Self-propelled wheelchairs cost between $1,500 and $25,000 and there may be substantial variation between therapists as to the needs of any one client (per Shoppers Home Care, personal conversation, 6 April 2004). D. Smillie, in *Wheels of Fortune*, described models costing up to $39,000 (Forbes Magazine, 24 November 2003, 46).

   In *Eldridge v. British Columbia (Attorney General)*, [1997] 3 S.C.R. 624, paras 4 and 87, the Court estimated the cost of providing sign language interpretation services for health care purposes to be $150,000 annually. The actual cost is now more than four times that amount (personal correspondence with Larry N. Austman, senior policy analyst, Strategic Policy and Re-search Division, Ministry of Health Services, Province of British Columbia).

84 Two other cases where the Court compelled the expenditure of money mentioned at para. 73 of *Eldridge* (1997) were also not included in Choudhry and Hunter's database.

85 See *supra*, note 71 and figure 12.4.

86 Roach, *Supreme Court, supra* note 75, at 160–8.

87 See, for example, P.W. Hogg, *Equality as a Charter Value in Constitutional Interpretation* (delivered at the 2002 Constitutional Cases conference, *supra* note 38, 4 *et seq.*).

88 QuickLaw search performed by the author.

89 See, for example, the following articles dealing with the costs and benefits

of changing, or declining to change the law: T.R. Lee, *Stare Decisis in Economic Perspective: An Economic Analysis of the Supreme Court's Doctrine of Precedent*, (2000) 78 N.C.L. Rev. 643; J.R. Macey, *The Internal and External Costs and Benefits of Stare Decisis*, (1989) 65 Chi.-Kent L. Rev. 93; L.A. Kornhauser, *Response to Macey*, (1989) 65 Chi.-Kent L. Rev. 115; and L.A. Kornhauser, *An Economic Perspective on Stare Decisis*, (1989) 65 Chi.-Kent L. Rev. 63

90 A.C. Hutchinson, *Work in Progress: Evolution and the Common Law* (Cambridge: Cambridge University Press), 157.

91 Brian Dickson, as quoted by Sharpe and Roach, in *Brian Dickson: A Judge's Journey* (Toronto: Osgoode Society for Canadian Legal History and University of Toronto Press, 2003), 237.

92 A.W.B. Simpson, 'The Common Law and Legal Theory,' in A.W.B. Simpson, ed., *Oxford Essays in Jurisprudence*, 2nd ser. (Oxford: Clarendon Press, 1973).

93 See K. Makin, *Top Court to Review Jurist Role in Budgets*, Globe and Mail, 16 May 2003, A8; Makin, *Top Court to Consider Self-Defence Argument*, Globe and Mail, 16 January 2004, A-7; Makin, *Third-Party Ad Spending off to Top Court*, Globe and Mail, 9 February 2004, A-4; and T. MacCharles, *Naming Process Draws Fire*, Toronto Star, 25 August 2004, A4. Hutchinson, despite the fact that he thinks the whole debate to be ill founded, eloquently describes the democratic deficit in *Judges and Politics, supra* note 2 at 292–3.

94 See, for example, A. Young, *Judiciary Fills Legislative Void*, Toronto Star, 6 July 2003, F7.

95 For a discussion of this issue in the American context, see L.C. Marshall, *'Let Congress Do It': The Case for an Absolute Rule of Statutory State Decisis*, (1989) 88 Mich. L. Rev. 177, and T.E. Freed, *Is Stare Decisis Still the Lighthouse Beacon of Supreme Court Jurisprudence? A Critical Analysis*, (1996) 57 Ohio St. L.J. 1767.

96 Monahan, *Politics and the Constitution, supra* note 29, at 137 (emphasis added).

97 See, for example, *Figueroa v. Canada (Attorney General)*, [2003] 1 S.C.R. 912.

98 See Morton & Knopff, *Charter Revolution, supra* note 17, at 24.

99 See, for example, C.P. Banks, *Reversals of Precedent, supra* note 10; C.J. Cooper, *Stare Decisis: Precedent and Principle in Constitutional Adjudication*, (1988) 73 Cornell L. Rev. 401; T.R. Lee, *Stare Decisis in Historical Perspective: From the Founding Era to the Rehnquist Court*, (1999) 52 Vand. L.R. 647; R.H. Fallon, Jr., *Stare Decisis and the Constitution: An Essay on Constitutional Methodology*, (2001) 76 N.Y.U.L.R. 570; and E.G. Lee III, *Overruling Rhetoric:*

The Court's New Approach to Stare Decisis in Constitutional Cases, (2002) 33 U. Tol. L. Rev. 581.

At least two of the American Justices have written on the topic: J.C. Rehnquist, *The Power That Shall Be Vested in a Precedent: Stare Decisis, the Constitution and the Supreme Court*, (1986) 66 B.U.L. Rev. 345; J.P. Stevens, *The Life Span of a Judge-Made Rule*, (1983) 58 N.Y.U.L. Rev. 1.

Chapter 13

1 P. Weiler, *In the Last Resort: A Critical Study of the Supreme Court of Canada* (Toronto: Carswell, 1974), 227.
2 P. Monahan, *The Supreme Court of Canada in the 21st Century*, (2001) 80 Can. Bar Rev. 374.
3 See page 30.
4 See L. Epstein & G. King, *The Rules of Inference*, (2002) 69 U. Chi. L. Rev. 1.
5 R.L. Revesz, *Empirical Research and the Goals of Legal Scholarship: A Defense of Empirical Legal Scholarship*, (2002) 69 U. Chi. L. Rev. 169.
6 See M. Heise, *The Past, Present, and Future of Empirical Legal Scholarship: Judicial Decision Making and the New Empiricism*, (2002) U. Ill. L. Rev. 819.
7 It may still be overrun by this type of writing, but that is another story...
8 J. Losee, *A Historical Introduction to the Philosophy of Science*, 4th ed. (Oxford: Oxford University Press, 2001), 202.
9 See T.S. Kuhn, *The Structure of Scientific Revolutions*, 3rd ed. (Chicago: University of Chicago Press, 1996).
10 S.M. Sugunasiri, *Contextualism: The Supreme Court's New Standard of Judicial Analysis and Accountability*, (1999) 22 Dalhousie L.J. 126. Sugnuasiri cites just under seventy cases in her article, not all of which are examples of contextual interpretation. During the relevant period, there were likely over two hundred cases of doctrinal interpretation. She could have written an article claiming that the Court was moving towards doctrinal interpretation by citing only one-third of the Court's use of doctrinal interpretation.
11 By 'petered out' I mean to indicate that these movements, once at the forefront of legal thought, have receded into the background. In their heyday, each of these movements asserted that it represented the most accurate descriptive paradigm, but each failed to live up to its promise. Lord Lloyd's tome describes Legal Realism as being a movement located primarily in the United States, and to a lesser extent in Scandinavia, and having its heyday in the period between 1920 and 1940. Thereafter, it

faded into the background. In some ways, Critical Legal Studies was an attempt to revive Legal Realism. Legal Realism is no longer a dominant paradigm, but it continues to provide a worthwhile perspective by which to analyse both jurisprudential theories and particular judicial decisions. See M.D.A Freeman, *Lloyd's Introduction to Jurisprudence*, 7th ed. (London: Sweet & Maxwell Ltd., 2001) esp. 1055 and more generally at 1040 *et seq.*, 799 *et seq.*, and 855 *et seq.*

12 The attribution to a philosopher was meant to be tongue-in-cheek. One of my reviewers noted that the shortened phrase I use here is actually a newspaper headline from the 1950s. The classical version of the saying, 'the proof of the pudding is in the tasting' is usually attributed to Miguel de Cervantes. But the reviewer noted that de Cervantes was a writer, not a philosopher, and that in any event the proverb predates de Cervantes by several centuries.

Glossary (Selected and Summarized)

Bright line test. A test that prescribes a specific demarcation between two alternatives. (See 'Open standard' below and chapter 7.)

Close Call. A legal decision decided by a panel fractured by a substantial number of dissenting judges. (See chapter 8.)

Contextual interpretation. Mode of judicial reasoning utilizing a wide range of materials and viewpoints. (See chapter 5.)

Doctrinal reconciliation. Mode of judicial reasoning which seeks to unite various legal doctrines under one guiding principle. (See chapter 5.)

Formal legal reasoning. The application of a proposition to a set of facts to arrive at an answer. (See chapter 5.)

Foundational. Based on a set of established ground rules. (See 'Non-foundational' below and chapters 1 and 7.)

Hard distinguishing. Judicial rationalization which is questionable or convoluted. (See chapter 6.)

Legal principle. A general guideline capable of being applied to many situations. (See chapters 5 and 7.)

Legal proposition. A specific statement of law. (See chapters 4, 5, and 7.)

Non-foundational. A search for answers without overbearing restrictions. (See 'Foundational' above and chapters 1 and 7.)

Open standard test. A test that promulgates flexible criteria or models. (See 'Bright line' above and chapter 7.)

Overruling. The refusal to follow legal precedent. (See chapter 6.)

Stare Decisis. The dogma which requires courts to follow precedent.

Bibliography

Abraham, H.J. *The Judicial Process*, 7th ed. New York: Oxford University Press, 1998

Adams, D.M. *Skepticism and the Apologetics of Law*. (1990) 3 C.J.L.J. 69

Agresto, J. *The Supreme Court and Constitutional Democracy*. Ithaca, NY: Cornell University Press, 1984

Allan, J. *Positively Fabulous: Why It Is Good to Be a Legal Positivist*. (1997) 10 C.J.L.J. 231

Altman, A. *Legal Realism, Critical Legal Studies, and Dworkin*. (1986) 15 Philosophy and Public Affairs 205

Anglin, F.A. *Stare Decisis and Other Subjects as Viewed in the Civil Law and at Common Law*. Address given to the Jeune Barreau de Québec, Ottawa, 2 February 1922

Archibald, B.P. *The Canadian Hearsay Revolution: Is Half a Loaf Better Than No Loaf at All?* (1999) 25 Queen's L.J. 1

Arthurs, H. (Chair). *Law and Learning*. Report to the Social Sciences and Humanities Research Council of Canada by the Consultative Group on Research and Education in Law. Ottawa; Minister of Supply and Services Canada, 1983

Austin, A. *The Empire Strikes Back: Outsiders and the Struggle over Legal Education*. New York: New York University Press, 1998

Bahá'u'lláh. *The Hidden Words*. Wilmette, IL: Baha'i Publishing Trust, 1982

Balcome, R. et al. *Supreme Court of Canada Decision-Making: The Benchmarks of Rand, Kerwin and Martland*. Toronto: Carswell, 1990

Balkin, J.M. *Deconstructive Practice and Legal Theory*. (1987) 96 Yale L.J. 743

Band, P. *Stare Decisis: Are Appellate Courts Bound by Their Previous Decisions?* (1998) 20 Advocates Quarterly 345

Banks, C.P. *Reversals of Precedent and Judicial Policy-Making: How Judicial Conceptions of Stare Decisis in the U.S. Supreme Court Influence Social Change.* (1999) 32 Akron L. Rev. 233

Barron, S. *Supreme Life.* (1998) 12 (no. 7) Canadian Lawyer, 20

Bastarache, M. *Supreme Advice to the Successful Litigator: Advocacy in the Supreme Court of Canada.* Address to the County of Carleton Law Association. Ottawa and Quebec, 6 and 7 November, 1998

Bateman, T. *Rights Application Doctrine and the Clash of Constitutionalisms in Canada.* (1998) 31 Can. J. Pol. Sci. 3

Batten, J. *Judges.* Toronto: Macmillan, 1986

Bayefsky, A.F. ed. *Legal Theory Meets Legal Practice.* Edmonton: Academic Printing and Publishing, 1988

Beatty, D. *Constitutional Conceits: The Coercive Authority of Courts.* (1987) 37 U.T.L.J. 183

Beatty, D.M. *Talking Heads and the Supremes.* Toronto: Carswell, 1990

Beaudoin, G-A. ed. *The Supreme Court of Canada: Proceedings of the October 1985. Conference.* Cowansville, QC: Les Editions Yvon Blais Inc., 1986

Bell, J. *Policy Arguments in Judicial Decisions.* Oxford: Clarendon Press, 1983

Belliotti, R.A. *The Rule of Law and the Critical Studies Movement.* (1986) 24 U.W.O.L.R. 67

Benoit, W.L. *Attorney Argumentation and Supreme Court Opinions.* (1989) 26 Argumentation and Advocacy 22

Benseh, S.C., & Reddick, M. *Overruled: An Event History Analysis of Lower Court Reaction to Supreme Court Alteration of Precedent.* (2002) 64 J. of Politics 534

Binnie, I. *A Survivor's Guide to Advocacy in the Supreme Court of Canada.* (1999) 18 Advocates' Soc. J. 13

Bix, B. *The Application (and Mis-Application) of Wittgenstein's Rule-Following Considerations to Legal Theory.* (1990) 3 C.J.L.J. 107

Boeddu, G., & Haigh, R. *Terms of Convenience: Examining Constitutional Over-rulings by the High Court.* (2003) 31 Fed. L. Rev. 167

Bourdieu, P., & Terdiman, R. *The Force of Law: Toward a Sociology of the Juridical Field.* (1987) 38 Hastings L.J. 805

Bowen, D.R. *Sociological Characteristics of Judges.* (unpublished manuscript)

Bowman, S.W. *Interpretation of Tax Legislation: The Evolution of Purposive Analysis.* (1995) 43 Cdn. Tax J. 1167

Braithwaite, J. *Rules and Principles: A Theory of Legal Certainty.* (2002) 27 Australian J. of Legal Philosophy 46

Bratz, D.C. *Stare Decisis in Lower Courts: Predicting the Demise of Supreme Court Precedent.* (1984) 60 Wash. L. Rev. 87

Brenner, S., & Spaeth, H.J. *Stare Indecisis: Alteration of Precedent in USSC, 1946–1992.* New York: Cambridge University Press, 1995

Brenner, S.W. *Precedent Inflation.* New Brunswick, NJ: Transaction Publishers, 1992

Breslin, J.M. *Making Inclusive Positivism Compatible with Razian Authority.* (2001) C.J.L.J. 133

Brewer, S., ed. *Evolution and Revolution in Theories of Legal Reasoning: Nineteenth Century through the Present.* New York: Garland Publishing, 1998

Brewer, S., ed. *Logic, Probability, and Presumptions in Legal Reasoning.* New York: Garland Publishing, 1998

Brewer, S., ed. *Precedents, Statutes, and Analysis of Legal Concepts.* New York: Garland Publishing, 1998

Brewer, S., ed. *Moral Theory and Legal Reasoning.* New York: Garland Publishing, 1998

Brewer, S., ed. *Scientific Models of Legal Reasoning: Economics, Artificial Intelligence, and the Physical Sciences.* New York: Garland Publishing, 1998

Brodie, I., *Friends of the Courts: The Privileging of Interest Group Litigants in Canada.* Albany, NY: State University of New York Press, 2002

Brown, H.S., Crane, B.A., & Allard, L. *Leave to Appeal Applictions: The 1993–94 Term.* (1995) 6 Sup. Ct. L. Rev. (2nd) 545

Brown, H.S., Crane, B.A., & Date, C.J. *Annual Report on Applications for Leave to Appeal to the Supreme Court of Canada, 1996–97.* (1998) 9 Sup. Ct. L. Rev. (2nd) 431

Brown, H.S., Crane, B.A., & Ebos, M.R. *Annual Report on Applications for Leave to Appeal to the Supreme Court of Canada, 1997–98.* (1999) 10 Sup. Ct. L. Rev. (2nd) 513

Brown, H.S. Crane, B.A., & Imerti, V. *Annual Report on Applications for Leave to Appeal to the Supreme Court of Canada, 1995–1996.* (1997) 8 Sup. Ct. L. Rev. (2nd) 500

Brown, H.S., Crane, B.A., & Jolicoeur, M. *Annual Report on Applications for Leave to Appeal to the Supreme Court of Canada: The 1992–93 Term.* (1994) 5 Sup. Ct. L. Rev. (2nd) 1

Brown, H.S. Crane, B.A., & Lemieux, K. *Leave to Appeal Applications: The 1994–95 Term.* (1996) 7 Sup. Ct. L. Rev. (2nd) 421

Brown, H.S., Crane, B.A., & McNulty, C. *Annual Report on Applications for Leave to Appeal to the Supreme Court of Canada, 1999–2000.* (2000) 13 Sup. Ct. L. Rev. (2nd) 335

Brown, H.S., Crane, B.A., & Tourigny, C. *Annual Report on Applications for Leave to Appeal to the Supreme Court of Canada, 1998–99.* (2000) 11 Sup. Ct. L. Rev. (2nd) 517

Brown, H.S., Crane, B.A., & Zubec, J.-P. *Annual Report on Applications for Leave to Appeal to the Supreme Court of Canada, 2001–2002.* (2002) 18 Sup. Ct. L. Rev. (2nd) 413

Bryant, A.W., Gold, M., Stevenson, H.M., & Northrup, D. *Public Attitudes toward the Exclusion of Evidence: Section 24(2) of the Canadian Charter of Rights and Freedoms.* (1990) 69 Can. Bar Rev. 1

Burton, S.J. *Judging in Good Faith.* Oakleigh, Australia: Cambridge University Press, 1992

Bushnell, S.I., *The Captive Court: A Study of the Supreme Court of Canada.* Montreal and Kingston: McGill-Queen's University Press, 1992

Bushnell, S.I. *Leave to Appeal Applications to the Supreme Court of Canada: A Matter of Public Importance.* (1982) 3 Sup. Ct. L. Rev. 479

Bushnell, S.I. *Leave to Appeal Applications: The 1985–86 Term.* (1987) 9 Sup. Ct. L. Rev. 467

Bushnell, S.I. *Leave to Appeal Applications: The 1986–87 Term.* (1988) 10 Sup. Ct. L. Rev. 361

Bushnell, S.I. *Leave to Appeal Applications: The 1987–88 Term.* (1989) 11 Sup. Ct. L. Rev. 383

Callen, C.R. *From Theory to Practice: 'Intelligent' Procedures for Drawing Inferences in Static and Dynamic Legal Environments. Othello Could not Optimize: Economics, Hearsay, and Less Adversary Systems.* (2001) 22 Cardozo L. Rev. 1791

Cameron, J. *Dialogue and Hierarchy in Charter Interpretation: A Comment on R. v. Mills.* (2001) 38 Alta. L. Rev. 1051

Campbell, T., and Goldsworthy, J. eds. *Judicial Power, Democracy and Legal Positivism.* Aldershot, U.K.: Ashgate, 2000

Canadian Bar Association. *Report on the Appointment of Judges in Canada.* Ottawa: Canadian Bar Foundation, 1985

Canadian Bar Association. *Report on the Independence of the Judiciary.* Ottawa: Canadian Bar Foundation, 1985

Canadian Bar Review. *The Supreme Court of Canada: Legacy and Challenges.* Commemorative edition on the 125th Anniversary of the Supreme Court of Canada. (2000) 79–80 Can. Bar Rev.

Caparros, E. *Le travail de la femme d'un 'rancher': Une décision renversante de la Cour Suprême.* (1974) 15 C. de D. 180

Capurso, T.J. *How Judges Judge: Theories on Judicial Decision Making.* (1999) 29 U. Balt. L.F. 5

Carroll, H.N. *Stare Decisis and Supreme Court of Canada.* Master of law thesis, University of Manitoba, 1964

Case, R. *Understanding Judicial Reasoning.* Toronto: Thompson Educational Publishing, 1997

Cass, R.A. *Judging: Norms and Incentives of Retrospective Decision-Making.* (1995) 75 B.U.L. Rev. 941

Casswell, D. *A Prescriptive Model for Decision-Making in the Supreme Court of Canada.* (1982) 14 Ottawa L. Rev. 126

Choudhry, S., & Hunter, C.E. *Measuring Judicial Activism on the Supreme Court of Canada: A Comment on Newfoundland (Treasury Board) v. NAPE.* (2003) 48 McGill L.J. 525, 546

Clayton, C.W., & Gillman, H., eds. *Supreme Court Decision-Making.* Chicago: University of Chicago Press, 1999

Conley, J.M., & O'Barr, W.M. *Rules versus Relationships: The Ethnography of Legal Discourse.* Chicago: University of Chicago Press, 1990

Cooper, C.J. *Stare Decisis: Precedent and Principle in Constitutional Adjudication.* (1988) 73 Cornell L. Rev. 401

Corsi, J.R. *Judicial Politics.* Englewood Cliffs, NJ: Prentice-Hall, 1984

Coser, L.A. *Masters of Sociological Thought: Ideas in Historical and Social Context.* 2nd ed. New York: Harcourt Brace Jovanovich, 1977

Crane, B.A., & Brown, H.S., *Leave to Appeal Applications: The 1988–89 Term.* (1990) 1 Sup. Ct. L. Rep. (2nd) 483

Crane, B.A., & Brown, H.S. *Leave to Appeal Applications: The 1989–90 Term.* (1991) 2 Sup. Ct. L. Rev. (2nd) 473

Crane, B.A. & Brown, H.S., *Leave to Appeal Applications: The 1990–91 Term.* (1992) 3 Sup. Ct. L. Rev. (2nd) 381

Crane, B.A., Brown, H.S., & Thompson, G. *Leave to Appeal Applications: The 1991–92 Term.* (1993) 4 Sup. Ct. L. Rev. (2nd) 27

Cross, F.B. *Decisionmaking in the U.S. Circuit Courts of Appeals.* (2003) 91 Cal. L. Rev. 1457

CTV. *A Gift of Freedom,* W5, 8 June 1986

Dawkins, R. *Bees Are Easily Distracted.* (1969) 165 Science 751

DeCoste, F.C. *Political Corruption, Judicial Selection, and the Rule of Law.* (2000) 38 Alta. L. Rev. 654

DeCoste, F.C. *Redeeming the Rule of Law: Constitutional Justice: A Liberal Theory of the Rule of Law, T.R.S. Allan.* (2002) 39 Alta. L. Rev. 1004

Delisle, R.J. *Collins: An Unjustified Distinction.* (1987) 56 C.R. (3rd) 216

Des Rosiers, N. *The Courts in a Deliberative Democracy ... Asking the Right Questions.* Notes for a speech given on 24 April 2001 to the Conference of appeal courts organized by the National Judicial Institute, Montreal. Available online at http://www.lcc.gc.ca/en/pc/speeches/20010424.asp

Devlin, P. *The Judge.* Oxford: Oxford University Press, 1979

Devlin, R., ed. *Canadian Perspectives on Legal Theory.* Toronto: Emond Montgomery Publications Ltd., 1991

Devlin, R., MacKay, A.W., & Kim, N. *Reducing the Democratic Deficit: Representation, Diversity and the Canadian Judiciary, or Towards a 'Triple P' Judiciary.* (2000) 38 Alta. L. Rev. 734

Devlin, R.F., *Jurisprudence for Judges: Why Legal Theory Matters for Social Context Education.* (2001), 27 Queen's L.J. 161

Devlin, R.F. *Mapping Legal Theory.* (1994) 32 Alta. L. Rev. 602

Dickson, B. *The Judiciary: Law Interpreters or Law Makers.* (1983) Man. L.J. 1

Dickson, B. *The Role and Function of Judges.* (1980) 14 Gazette 138

Doering, R.L. *Murdoch v. Murdoch and the Law of Constructive Trusts.* (1974) 6 Ottawa L. Rev. 568

Douzinas, C., Warrington, R., & McVeigh, S. *Postmodern Jurisprudence: The Law of Text in the Texts of Law.* London and New York: Routledge, 1991

Dworkin, R. *Darwin's New Bulldog.* (1998) Harv. L. Rev. 1718

Dworkin, R. *Law's Empire.* Cambridge, MA: Belknap Press of Harvard University Press, 1986

Dworkin, R. *Taking Rights Seriously.* Cambridge, MA: Harvard University Press, 1978

Edinger, E. *Retrospectivity in Law.* (1995) 29 U.B.C.L. Rev. 5

Ehrcke, W.F., *Stare Decisis.* (1995) 53 Advocate 847

Epp, C. *Do Bills of Rights Matter? The Canadian Charter of Rights and Freedoms.* (1996) 90 Am. Pol. Sci. Rev. 765

Epstein, L., et al. *The Supreme Court Compendium: Data, Decisions and Development.* 3rd ed. Washington, DC: CQ Press, 2003

Epstein, L., & King, G. *The Rules of Inference.* (2002) 69 U. Chi. L. Rev. 1

Eskridge, W.N., Jr. *Overriding Supreme Court Statutory Interpretation Decisions.* (1991) 101 Yale L. J. 331

Eskridge, W.N., Jr. *Reneging on History? Playing the Court/Congress/President Civil Rights Game.* (1991) 79 Cal. L. Rev. 613

Fallon, R.H., Jr. *Stare Decisis and the Constitution: An Essay on Constitutional Methodology.* (2001) 76 N.Y.U. Law Rev. 570

Feldman, S.M., *American Legal Thought from Premodernism to Postmodernism: An Intellectual Voyage.* New York: Oxford University Press, 2000

Fish, S. *Doing What Comes Naturally.* Durham, NC: Duke University Press, 1989

Fish, S. *The Trouble with Principle.* Cambridge, MA: Harvard University Press, 1999

Flemming, R.B. *Tournament of Appeals: Granting Judicial Review in Canada.* Vancouver; UBC Press, 2004

Flemming, R.B., & Krutz, G.S. *Repeat Litigators and Agenda Setting on the Supreme Court of Canada.* (2002) 35 Can. J. of Pol. Sci. 811

Flemming, R.B., & Krutz, G.S. *Selecting Appeals for Judicial Review in Canada: A Replication of the Multivariate Test of American Hypotheses.* (2002) 64 J. of Politics 232

Fletcher, J.F., & Howe, P. *Canadian Attitudes towards the Charter and the Courts in Comparative Perspective.* (2000) 6 (no. 3) Choices 11

Fletcher, J.F., & Howe, P. *Supreme Court Cases and Court Support: The State of Canadian Public Opinion.* (2000) 6 (no. 3) Choices 30

Freed, T.E. *Is Stare Decisis Still the Lighthouse Beacon of Supreme Court Jurisprudence? A Critical Analysis.* (1996) 57 Ohio St. L.J. 1767

Freeman, M.D.A. *Lloyd's Introduction to Jurisprudence.* 7th ed. London: Sweet and Maxwell, 2001

Friedland, M.L. *A Place Apart: Judicial Independence and Accountability in Canada.* Ottawa: Canadian Judicial Council, 1995

Gambrill, D. *Historian Has a Few Words on Court's 125th Anniversary: Supreme Court Has Legitimacy Problems.* (2001) Law Times, 16 October, xx.

George, R.P., ed., *The Autonomy of Law: Essays on Legal Positivism.* Oxford: Oxford University Press, 1996

Gibson, D. *Judges as Legislators: Not Whether but How.* (1987) 25 Alta. L. Rev. 249

Gibson, D. & Baldwin, J.K., eds, *Law in a Cynical Society? Opinion and Law in the 1980s.* Vancouver: Carswell Legal Publications, 1985

Gibson, J.L. & Caldeira, G.A. *The Etiology of Public Support for the Supreme Court.* (1992) 36 Am. J. Pol. Sci. 638

Gibson, J.L., Caldeira, G.A., & Baird, V.A. *On the Legitimacy of National High Courts.* (1998) 92 Am. Pol. Sci. Rev. 343

Gibson, J.L., Caldeira, G.A., & Spence, L.K. *Measuring Attitudes towards the United States Supreme Court.* (2003) 47 Am. J. Pol. Sci. 354

Gibson, J.L., Caldeira, G.A., & Spence, L.K. *The Supreme Court and the U.S. Presidential Election of 2000: Wounds, Self-Inflicted or Otherwise?* (2003) 33 Br. J. Pol. Sci. 535.

Giudice, M. *Unconstitutionality, Invalidity, and Charter Challenges.* (2002) 15 Can. J.L. & Juris. 69

Gold, M., et al. *Public Support for the Exclusion of Unconstitutionally Obtained Evidence.* (1990) 1 Sup. Ct. L. Rev. (2d) 555

Gold, M.E. *The Mask of Objectivity: Politics and Rhetoric in the Supreme Court of Canada.* (1985) 7 Sup. Ct. Law Rev. 455

Golding, M.P. *Legal Reasoning.* New York: Alfred A. Knopf, 1984

Goldman, S. *Politics, Judges and the Administration of Justice.* Unpublished manuscript

Goldstein, L.. ed. *Precedent in Law.* Oxford: Clarendon Press, 1987

Goodrich, P. *Historical Aspects of Legal Interpretation*. (1986) 61 Ind. L.J. 331

Goodrich, P. *Legal Discourse: Studies in Linguistics, Rhetoric and Legal Analysis*. New York: St Martins Press, 1987

Goodrich, P. *Reading the Law: A Critical Introduction to Legal Method and Techniques*. Oxford: Basil Blackwell, 1986

Greene, I. *The Charter of Rights*. Toronto: Lorimer, 1989

Greene, I. *The Doctrine of Judicial Independence Developed by the Supreme Court of Canada*. (1988) O.H.L.J. 177

Greene, I., et al. *Final Appeal: Decision-Making in Canadian Courts of Appeal*. Toronto: Lorimer, 1998

Guest, S. ed. *Positivism Today*. Aldershot, UK: Dartmouth Publishing, 1996

Guest, S. *Ronald Dworkin*. 2nd ed. Edinburgh: Edinburgh University Press, 1997

Guthrie, C. Rachlinski, J.J., & Wistrich, A.J. *Inside the Judicial Mind*. (2001) 86 Cornell L. Rev. 777

Haigh, R. *A Kindler, Gentler Supreme Court? The Case of Burns and the Need for a Principled Approach to Overruling*. (2001) 14 Sup. Ct. L. Rev. (2d) 139

Halewood, P.H. *Performance and Pragmatism in Constitutional Interpretation*. (1990) 3 C.J.L.J. 91

Halpin, A. *Reasoning with Law*. Oxford: Hart Publishing, 2001

Hamner Hill, H. *H.L.A. Hart's Hermeneutic Positivism: On Some Methodological Difficulties in 'The Concept of Law.'* (1990) 3 C.J.L.J. 113

Hart, H.L.A. *American Jurisprudence through English Eyes: The Nightmare and the Noble Dream*. (1977) 11 Georgia Law Rev. 969

Hart, H.L.A. *The Concept of Law*. 2nd ed. Oxford: Clarendon Press, 1994

Heard, A.D. *The Charter of Rights and the Supreme Court of Canada: The Importance of Which Judges Hear an Appeal*. (1991) 24 Can. J. of Pol. Sci. 289

Heise, M. *The Past, Present, and Future of Empirical Legal Scholarship: Judicial Decision Making and the New Empiricism*. (2002) U. Ill. L. Rev. 819

Hellman, D. *The Importance of Appearing Principled*. (1995) 37 Ariz. L. Rev. 110

Hiebert, J.L. *Charter Conflicts: What is Parliament's Role?* Montreal and Kingston: McGill-Queen's University Press, 2002

Hogg, P.W. *Constitutional Law of Canada*, Loose-leaf ed. Toronto: Carswell Thomson, 1997

Hogg, P.W. *Equality as a Charter Value in Constitutional Interpretation*. Paper delivered at the Sixth Annual Analysis of the Constitutional Decisions of the Supreme Court of Canada: 2002 Constitutional Cases, Osgoode Hall Law School, Toronto, 4 April 2003

Hogg, P.W., & Bushell, A.A. *The Charter Dialogue between Courts and Legisla-*

tures (Or Perhaps the Charter of Rights Isn't Such a Bad Thing After All). (1997) 35 O.H.L.J. 75

Hogg, P.W., & Thornton, A.A. *The Charter Dialogue between Courts and Legislatures.* Policy Options april 1999 at 19

Howe, P., & Russell, P. *Judicial Power and Canadian Democracy.* Montreal and Kingston: McGill-Queen's University Press, 2001

Hughes, P. *Judicial Independence: Contemporary Pressures and Appropriate Responses.* (2000) 80 Can. Bar Rev. 181

Hunt, A. ed. *Reading Dworkin Critically.* New York: Berg, 1992

Hunter, D. *Reason Is Too Large: Analogy and Precedent in Law.* (2001) 50 Emory L.J. 1197

Huscroft, G., & Brodie, I., eds. *Constitutionalism in the Charter Era.* Markham, ON: LexisNexis/Butterworths, 2004

Hutchinson, A.C. *Casaubon's Ghosts: The Haunting of Legal Scholarship.* (2001) 21 Legal Studies 65

Hutchinson, A.C. *Hermeneutics and Critique in Legal Practice. Work-In-Progress: Gadamer, Tradition, and the Common Law.* (2000) 76 Chi.-Kent L. Rev. 1015

Hutchinson, A.C. *It's All in the Game: A Non-Foundational Account of Law and Adjudication.* Durham, NC: Duke University Press, 2000

Hutchinson, A.C. *Of Judges, Democracy and Bus Driving.* (1982) 26 L.S. Gazette 26

Hutchinson, A.C. *Judges and Politics: An Essay from Canada.* (2004) 24 Legal Studies 275

Hutchinson, A.C. *A Postmodern's Hart: Taking Rules Sceptically.* (1995) 58 Modern Law Rev. 788

Hutchinson, A.C. *Towards Judicial Accountability: Are the Excuses Getting Lamer?* (1996) 45 U.N.B.L.J. 97

Hutchinson, A.C. *Work in Progress: Evolution and the Common Law.* Cambridge: University Press, 2005

Hutchinson, A.C., & Monahan P.J., eds. *The Rule of Law: Ideal or Ideology.* Toronto: Carswell, 1987

Iacobucci, F. *The Supreme Court of Canada: Its History, Powers and Responsibilities.* (2002) 4 J. App. Prac. & Process 27

Jackson, B.S. *Law, Fact and Narrative Coherence.* Merseyside, UK: Deborah Charles Publications, 1988

Jacobson, P. *Murdoch v. Murdoch: Just about What the Ordinary Rancher's Wife Does.* (1974) 20 McGill L.J. 308

Jennex, D. *Dworkin and the Doctrine of Judicial Discretion.* (1992) 14 Dal. L.J. 473

Johnson, R. *Taxing Choices: The Intersection of Class, Gender, Parenthood and the Law.* Vancouver: UBC Press, 2002

Kairys, D., ed. *The Politics of Law: A Progressive Critique.* 3rd ed. New York: Basic Books, 1998

Kaye, P. *Parliament and the Courts: Who's Legislating Whom?* (1998) Research at the Ontario Legislative Library

Keeton, R.E. *Venturing to Do Justice, Reforming Private Law.* Cambridge, MA: Harvard University Press, 1969

Kennedy, D. *A Critique of Adjudication: fin de siècle* Cambridge, MA: Harvard University Press, 1997

Kennedy, D. *Freedom and Constraint in Adjudication: A Critical Phenomenology.* (1986) 36 J. of Legal Education 518

Kelly, J.B. *Bureaucratic Activism and the Charter of Rights and Freedoms: The Department of Justice and Its Entry into the Centre of Government.* (1999) 42 Can. Public Administration 476

Kelly, J.B. *The Charter of Righs and Freedoms and the Rebalancing of Liberal Constitutionalism in Canada, 1982–1997.* (1999) 37 O.H.L.J. 625

Kornhauser, L.A. *An Economic Perspective on Stare Decisis.* (1989) 65 Chi.-Kent L. Rev. 63

Kornhauser, L.A. *Response to Macey.* (1989) 65 Chi.-Kent L. Rev. 115

Kramer, M. *Also among the Prophets: Some Rejoinders to Ronald Dworkin's Attacks on Legal Positivism.* (1999) 12 C.J.L.J. 53

Kramer, M.H. *In Defense of Legal Positivism.* Oxford: Oxford University Press, 1999

Kress, K.J. *Legal Reasoning and Coherence Theories: Dworkin's Rights Thesis, Retroactivity, and the Linear Order of Decisions.* (1984) 72 Cal. L. Rev. 369

Kuhn, T.S. *The Structure of Scientific Revolutions.* 3rd ed. Chicago: University of Chicago Press, 1996

L'Heureux-Dubé, C. *By Reason of Authority or by Authority of Reason.* (1993) 27 U.B.C. Law Rev. 1

L'Heureux-Dubé, C. *The Dissenting Opinion: Voice of the Future?* (2000) 38 Osgoode Hall L.J. 495

L'Heureux-Dubé, C. *What a Difference a Decade Makes: The Canadian Constitution and the Family since 1991.* (2001) 27 Queen's L.J. 361

La Forest, G.V. *Judicial Lawmaking, Creativity and Constraints.* Address to symposium. Gérard V. La Forest at the Supreme Court of Canada 1985–1997, University of New Brunswick, 2002

Lambert, D. *Ratio Decidendi and Obiter Dicta.* (1993) 51 Advocate 689

Landes, W., & Posner, R.A. *Legal Precedent: A Theoretical and Empirical Analysis.* (1976) 19 J. of Law and Economics 249, 271

Laskin, B. *Judicial Integrity and the Supreme Court of Canada.* (1978) 12 Gazette 116

Lazarus, E. *Closed Chambers: The Rise, Fall and Future of the Modern Supreme Court.* New York: Penguin Books, 1999

Lee, S. *Judging Judges.* London: Faber and Faber, 1988

Lee, E.G., III. *Overruling Rhetoric: The Court's New Approach to Stare Decisis in Constitutional Cases.* (2002) 33 U. Tol. L. Rev. 581.

Lee, T.R. *Stare Decisis in Economic Perspective: An Economic Analysis of the Supreme Court's Doctrine of Precedent.* (2000) 78 N.C.L. Rev. 643

Lee, T.R. *Stare Decisis in Historical Perspective: From the Founding Era to the Rehnquist Court.* (1999) 52 Vand. L. Rev. 647

Leiter, B. *Positivism, Formalism, Realism: Legal Positivism in American Jurisprudence.* (1999) 99 Colum. L. Rev. 1138

Levinson, B.M. *Deuteronomy and the Hermeneutics of Legal Innovation.* New York: Oxford University Press, 1997

Levinson, S., & Mailloux, S., eds. *Interpreting Law and Literature: A Hermeneutic Reader.* Evanston, IL: Northwestern University Press, 1988

Levmore, S. *Ruling Majorities and Reasoning Pluralities.* (2002) 3 Theoretical Inquiries into Law 87

Leyh, G., ed. *Legal Hermeneutics: History, Theory and Practice.* (Berkeley and Los Angeles: University of Californai Press, 1992

Lien, M.W. *Technocentrism and the Soul of the Common Law Lawyer.* (1998) 48 Am. U.L. Rev. 85

Lim, Y. *An Empirical Analysis of Supreme Court Justices' Decision Making.* (2000) 29 J. Legal Stud. 721

Llewellyn, K. 'The Bramble Bush.' In *Introduction to Legal Studies,* ed. N. Sargent et al., North York, ON: Captus Press, 1990

Llewellyn, K.N. *Remarks on the Theory of Appellate Decision and the Rules or Canons about How Statutes Are to Be Construed.* (1950) 3 Vand. L. Rev. 395

Lloyd, Lord of Hampstead, & Freeman, M.D.A. *Lloyd's Introduction to Jurisprudence.* 5th ed. London: Stevens and Sons, 1985

Losee, J. *A Historical Introduction to the Philosophy of Science.* 4th ed. Oxford: Oxford University Press, 2001

Lyons, D. *Moral Aspects of Legal Theory: Essays on Law, Justice and Political Responsibility.* Cambridge: Cambridge University Press, 1993

MacCormick, N. *Contemporary Legal Philosophy: The Rediscovery of Practical Reason.* (1983) 10 J. Law & Soc. 1

MacCormick, N. *H.L.A. Hart.* London: Edward Arnold 1981

MacCormick, N. *Legal Reasoning and Legal Theory.* Oxford: Clarendon Press, 1978

MacCormick, N. *Reconstruction after Deconstruction: A Response to CLS.* (1990) 10 Oxford J. Leg. Studies 539

MacCormick, N., & Summers, R.S. *Interpreting Precedents: A Comparative Study.* Aldershot, UK: Ashgate/Dartmouth, 1997

Macey, J.R. *The Internal and External Costs and Benefits of Stare Decisis.* (1989) 65 Chi.-Kent. L. Rev. 93

MacGuigan, M. *Precedent and Policy in the Supreme Court of Canada.* (1967) 45 Can. Bar Rev. 627

MacKay, A.W., *The Supreme Court of Canada and Federalism: Does/Should Anyone Care Anymore?* (2000) 80 Can. Bar Rev. 241

MacPherson, J. *Canadian Constitutional Law and Madame Justice Bertha Wilson: Patriot, Visionary and Heretic.* (1992) 15 Dalhousie L.J. 217

Malleson, K. *The New Judiciary: The Effects of Expansion and Activism.* Aldershot, UK: Ashgate/Dartmouth, 1999

Mandel, M. *The Charter of Rights and the Legalization of Politics in Canada.* Toronto: Thompson Educational Publishing, 1992

Manfredi, C.P. *Judicial Power and the Charter: Canada and the Paradox of Liberal Constitutionalism.* Toronto: McClelland and Stewart, 1993

Manfredi, C.P. *Feminist Activism in the Supreme Court.* Vancouver: UBC Press, 2004

Manfredi, C.P. *Judicial Power and the Charter: Canada and the Paradox of Liberal Constitutionalism.* 2nd ed. Don Mills, ON: Oxford University Press, 2001

Manfredi, C.P. *Judicial Power and the Charter: Three Myths and a Political Analysis.* (2001) 14 Sup. Ct. L. Rev. (2d) 331

Marmor, A. *Interpretation and Legal Theory.* Oxford: Clarendon Press, 1992

Marmor, A. *No Easy Cases.* (1990) 3 C.J.L.J. 61

Marshall, L.C. *'Let Congress Do It': The Case for an Absolute Rule of Statutory State Decisis.* (1989) 88 Mich. L. Rev. 177

Marshall, T.D. *Judicial Conduct and Accountability.* Toronto: Carswell, 1995

Martin, S. *Balancing Individual Rights to Equality and Social Goals.* (2001) 80 Can Bar Rev. 299

Mayrand, A. *L'autorité du précédent au Québec.* (1994) 28 R.J.T. 761

McConnell, M.W. *Fidelity in Constitutional Theory, Fidelity as Integrity: The Importance of Humility in Judicial Review. A Comment on Ronald Dworkin's 'Moral Reading' of the Constitution.* (1997) 65 Fordham L. Rev. 1269

McCormick, P. *Canada's Courts.* Toronto: Lorimer, 1994

McCormick, P. *Second Thoughts: Supreme Court Citation of Dissents and Separate Concurrences, 1949–1996.* (2002) 81 Can. Bar Rev. 369

McCormick, P. *Supreme at Last: The Evolution of the Supreme Court of Canada.* Toronto: Lorimer, 2000

McCormick, P., and Greene, I., *Judges and Judging.* Toronto: Lorimer, 1990

McKinnon, C. *Toward a Feminist Theory of the State*. Cambridge, MA: Harvard University Press, 1989

McLachlin, B. *Courts, Legislatures, and Executives in the Post-Charter Era*. Policy Options, June 1999, at 42

Mellinkoff, D. *The Language of the Law*. Boston: Little, Brown, 1963

Mellon, H., & Westmacott, M. *Political Dispute and Judicial Review: Assessing the Work of the Supreme Court of Canada*. Scarborough, ON: Nelson Thomson Learning, 2000

Miller, G.P. *Pragmatics and the Maxims of Interpretation*. (1990) Wis. L. Rev. 1179

Miller, M.C. *A Comparison of the Judicial Role in the United States and in Canada*. (1998) 22 Suffolk Transnat. L. Rev. 1

Mitchell, G.G. *Developments in Constitutional Law, the 1997–98 Term: Activism and Accountability*. (1999) 10 Sup. Ct. L. Rev. (2d) 84

Mitchell, W.J.T. ed. *The Politics of Interpretation*. Chicago: University of Chicago Press, 1982

Modak-Truran, M.C. *A Pragmatic Justification of the Judicial Hunch*. (2001) 35 U. Rich. L. Rev. 55

Moles, R.N. *Definition and Rule in Legal Theory: A Reassessment of H.L.A. Hart and the Positivist Tradition*. Oxford: Basil Blackwell, 1987

Monahan, P.J. *The Charter of Rights and Public Policy in Canada*. (1992) 30 O.H.L.J. 501

Monahan, P.J. *The Doctrines of Canadian Federalism*. Unpublished essay

Monahan, P.J. *Doing the Rules: An Assessment of the Federal 'Clarity Act' in Light of the Quebec Secession Reference*. C.D. Howe Institute Commentary No. 135. Toronto: C.D. Howe Institute, 2000

Monahan, P.J. *Judicial Review and Democracy: A Theory of Judicial Review*. (1987) 21 U.B.C. Law Rev. 87

Monahan, P.J. *Politics and the Constitution*. Toronto: Carswell, 1987

Monahan, P.J. *The Law and Politics of Quebec Secession*. (1995) 33 O.H.L.J. 1

Monahan, P.J. *The Public Policy Role of the Supreme Court of Canada in the Secession Reference*. (1999) 11 N.J.C.L. 65

Monahan, P.J. *The Law and Politics of Quebec Secession*. (1995) 33 O.H.L.J. 1

Monahan, P.J. *The Supreme Court of Canada's Constitutional Decisions in 2001: An Overview*. Paper presented at Constitutional Cases Conference, Osgoode Hall Law School, Toronto, 12 April 2002

Monahan, P.J. *The Supreme Court of Canada in the 21st Century*. (2001) 80 Can. Bar Rev. 376

Monahan, P.J. *The Supreme Court and the Economy*. Royal Commission on the

Economic Union and Development Prospects for Canada. Toronto: Osgoode Hall Law School, 1984

Monahan, P.J. *The Supreme Court's 1998 Constitutional Cases: The Debate over Judicial Activism Heats Up.* (1999) 7 (nos 4–5) Canada Watch. Available online at http://www.robarts.yorku.ca/canadawatch/vol_7_4-5/default.htm. (accessed 4 March 2004)

Monahan, P.J. & Forbes, S.A., eds. *Peter Cory at the Supreme Court of Canada 1989–1999.* Winnipeg: Supreme Court of Canada Historical Society, 2001

Monahan, P.J. The Supreme Court's Constitutional Decisions 2003, at the Seventh Annual Analysis of the Constitutional Decisions of the Supreme Court of Canada: 2003 Constitutional Cases. Osgoode Hall Law School, Toronto, 2 April 2004

Monopoli, W. *Dickson Warns Judges Not to Be Legislators.* (1985) 12 (no. 8) National 17

Morawetz, T. *The Epistemology of Judging: Wittgenstein and Deliberative Practices.* (1990) 3 C.J.L.J. 35

Morawetz, T. *Law's Premises, Law's Promise: Jurisprudence after Wittgenstein.* Aldershot UK: Ashgate/Dartmouth, 2000

Morrison, W. *Jurisprudence: From the Greeks to Post Modernism.* London: Cavendish, 1997

Morton, F.L., ed. *Law, Politics and the Judicial Process in Canada.* Calgary: University of Calgary Press, 1992

Morton, F.L., ed. *Law, Politics and the Judicial Process in Canada,* 3rd ed. Calgary: University of Calgary Press, 2002

Morton, F.L., & Knopff, R. *The Charter Revolution and the Court Party.* Peterborough, ON: Broadview Press, 2000

Morton, F.L., Russell, P.H., & Riddell, T. *The Canadian Charter of Rights and Freedoms: A Descriptive Analysis of the First Decade, 1982–1992.* (1996) 5 N.J.C.L. 1

Muldoon, P.R. *Law of Intervention: Status and Practice.* Aurora, ON: Canada Law Book, 1989

Murphy, J.D., & Rueter, R. *Stare Decisis in Commonwealth Appellate Courts.* Toronto: Butterworths, 1981

Nagel, S.S., *Judicial Characteristics and Judicial Decision-Making.* PhD diss., Northwestern University, 1961

O'Brien, D.M. *Judges on Judging: Views from the Bench.* Chatham, NJ: Chatham House Publishers, 1997

O'Hara, E. *Social Constraint or Implicit Collusion? Toward a Game Theoretic Analysis of Stare Decisis.* (1993) 24 Seton Hall L. Rev. 736

Ó Súilleabháin, M., ed. *Legal Theory and Cases: Shifting Frontiers*. Munich: Rainer Hampp Verlag, 1994

Peck, S.R. *The Supreme Court of Canada, 1958–1966: A Search for Policy through Scalogram Analysis*. (1967) 65 Can. Bar Rev. 666

Perell, P. *Stare Decisis and Techniques of Legal Reasoning and Legal Argument*. (1987) Legal Research Update 11

Perry, S.R. *Judicial Obligation, Precedent and the Common Law*. Toronto: Centre for Research on Public Law and Public Policy, 1987

Philipps, L. *The Supreme Court of Canada's Tax Jurisprudence: What's Wrong with the Rule of Law*. (2000) 79 C.B.R. 126

Pond, D.J. *The Supreme Court of Canada and the Politics of Public Law*. PhD diss., University of Toronto, 1992

Posner, R. *The Problems of Jurisprudence*. Cambridge, MA: Harvard University Press, 1990

Posner, R.A. *Legal Precedent: A Theoretical and Empirical Analysis*. (1976) 19 J. of Law and Economics 249

Posner, R.A. *Overcoming Law*. Cambridge, MA: Harvard University Press, 1995

Posner, R.A. *The Problematics of Moral and Legal Theory*. Cambridge, MA: The Belknap Press of Harvard University Press, 1999

Raz, J. *The Authority of Law: Essays on Law and Morality*. Oxford: Clarendon Press, 1979

Rehnquist, J.C. *The Power That Shall Be Vested in a Precedent: Stare Decisis, the Constitution and the Supreme Court*. (1986) 66 B.U.L. Rev. 345

Revesz, R.L. *Empirical Research and the Goals of Legal Scholarship: A Defense of Empirical Legal Scholarship*. (2002) 69 U. Chi. L. Rev. 169

Roach, K. *Constitutional and Common Law Dialogues between the Supreme Court and Canadian Legislatures*. (2001) 80 Can. Bar Rev. 48

Roach, K. *The Myths of Judicial Activism*. (2001) 14 Sup. Ct. L. Rev. (2d) 297

Roach, K. *The Supreme Court on Trial*. Toronto: Irwin Law, 2001

Rosenberg, G.N. *Incentives, Reputation, and the Glorious Determinants of Judicial Behavior*. (2000) 68 U. Cin. L. Rev. 637

Rotenberg, C.L., & Lam, M. *Stare Decisis: Oh Where Have You Gone?* 28 Imm. L. Rev. (2d) 214

Rowland, C.K., &. Carp, R.A. *Politics and Judgment in Federal District Courts*. Lawrence: University of Kansas Press, 1996

Russell, J.S. *The Critical Legal Studies Challenge to Contemporary Mainstream Legal Philosophy*. (1986) 18 Ottawa L. Rev. 1

Russell, P.H. *The Judiciary in Canada: The Third Branch of Government*. Toronto: McGraw-Hill Ryerson, 1987

Russell, P.H. *The Political Role of the Supreme Court of Canada in Its First Century.* (1975) 53 Can. Bar Rev. 576

Salmond, J.W. *The Theory of Judicial Precedents.* (1900) 16 Law Quarterly Rev. 376, 381–2

Saunders, C., ed. *Courts of Final Jurisdiction: The Mason Court in Australia.* Annandale, NSW: Federation Press, 1996

Saywell, J.T. *The Lawmakers: Judicial Power and the Shaping of Canadian Federalism.* Toronto: Osgoode Society for Canadian Legal History, University of Toronto Press, 2002

Schauer, F. *Incentives, Reputation, and the Inglorious Determinants of Judicial Behavior.* (2000) 68 U. Cin. L. Rev. 615

Schauer, F. Review of *The Jurisprudence of Reasons: Law's Empire,* by Ronald Dworkin. (1987) 85 Mich. L. Rev. 847

Schlag, P. *Cannibal Moves: An Essay on the Metamorphoses of the Legal Distinction.* (1988) 40 Stan. L. Rev. 929

Schmitz, C. *'Activism' Critics Posing Threat to Judicial Independence: Dubé.* (1999) 19 (no. 16) Lawyer's Weekly 1

Schubert, G., & Danelski, D., eds. *Comparative Judicial Behaviour: Cross-Cultural Decision-Making in the East and West.* Toronto: Oxford University Press; 1969

Schubert, G.A. *The Judicial Mind: The Attitudes and Ideologies of Supreme Court Justices 1946–1963.* Evanston, IL: Northwestern University Press, 1965

Sebok, A.J. *Legal Positivism in American Jurisprudence.* Cambridge: Cambridge University Press, 1998

Segal, J.A., & Spaeth, H.J. *The Supreme Court and the Attitudinal Model.* Cambridge: Cambridge University Press, 1993

Segal, J.A., & Spaeth, H.J. *The Supreme Court and the Attitudinal Model Revisited.* Cambridge: Cambridge University Press, 2002

Sharpe, R.J., & Roach, K. *Brian Dickson: A Judge's Journey.* Toronto: Osgoode Society for Canadian Legal History, University of Toronto Press, 2003

Siltala, R. *A Theory of Precedent: From Analytical Positivism to a Post-Analytical Philosophy of Law.* Oxford: Hart Publishing, 2000

Simpson, A.W.B., ed. *Oxford Essays in Jurisprudence.* 2nd ser. Oxford: Clarendon Press, 1973

Singer, J.W. *The Player and the Cards: Nihilism and Legal Theory.* (1984) 94 Yale L.J. 1

Sisk, G.K., & Heise, M. *Judges and Ideology: Public and Academic Debates about Statistical Measures.* (2005) 99 Nw. U.L. Rev. 743, 759

Sittiwong, P. *Canadian Supreme Court Decisions, 1949–1980.* MA thesis, North Texas University, 1985

Slattery, B. *Are Constitutional Cases Political?* (1989) 2 Sup. Ct. Rev. (2nd) 507

Smith, G.A. *Wittgenstein and the Sceptical Fallacy*. (1990) 3 C.J.L.J. 155

Snell, J.G., & Vaughan, F. *The Supreme Court of Canada: History of the Institution*. Toronto: Osgoode Society, 1985

Solan, L.M. *The Language of Judges*. Chicago: Chicago University Press, 1993

Songer, D.R., & Johnson, S.W. *Attitudinal Decision Making in the Supreme Court of Canada*. Paper delivered at the Annual Meeting of the Midwest Political Science Association, Chicago, 25–8 April 2002

Soper, P. *A Theory of Law*. Cambridge, MA: Harvard University Press, 1984

Spaeth, H.J., & Segal, J.A. *Majority Rule or Minority Will: Adherence to Precedent on the U.S. Supreme Court*. Cambridge: Cambridge University Press, 1999

Stearns, M.L. *The Condorcet Jury Theorem and Judicial Decisonmaking: A Reply to Saul Levmore*. (2002) 3 Theoretical Inquiries into Law 125

Sterett, S. *Politics and Jurisprudence in the British Courts*. (1988) 1 C.J.L.J. 173

Stevens, J.P. *The Life Span of a Judge-Made Rule*. (1983) 58 N.Y.U.L. Rev. 1

Stone, J. *Precedent and Law: Dynamics of Common Law Growth*. Sydney, NSW; Butterworths, 1985

Stratman, J.F. *Investigating Persuasive Processes in Legal Discourse in Real Time: Cognitive Biases and Rhetorical Strategy in Appeal Court Briefs*. (1994) 17 Discourse Processes 1

Stravopoulos, N. *Objectivity in Law*. Oxford: Clarendon Press, 1996

Stuart, D. *Charter Justice in Canadian Criminal Law*. Toronto: Carswell, 2001

Stuart, D. *Zigzags on Rights of Accused: Brittle Majorities Manipulate Weasel Words of Dialogue, Deference and Charter Values*. Paper prepared for the Sixth Annual Analysis of the Constitutional Decisions of the Supreme Court of Canada Conference, Osgoode Hall Law School, Toronto, 4 April 2003

Sturgess, G., & Chubb, P. *Judging the World: Law and Politics in the World's Leading Courts*. Sydney, NSW: Butterworths, 1988

Sugarman, S.D. *A New Approach to Tort Doctrine: Taking the Best from the Civil Law and Common Law of Canada*. (2002) 17 Sup. Ct. L. Rev. 375

Sugunasiri, S.M. *Contextualism: The Supreme Court's New Standard of Judicial Analysis and Accountability*. (1999) 22 Dalhousie L.J. 126

Sullivan, R. *Statutory Interpretation in the Supreme Court of Canada* (1998–9) 30 Ottawa L. Rev. 175

Summers, R.S. *Instrumentalism and American Legal Theory*. Ithaca, NY: Cornell University Press, 1982

Sunstein, C.R. *Of Artificial Intelligence and Legal Reasoning*. (2001) 8 U. Chi. L. Sch. Roundtable 29

Sunstein, C.R. *Legal Reasoning and Political Conflict*. New York: Oxford University Press, 1996

Tibbets, J. *Farewell Claire*. Canadian Lawyer, September 2002, at 38

Tiersma, P.M. *Linguistic Issues in the Law.* (1993) 69 Language 113

Twining, W. *Law in Context: Enlarging a Discipline.* Oxford: Clarendon Press, 1997

Unger, R.M. *The Critical Legal Studies Movement* (1983) 96 Harv. L. Rev. 561

von Frisch, K. *Honeybees: Do They Use Direction and Distance Information Provided by Their Dances?* (1967) 158 Science 1072

Walker, L., & Monahan, J. *Social Facts: Scientific Methodology as Legal Precedent.* (1988) 76 Calif. L. Rev. 877

Waluchow, W. J. *Inclusive Legal Positivism.* Oxford: Clarendon Press, 1994

Wasserstrom, R. A. *The Judicial Decision: Toward a Theory of Legal Justification.* London: Oxford University Press, 1961

Weber, M. *The Protestant Ethic and the Spirit of Capitalism.* Trans. T. Parsons. London: Routledge, 1992,

Weiler, P. *In the Last Resort: A Critical Study of the Supreme Court of Canada.* Toronto: Carswell, 1974

Weiler, P. *Two Models of Judicial Decision-Making.* (1968) 46 Can. Bar Rev. 407

Weiler, P.C. *The Supreme Court of Canada and Canadian Federalism.* (1973) 11 O.H.L.J. 225

Weinrib, E.J. *The Idea of Private Law.* Cambridge, MA: Harvard University Press, 1995

Wenner, A.M., & Johnson, D.L. *Reply to Karl von Frisch.* (1967) 158 Science 1076

Wenner, A.M., Wells, P.H., & Johnson, D.L. *Honey Bee Recruitment to Food Sources: Olfaction or Language?* (1969) 158 Science 84

Wilson, B. *Decision-Making in the Supreme Court.* (1986) U.T.L.J. 227

Wilson, B. *Will Women Judges Really Make a Difference?* (1990) 28 O.H.L.J. 507

Woodward, B., & Armstrong, S. *The Brethern: Inside the Supreme Court.* New York: Avon Books, 1981

Wrightsman, L.S. *Judicial Decision Making: Is Psychology Relevant?* New York: Kluwer Academic/Plenum Publishers, 1999

Yablon, C. *Are Judges Liars? A Wittgensteinian Critique of 'Law's Empire.'* (1990) 3 C.J.L.J. 123

Index